RESTORING
THE GATES
THAT PREVAIL

DR. JOAQUIN G. MOLINA

CREATION
HOUSE
A STRANG COMPANY

RESTORING THE GATES THAT PREVAIL by Dr. Joaquin G. Molina
Published by Creation House
A Strang Company
600 Rinehart Road
Lake Mary, Florida 32746
www.creationhouse.com

Unless otherwise noted, all Scripture quotations are from the King James
Version of the Bible.

Scripture quotations marked NKJV are from the New King James Version of
the Bible. Copyright © 1979, 1980, 1982 by Thomas Nelson, Inc., publishers.
Used by permission.

Cover design by Terry Clifton

Library of Congress Control Number: 2006926811
International Standard Book Number: 978-1-59979-024-4

First Edition

07 08 09 10 11 — 987654321
Printed in the United States of America

This book is dedicated to my beloved wife, Yvette, a virtuous woman and perfect helper. Without you, I could never fulfill God's call to change the world.

To my four godly children, Nicholas, Joshua, Brandon, and Christina. Continue walking in the fear and wisdom of God by obeying His Word.

To all my brothers and sisters at Spring of Life Fellowship, may our lives be an example to the body of Christ, proving that with God all things are possible.

ACKNOWLEDGMENTS

To God the Father, Jesus Christ His Son, and the Holy Spirit I offer my highest acknowledgment for His unceasing grace and mercy that flow towards this ministry allowing us the privilege to serve the body of Christ.

I would like to extend my warmest, heartfelt acknowledgment to every member in the body of Christ that has imparted their grace, prayers, love, and truth into my life and ministry. I am fully aware and acknowledge how God was able to use many godly brothers and sisters in Christ too numerous to list, who inspired my walk and faithfulness to the Lord Jesus Christ. I will never forget the words of wisdom, warm embraces, and examples given to me at different and crucial times in my life, allowing me to attain and fulfill the call of God for my life. This book is a harvest for the glory of God made possible by the many seeds of godly men and women who sowed God's truth and love into my heart during the past two decades.

I thank God for my parents, Dr. Raul G. Molina and Julieta Molina, for their love and support, and for showing an example through their lives of walking in wisdom and the fear of the Lord.

I am also forever grateful to Dr. R. T. and Louise Kendall, together with the Creation House staff, for your help and continued words of encouragement.

Many thanks to Yvette, Vicente, Silvia, Kaye Whitney, and others who helped so much with the particular manuscripts in the development process of writing this book.

I would like to acknowledge and honor those in the body of Christ called to lead; may God always allow you to be diligent examples, showing yourselves to be approved and faithful to God so that you need not be ashamed upon Christ's return.

If I forget thee, O Jerusalem, let my right hand forget her cunning. If I do not remember thee, let my tongue cleave to the roof of my mouth; if I prefer not Jerusalem above my chief joy.

—PSALM 137:5–6

CONTENTS

FOREWORD

Dr. Joaquin G. Molina is an unusual man. With the encouragement and support of his wife Yvette, he recently gave up a lucrative law practice in the United States to enter the ministry of the gospel of Jesus Christ, not knowing how he and his family would cope. It was a major step of faith. This move was in some ways akin to that of my predecessor at Westminster Chapel, Dr. Martyn Lloyd-Jones, who gave up a medical practice in England to enter the ministry.

Dr. Molina is now the senior pastor and founder of the thriving Spring of Life Fellowship church in Miami, Florida, a substantial and ever-increasing international congregation. It has been a joy to preach for his congregation. The services are in English, but there is always an interpreter for the preaching and worship to ensure that all present receive the Word of God. What impressed me most however, was the spirituality of the church. I do not merely mean a lively worship, but also a warm receptivity to the Word. These people want *God* more than anything and will do what it takes to have more of *Him*. Such devotion could only come because of a pastor's heart that has led people to aspire to God like that.

It is for this reason I am delighted to write a commendation for Dr. Molina's book, *Restoring the Gates That Prevail*. It is a very different kind of book, applying the Book of Nehemiah in a manner I have never thought of. The Book of Nehemiah is one of my favorite books in the Old Testament, but I have not thought of the unique manner in which Joaquin draws the fascinating chapter headings and ideas from Nehemiah.

You should know that it is Pastor Molina's burden to change the world with the gospel, particularly among those who lead their local church. He desires to reach them with necessary correctives on certain issues. He is aware that people in the pulpit in these perilous times are not always very balanced, and often speak too much to people's wishes rather than have any desire for the glory of God. Pastor Molina fears that the excesses of some teachers have misled sincere Christians by appealing to a "What's in it for me?" attitude, rather than "What's in it for God?"

I applaud his burden, and I believe you will enjoy this book. His applications are most interesting; he has come up with thoughts that are needed right now. I pray this book will bless you, edify you, encourage you, and most of all, bring great honor and glory to God.

—Dr. R. T. Kendall
Key Largo, Florida
April 2006
Former Minister, Westminster Chapel
London, England

PREFACE

After two decades of participating in Christian ministry and witnessing the work of God within the local church, God has unfolded hidden truths that led to the writing of this book. This book is entrusted to all church pastors, elders, leaders, officers, and ministers within the body of Christ that have the responsibility to care, train, equip, oversee, and shepherd the church of our Lord. Each chapter in this book focuses on the vital aspects of local church ministry that allows the church to arise efficiently as the epicenter of God's redemption plan for mankind. I hope godly leaders realize that God's purpose was that unto all powers that be, might be known by the church the manifold wisdom of God; in other words, that the church would display the multiform wisdom of God in all things. In recent years, the foolishness of the local church has been more widespread and openly displayed than the wisdom of God.

This book was written to provide the body of Christ with practical application and truth that could assist those who participate in local church ministry. The work entrusted by God to the local church is totally exclusive, vitally important, and nontransferable. No other entity in the world has been given a more serious task or responsibility. Church leaders cannot afford to be negligent and dismissive as divine stewards of the mysteries of God and administrators of the riches of His grace. While many in the local church are lacking the understanding and aptitude to fulfill their ministry, this book will challenge the leadership in the local church to restore and repair specific aspects of church ministry so that Christ's church returns to her place as a strong, fortified, and glorious city.

Remember that God desires the church to become the joy of all the earth. In past years, the church has suffered an identity crisis, not being able to walk in her calling to overcome victoriously and lead the nations as God intended. The church's glorious identity has been tremendously damaged and still remains in ill repute. The price paid by God on Calvary's cross was that Jesus might present unto Himself a glorious bride, having no spot or wrinkle or any such thing (see Eph. 5:27). The world should not perceive the local church as an irrelevant and obscure embarrassment. God intended for the church to be arrayed and adorned in fine linen, reflecting the splendor, glory, and wisdom of her King. God's desire is that the local church would embrace her legacy to prevail against the gates of hell. Jesus promised in Matthew 16:18, "I will build my church; and the gates of hell shall not prevail against it."

Upon reading this book, I am sure that many local church leaders will be changed forever. I hope this book motivates other leaders to address the essential aspects of local church ministry that have been abandoned and forsaken for too long. The local church is ultimately an expression of the effort, diligence, and competence of its leaders. Nehemiah's legacy shows leaders that they can rebuild the church walls and gates to prevent further embarrassment and reproach to their families and congregations. The commitment to restore these gates will bless a multitude of families for many generations by providing a safe haven for those within the church. I pray that this book will be read prayerfully, with all spiritual maturity and reflection.

MAP OF ANCIENT CITY OF JERUSALEM

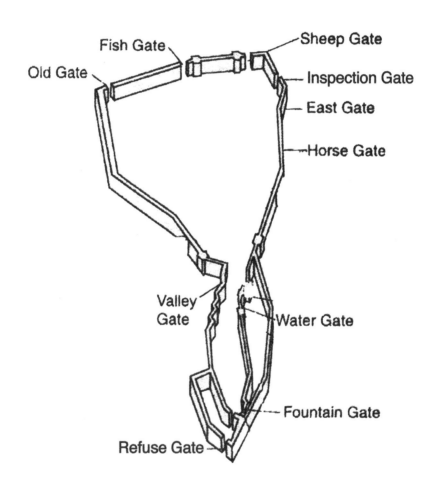

Fish Gate

Sheep Gate

Old Gate

Inspection Gate

East Gate

Horse Gate

Valley Gate

Water Gate

Fountain Gate

Refuse Gate

INTRODUCTION

> *Lift up your head, O ye gates; and be ye lift up, ye everlasting doors; and the King of glory shall come in. Who is this King of glory? The LORD strong and mighty, the LORD mighty in battle. Lift up your heads, O ye gates; even lift them up, ye everlasting doors; and the King of glory shall come in. Who is this King of glory? The LORD of hosts, he is the King of glory. Selah.*
>
> —PSALM 24:7–10

My earnest desire is that those responsible for the church and its condition will begin to change the world by lifting up the gates and walls that surround and protect the body of Christ. The Book of Psalms has a prophetic announcement that if the gates be lifted up, the King of glory will come marching in strong and mighty (see Ps. 24:7–10). Every word of *Restoring the Gates That Prevail* was written to change the present state of affairs in the body of Christ. This book was written for every minister and ministry anointed by God's Spirit and zeal, having the desire to rebuild and restore the Christian church.

Sadly enough today, the Christian church in many places has become lifeless, heartless, passionless, and reproachful houses of worship—but the time has come for God to turn the local churches' mourning into dancing. The lack of obedience to God's Word and the absence of the Holy Spirit's power have opened the doors of many local churches to ungodly, heathen-inspired, and worldly influences that invade God's inheritance and thereby defile the house of God and His children.

> O God, the heathen are come into thine inheritance; thy holy temple have they defiled; they have laid Jerusalem on heaps.
> —PSALM 79:1

I hope this book challenges church leaders to restore their houses of worship from heaps of desolate ruins to strong, fully-restored, fortified gates. The church was called to prevail against the gates of hell, which include wicked forces and all influence of ungodliness and worldliness that contend fiercely against God's people. A genuine movement of God's Spirit will always bring about renewal and regeneration to the body of Christ.

Upon reading 2 Chronicles 36:14–23, I began to see that today's Christian church is suffering the same peril and destruction that Israel experienced in those times. As a result of great apostasy and incredible spiritual indifference, Jerusalem and her inhabitations were attacked and taken captive by surrounding enemies who hated God's dwelling place and longed for the destruction of all her precious possessions.

> Then they burned the house of God, broke down the wall of Jerusalem, burned all its palaces with fire, and destroyed all its precious possessions.
> —2 CHRONICLES 36:19, NKJV

However, I believe that at God's appointed time, God will impart the necessary wisdom, skill, and grace to motivate godly leaders everywhere in a mighty work of restoration. God's Spirit will move zealously in the hearts of men and women to restore and lift up the integrity and character of His church. During the next several years, God will allow believers to rise and follow the example and efforts of Zerubabel, Ezra, and Nehemiah. These young men moved with passion and zeal to restore the city of God that lay in ruins for seventy years.

In its present state, the church is suffering continued plunder and devastation by rebellious and wayward leaders and believers who fail to understand their calling to lead the body of Christ by example. Church leadership and elders have forsaken their places at the gates, thus permitting vandalism and destruction—the walls and gates of the church are broken, burned, and failing to protect those seeking refuge behind church walls.

The Bible states, "Where there is no vision, the people perish" (Prov. 29:18). I pray that today's church leaders can see the practical truths behind each gate depicted in Nehemiah, and begin to see that God desires the church to prevail against this present darkness.

Many aspects of this book will assist leaders in following God's divine architectural blueprint to restore the Christian church. Through this book, godly leaders will be able to discern God's heart and restore specific gates that serve to protect God's people. Similar to the rebuilding of the ancient city of Jerusalem, examining the Sheep Gate, Fish Gate, Old Gate, Valley Gate, Refuse Gate, Fountain Gate, Water Gate, Horse Gate, East Gate, and Inspection Gate will give every church a refreshing new look at God's design. Each gate has the essence of God's heart and His desire to define the dwelling place where His people presently abide. As the new Jerusalem is restored, the church shall arise to fulfill her calling and become the joy of all the earth.

Restoring the Gates That Prevail shall serve as a tremendous contribution and encouragement to those whose task it is of perfecting the saints for the work of ministry. The Christian church needs to begin exhibiting the character of those having attained the measure of the stature and fullness of Christ. Each gate will provide practical insight that will strengthen and encourage every believer. A city without walls shall perish, and a city with nonfunctioning gates is at peril. My desire is to help leaders in the body of Christ to move with all deliberate and passionate zeal toward restoring the church to reflect God's glory, wisdom, and grace. I pray all Christian leaders accept this challenge to change the world by restoring the gates that prevail, and in so doing present the church as a glorious and beautiful chaste virgin and bride unto Christ.

—Dr. Joaquin G. Molina
June 2006

1

THE SHEEP GATE

Then said Jesus unto them again, Verily, verily, I say unto you, I am the door of the sheep. All that ever came before me are thieves and robbers: but the sheep did not hear them. I am the door: by me if any man enter in, he shall be saved, and shall go in and out, and find pasture.

—JOHN 10:7–9

The journey toward the restoration of the ancient city of Jerusalem begins in Nehemiah 3:1, where Nehemiah made a call to arms so that the city's inhabitants would gather to rebuild a city that had laid in ruins for seventy years. For purposes of this book, the reader should consider ancient Jerusalem as a shadow and type of the local church. This book follows the order in which the gates are mentioned in chapter three of the Book of Nehemiah.

The specific order in which the gates are listed may hold some divine significance. The very first verse in chapter three mentions a surrounding gate known as the Sheep Gate. The Sheep Gate is important to the effort of church restoration because this gate concerns those most benefited by the restoration—God's sheep. God's people need to be aware that He always proceeds in a specific order to fulfill His sovereign design and divine plan.

For seventy years, the city of God had broken gates that allowed strangers, thieves, and robbers easy access to take what belonged to God's people. Many people believe that bandits damaged some gates more than others. Enemy attacks at some of the gates allowed easier access and swifter conquest of the city than at other gates. As the reconstruction effort was realized in ancient Jerusalem, the high priest rose up to build the sheep gate. Likewise, at the forefront of God's concern are His people. The beginning of the restoration begins with this verse in Nehemiah 3:1:

> Then Eliashib the high priest rose up with his brethren the priests, and they builded the sheep gate; they sanctified it, and set up the doors of it; even unto the tower of Meah they sanctified it, unto the tower of Hananeel.

The Sheep Gate is located at the northeast section of the city. The repairs began at the Sheep Gate and then proceeded all the way around the city counterclockwise, until all ten gates were restored. Between each city gate, walls were lifted and fortified so that the city was fully enclosed without any gaps or holes.

The restoration efforts involved both men and women without distinction to particular abilities or skills. Nehemiah invited everyone to participate in realizing the restoration efforts; including the Jews, priests, nobles, rulers, and all ordinary or common people. There were about forty-five different sections of gates and walls that were divided up so that each section was worked on in phases by different groups.

As the Sheep Gate is restored, those called to the pastorate should note that the central purpose for the city's existence was for the caring of sheep. The very essence of every local church function should be for the purpose of caring for the Lord's sheep. Any participation at the local church must focus on this special aspect of ministry, which is providing care and protection for the Lord's sheep. If the Sheep Gate is not repaired quickly, today's pastors will have lost the opportunity to honor and bring pleasure to the heart of God. In Psalm 100, we see that God's people are the sheep of His pasture:

> Make a joyful noise unto the LORD, all ye lands. Serve the LORD with gladness: come before his presence with singing. Know ye that the LORD he is God: it is he that hath made us, and not we ourselves; we are his people, and the sheep of his pasture. Enter into his gates with thanksgiving, and into his courts with praise: be thankful unto him, and bless his name. For the LORD is good; his mercy is everlasting; and his truth endureth to all generations.
>
> —PSALM 100

This passage emphasizes the priority of God's heart. God is genuinely concerned about the sheep of His pasture. Every effort to restore the local church must line up with God's heart to provide a peaceful pasture for the Lord's sheep. In other words, believers must learn from God's heart and begin to concern themselves with the matters that address God's desire. The greatest illustration of God's care and attention toward His people is found in the Bible through the illustration of a shepherd's constant care for his sheep. Throughout Scripture, vivid imagery reveals the Lord's desire to provide for and protect those under His watch.

Certain attributes describe a shepherd's constant care and attention for his sheep. As the model Shepherd, Jesus cares for His sheep in everything He does. To know God is to know first and foremost that He deals with His people as the sheep of His pasture. When the Lord Jesus came into the world, all the people were able to behold His genuine love for His sheep. As the Good Shepherd, Jesus continually concerned Himself with the well-being of His sheep. In the Gospel of Matthew, Jesus looks out over Jerusalem and is moved with compassion for the people by the fact that they had no shepherd:

And Jesus went about all the cities and villages, teaching in their synagogues, and preaching the gospel of the kingdom, and healing every sickness and every disease among the people. But when he saw the multitudes, he was moved with compassion on them, because they fainted, and were scattered abroad, as sheep having no shepherd.

—MATTHEW 9:35–36

Passing through the villages and teaching in the synagogues, Jesus visited His people as the Good Shepherd. He proclaimed the gospel of the kingdom and healed diseases among the people. When He saw the multitudes, He was moved with compassion for them because they were weary and scattered as sheep having no shepherd. The failure to restore the Sheep Gate will continue to render God's people fainted and scattered. This is what the Lord sees when He looks toward His people today.

The Lord's first concern is for the well-being of His sheep. Believers cannot say that they love the Lord if they do not love and feed His sheep. The pulse of God's heart beats for those who are genuinely concerned for His sheep. The church needs to restore this aspect of ministry. When Jesus came, He gave clear instruction concerning a good shepherd's efforts to protect and care for his sheep:

I am the good shepherd: the good shepherd giveth his life for the sheep. But he that is an hireling, and not the shepherd, whose own the sheep are not, seeth the wolf coming, and leaveth the sheep, and fleeth: and the wolf catcheth them, and scattereth the sheep. The hireling fleeth, because he is an hireling, and careth not for the sheep. I am the good shepherd, and know my sheep, and am known of mine.

—JOHN 10:11–14

Jesus provided the church the greatest example of a good shepherd when He gave His life for His sheep. Good shepherds—true shepherds—give their lives for their sheep. Restoring the Sheep Gate involves removing shepherds who are mere hirelings, or those motivated to take advantage of the sheep they care for and are never willing to lay down their lives for the flock.

How do church leaders know when the Sheep Gate is broken? Are the sheep scattered? Are the sheep weary, hungry, and thirsty? Are the sheep going off to the world to seek after other resources and provisions? Has the church failed to lead them beside still waters? How many years has it been since the sheep have eaten from green pastures? Are the sheep's souls being restored? Are the sheep failing to walk in the paths of righteousness? Have pastors fallen asleep during their watch? When pastors no longer see or perceive the needs of their fold and neglect caring and nourishing those in their trust, the church knows the Sheep Gate is fallen. Therefore, restoring the Sheep Gate is the responsibility of the entire church family.

Church members must concern themselves with restoring the Sheep Gate. Caring for the Lord's sheep is the chief duty of all believers. Caring for God's people must precede all other church activities. No activity in the church should override this principal and central facet of the church's purpose, which is to care for those entrusted to them by God. Often, many of the activities taking place in the church fail to consider the negative consequences that will befall the Lord's sheep as a result, and even continue to take place at the expense of these sheep. Church leaders must make full efforts to give attention to caring for the problems of God's flock and meeting their needs. This responsibility to protect and provide for God's people is a must until Jesus returns.

When God began looking for the perfect man to lead His people— Israel—He did not look for a man with great intellectual capacity, like a theologian or learned scholarly professor. Neither did He look for a mighty king with royal blood or nobility, nor did He look for somebody with great physical appearance or stature. God chose someone with the heart of a true shepherd. He found a young boy named David who concentrated all his efforts in being faithful to watch and care for his father's sheep. This young man would be just the man to entrust with ruling over God's people in Israel. God decided to train up this shepherd boy so that one day he would shepherd God's people. This young man did not have much experience, but he was willing to defend God's people by fighting courageously. David was always willing to lay down his life for the sheep whenever needed, regardless of the circumstance. Whenever the sheep were attacked by a wolf, lion, or bear, David would bravely defend the sheep, therefore God chose him to care for Israel.

> He chose David also his servant, and took him from the sheep-folds: From following the ewes great with young he brought him to feed Jacob his people, and Israel his inheritance. So he fed them according to the integrity of his heart; and guided them by the skilfullness of his hands.
> —PSALM 78:70–72

David was chosen by God because of his ability to shepherd God's people, even though they were weak and vulnerable, much like sheep. At the Sheep Gate, God reminds all those who shepherd the people of God to do so with integrity of heart and skillfulness of hands. God is always looking for those who are willing to provide genuine care for His sheep. Rather than looking for a position, title, or place of prominence, a real shepherd is focused on faithfully serving the One who entrusted him with the care of the sheep. As such, David was not seeking personal glory or recognition. His desire was only that none of God's sheep would be lost because of peril or by going astray.

In many of today's churches, the Sheep Gate has suffered much damage and loss by inept shepherds who have lost their understanding that the primary purpose of their call is to shepherd God's sheep. To restore the Sheep Gate, church leaders need to be prepared to stand up against those who want to abuse, neglect, hurt, and wrongfully take advantage of God's sheep. In some modern churches, the Sheep Gate is broken, destroyed, and burned. The Sheep Gate needs to be restored and defended against attacks from ravenous wolves, lions, and bears that seek to devour the sheep.

From an early age, David showed fierce concern for protecting God's people. In 1 Samuel chapter 17, this young shepherd boy approached his leaders and requested the opportunity to defend them against a giant who brought threats of harm against God's people:

> And David said unto Saul, Thy servant kept his father's sheep, and there came a lion, and a bear, and took a lamb out of the flock: And I went out after him, and smote him, and delivered it out of his mouth: and when he arose against me, I caught him by his beard, and smote him, and slew him. Thy servant slew both the lion and the bear: and this uncircumcised Philistine shall be as one of them, seeing he hath defied the armies of the living God.
>
> —1 SAMUEL 17:34–36

Those in leadership need to seriously consider the requisite mindset to achieve restoration of the Sheep Gate. Believers also need to understand that solemn efforts must be employed to fulfill this call of shepherding God's fold. Those who desire to become more effective in the restoration of the church must take their part in rebuilding the Sheep Gate. This task is not for cowards who are unwilling to take a courageous stand. Evangelical leaders cannot continue to look the other way while wolves in sheep's clothing continue to prey upon and devour the Lord's sheep. Those being trained up as shepherds must be willing to confront and overcome such predators that threaten the well-being of God's sheep. Only a courageous shepherd will be willing to defend his Father's sheep. God will not entrust His sheep to the care of those lacking the mental fortitude to protect and defend against preying beasts. Until church leaders accept this fact, they will not be seen as true servants of God.

The early church leaders understood the need to be sober and vigilant, knowing that the devil, as a roaring lion, was walking about seeking whom he could devour (see 1 Pet. 5:8). The apostle Peter wrote to the leaders of his day, encouraging them to be faithful in caring for and overseeing God's flock:

> The elders which are among you I exhort, who am also an elder, and a witness of the sufferings of Christ, and also a partaker of the glory that shall be revealed: *Feed the flock of God* which is among you, taking the oversight thereof, not by constraint, but willingly; not for filthy lucre, but of a ready mind; Neither as being lords over God's heritage, but *being ensamples to the flock.* And when the chief Shepherd shall appear, ye shall receive a crown of glory that fadeth not away.
>
> —1 PETER 5:1–4, EMPHASIS ADDED

The Lord considers good shepherds to be those who love His sheep. If you consider yourself as one who loves Jesus Christ, and He asks you, "Do you love Me?" you could reply, "Yes, Lord, I love You." Then He asks you again, "Do you love Me?" and you say, "Lord, what are You after?" When He asks you a third time, "Christian, do you love Me?" you say, "Lord, I don't understand what You're getting at." In each case, He responded to your answers focused on His sheep. He did not respond, *Do you love Me?—give Me tithes.* He did not say, *Do you love Me?—give Me offerings.* He did not say, *If you love Me, then have good attendance at church.* His focus is on His sheep, because when you truly love Jesus you will hear His voice asking you to show your love by caring for His sheep. When you tell the Lord you love Him, He expects you to show it by caring for His sheep. And when you love His sheep, you are not going to miss one church service. You are not going to be faulty with your tithes and offerings. You will be faithful in many areas when your primary motive is to love the Lord's sheep.

This is the hallmark of the Lord's desire for His people. What a tremendous thing it was that the last thing Jesus told Peter was, *Feed my lamb, shepherd my sheep, take care of my fold:*

So when they had eaten breakfast, Jesus said to Simon Peter, "Simon, son of Jonah, do you love Me more than these?" He said to Him, "Yes, Lord; You know that I love You." He said to him, "Feed My lambs." He said to him again a second time, "Simon, son of Jonah, do you love Me?" He said to Him, "Yes, Lord; You know that I love You." He said to him, "Tend My sheep." He said to him the third time, "Simon, son of Jonah, do you love Me?" Peter was grieved because He said to him the third time, "Do you love Me?" And he said to Him, "Lord, You know all things; You know that I love You." Jesus said to him, "Feed My sheep."

—John 21:15–17, NKJV

Herein lies the heartbeat of God. The true measure of love for God can be seen by constant care and attention to His sheep. God desires that pastors care for the least significant and the neediest among His people so that they receive the best attention and provision. Each pastor will have to give an account to the chief Shepherd concerning the well-being of God's sheepfold.

The greatest expression of a shepherd's care for His sheep is illustrated in Psalm 23. This psalm portrays the genuine efforts of a good shepherd who faithfully cares for his sheep so that they are fully restored:

The LORD is my shepherd; I shall not want. He maketh me to lie down in green pastures: he leadeth me beside the still waters. He restoreth my soul: he leadeth me in the paths of righteousness for his name's sake. Yea, though I walk through the valley of the shadow of death, I will fear no evil: for thou art with me; thy rod and thy staff they comfort me. Thou preparest a table before me in the presence of mine enemies: thou anointest my head with oil; my cup runneth over. Surely goodness and mercy shall follow me all the days of my life: and I will dwell in the house of the LORD for ever.

—Psalm 23

Every good shepherd affords proper care to his sheep by making sure that nothing is lacking. If God's people intend to repair the Sheep Gate so that churches are restored, they must be certain the sheep are lacking no good thing. All the essentials must be provided for the sheep of the Lord. Pastors should ask themselves whether they have made substantive efforts to provide protection, food, shelter, and proper grooming. The church may provide food to the poor from their pantry, but they need to provide spiritual nourishment also. Experts have documented that people usually become what they eat. If they eat junk food, they will become junk food addicts. This is no less true in the Christian walk. Therefore, shepherds must provide the necessary nourishment so that the sheep are well fed and kept free from ailments and infirmities.

People who are properly fed are stronger. A healthy appetite leads to a sound mind. When God's people are well fed, their attitudes and overall spiritual development improve. Malnourished and neglected sheep begin to wither away and experience all sorts of infirmities. One can easily distinguish between a sheep that lacks good nourishment from one that is well fed and fortified. The neglected sheep often deteriorate into negative attitudes and quickly lose stamina.

The Lord's sheep should never suffer from thirst or hunger. All thirst must be quenched from the springs of eternal life at the fountain of living waters. Those repairing the Sheep Gate must be able to lead the flock beside still waters so they may satisfy their thirst. Repairing the Sheep Gate will focus attention on assisting God's people in restoring their souls from excessive burdens and worries. The Lord desires undershepherds to restore the souls of those committed to their trust. They can rest assured that neither doctors nor therapists can minister to the needs within the soul of man. God desires to restore the wounds suffered in the church and He uses godly shepherds to heal them.

A good shepherd leads the sheep in paths of righteousness. The Lord desires for His sheep to have the opportunity to hear, "Come this way. I'll lead you in righteous paths." Fewer and fewer ministers are willing to say, "Come, follow me. Pattern yourself after my example. Follow my life. I am willing to lead you into righteousness for His namesake."

In John 10, Jesus says that a good shepherd is not a hireling, but will give his life for the sheep:

> I am the good shepherd: the good shepherd giveth his life for the sheep.
>
> —JOHN 10:11

The giving of one's life can take many different forms. One form is by offering time and attention. A person's time is the greatest part of his existence. People that are willing to repair the Sheep Gate must be willing to offer their time and attention to the sheep. The giving of personal time is the most sincere demonstration of a good shepherd's ability to watch over the flock. Pastors cannot be away from the sheep for too long before the sheep fall into harm's way. A shepherd must be committed to faithfully watching over the sheep at every moment:

> But he that is an hireling, and not the shepherd, whose own the sheep are not, seeth the wolf coming, and leaveth the sheep, and fleeth: and the wolf catcheth them, and scattereth the sheep. The hireling fleeth, because he is an hireling, and careth not for the sheep. I am the good shepherd, and know my sheep, and am known of mine. As the Father knoweth me, even so know I the Father: and I lay down my life for the sheep. And other sheep I have, which are not of this fold: them also I must bring, and they shall hear my voice; and there shall be one fold, and one shepherd.
>
> —JOHN 10:12-16

Believers can rejoice in the tenacity with which Jesus protects those under His care—not one will be lost. He is the good and omnipotent Shepherd.

The most common complaint these days regarding shepherds is

the reckless fleecing and swindling of the sheep. Many people today are reluctant to go to church because they fear becoming the victims of rash fleecing. For many, church pastors stand as ruthless workers eager to get their hands on people's money. Some think that a shepherd's purpose is only to make sure their sheep are continually fleeced. As soon as some pastors see a little fleece growing on their sheep, they bring the sheep in for a closer shave. This abuse might seem humorous to some, but the wrath of God will befall those shepherds who are scheming for their own personal gain. The Bible says in the Book of Jude that these dreamers will be eternally condemned. These wicked men are fooling only themselves and do not realize they are harming God's sheep.

> These are spots in your love feasts, while they feast with you without fear, serving only themselves. They are clouds without water, carried about by the winds; late autumn trees without fruit, twice dead, pulled up by the roots; raging waves of the sea, foaming up their own shame; wandering stars for whom is reserved the blackness of darkness forever.
> —JUDE 12–13, NKJV

The New International Version of the Bible translates this verse as "shepherds who feed only themselves," pointing to those who shepherd for their own personal gain

These verses show the travesty taking place in some churches, and how the people suffer from dysfunctional problems at the Sheep Gate. Many churches have failed to value God's people and serve Christ faithfully by genuinely caring for His sheep. While restoring the Sheep Gate, it is crucially important that all servants of God, who travel the world sharing the gospel of Jesus Christ, learn to turn their hearts back to the caring and protecting of God's sheep. The heart of every leader must beat with the tenacious zeal and passion of caring for God's elect. All leaders are instructed to shepherd and feed the church that Christ has purchased with His own blood:

Paul warned the believers of his day that they received the full counsel of God, and admonished the church to focus upon caring for the Lord's flock, which the Holy Spirit made them overseers to feed. Paul was an excellent shepherd who would not allow any ravenous wolf to show up while he was present. He was convinced that as soon as he departed, savage wolves would attack and devour the Lord's sheep.

> And now, behold, I know that ye all, among whom I have gone preaching the kingdom of God, shall see my face no more. Wherefore I take you to record this day, that I am pure from the blood of all men. For I have not shunned to declare unto you all the counsel of God. Take heed therefore unto yourselves, and to all the flock, over the which the Holy Ghost hath made you overseers, to feed the church of God, which he hath purchased with his own blood. For I know this, that after my departing shall grievous wolves enter in among you, not sparing the flock.
>
> —ACTS 20:25–29

There is a correlation between the presence of a good shepherd and the absence of savage wolves. The presence of a good shepherd diminishes the number of savage wolves. Paul warned believers that as soon as he departed, ravenous wolves would come in among them, and the wolves would not spare the flock.

Paul also warned that men would rise up among the church and twist things to draw disciples after themselves; even disciples are vulnerable to deceitful men. Some would like to think, *Surely not disciples. Maybe baby Christians or newborns, but not disciples.* How could deceitful men that twist things draw disciples away? Disciples? Being swallowed and devoured by wolves? When disciples are being drawn away the body of Christ is in deep trouble. Paul reminded the early believers to watch and remember how much emphasis he placed on caring for God's people when he was around:

17

Therefore watch, and remember, that by the space of three years I ceased not to warn every one night and day with tears.

—ACTS 20:31

Paul had the heart of a genuine shepherd who did not cease to watch and warn—night and day, with tears in his eyes—caring, overseeing, and protecting the Lord's sheep. Many people may ask, "How can a savage wolf rise up among God's people? How is it possible for a wolf to rise up in the midst of the church?" First of all, they must disguise themselves so that the shepherds do not easily spot them. The wolves must dress in sheep's clothing, having the outward appearance of a sheep. Is it possible for wolves to put on the apparel of sheep by taking up garments of wool? Can they take on the customary vestments and dress up like sheep? If so, shepherds need to pay more attention:

Beware of false prophets, which come to you in sheep's clothing, but inwardly they are ravening wolves.

—MATTHEW 7:15

Jesus warned about the reality of ministers who outwardly appear as ministers, but inwardly are ravenous wolves. The following is a test:

> ‣ Does it look like a sheep?
>
> ‣ Does it act like a sheep?
>
> ‣ Does this sheep have a track record of following their pastor's voice?
>
> ‣ Does it seem like this sheep has been groomed by a pastor?

There are many wolves dressed in sheep's clothing who appear to be following the Shepherd. In Matthew 7:15, Jesus said to beware of false prophets because they come in sheep's clothing. They look like sheep; they talk like sheep, but inside they are ravenous wolves. The best place to distinguish the difference between a sheep and a wolf is the mouth. Wolves have sharp teeth that they use to devour their prey. Likewise, the words spoken by the mouth of certain believers are often sharp and harsh. They demolish their victim with wicked words that serve only to destroy.

How can a believer recognize a wolf in sheep's clothing? These false prophets would be known by their fruit—except that they have none. Jesus asks, *Does a man go through a grapevine to get grapes in a thorn bush?* Do you find grapes on a thorn bush? No! Why? Thorn bushes do not have the ability to produce grapes. Are you going to find figs among thistles? No. Why not? Thistles do not produce figs. Jesus said, "A tree is known by its fruit" (Matt. 12:33, NKJV). Do ravenous wolves in sheep's clothing bear fruit? No. Then why do people follow them? People are led astray by the wolves' wicked ability to twist the truth and draw disciples after themselves.

Pastors must repair the Sheep Gate in their churches. From this moment on, the Christian church should be held out as a safe haven and refuge for the Lord's sheep. Those who understand the responsibility of restoring the Sheep Gate need to become expert under-shepherds. They must make sure that each sheep coming through the doors of the sanctuary will be safe. A pastor's close inspection can rid the church of those wolves hiding in sheep's clothing. Wolves know all the doctrines. Indeed, how could they pervert the truth if they did not know what the truth was?

The first question I ask believers that visit my congregation is, "Do you have a shepherd? If you do, then go back to that shepherd." I will not pastor people who have other shepherds and are just fugitive sheep hiding from accountability. Recently I told a young man I had known for over fifteen years, "You refuse to be shepherded and you do not like shepherds." In the last couple of years that I have been his pastor, he avoided any type of personal accountability. It is difficult to shepherd sheep who no longer desire to be shepherded. Some sheep do not follow their pastor's counsel and constantly go astray seeking their own ways, getting lost, and moving elsewhere from fold to fold, all the while avoiding discipline and correction. It is difficult to shepherd sheep who refuse to be taken care of, which is evidenced by their constant rebellion and defiance.

Regardless of the many opportunities provided, some sheep cannot recognize the importance of listening to their shepherd's voice. The sheep must be instructed to seek godly counsel from those who will one day give an account to God for their souls. Every church should teach their sheep the importance of seeking their pastors for guidance. A pastor's desire should be to acquaint the church with the importance of caring for the sheep in his fold.

This is the heart of God. This is what He thinks about the disrepair of the Sheep Gate:

> My people hath been lost sheep: their shepherds have caused them to go astray, they have turned them away on the mountains: they have gone from mountain to hill, they have forgotten their restingplace. All that found them have devoured them: and their adversaries said, We offend not, because they have sinned against the LORD, the habitation of justice, even the LORD, the hope of their fathers.
>
> —JEREMIAH 50:6–7

God does not change. Throughout the Bible, serious admonition and warnings are directed at those entrusted with caring for the Lord's sheep. The Lord continues to be the same yesterday, today, and forever. God's heart is always attentive to the genuine care of His sheep. The following text reveals God's concern for the safety and care of His sheep:

> And the word of the LORD came unto me, saying, Son of man, prophesy against the shepherds of Israel, prophesy, and say unto them, Thus saith the Lord GOD unto the shepherds; Woe be to the shepherds of Israel that do feed themselves! should

not the shepherds feed the flocks? Ye eat the fat, and ye clothe you with the wool, ye kill them that are fed: but ye feed not the flock. The diseased have ye not strengthened, neither have ye healed that which was sick, neither have ye bound up that which was broken, neither have ye brought again that which was driven away, neither have ye sought that which was lost; but with force and with cruelty have ye ruled them. And they were scattered, because there is no shepherd: and they became meat to all the beasts of the field, when they were scattered. My sheep wandered through all the mountains, and upon every high hill: yea, my flock was scattered upon all the face of the earth, and none did search or seek after them. Therefore, ye shepherds, hear the word of the LORD; As I live, saith the Lord GOD, surely because my flock became a prey, and my flock became meat to every beast of the field, because there was no shepherd, neither did my shepherds search for my flock, but the shepherds fed themselves, and fed not my flock; Therefore, O ye shepherds, hear the word of the LORD; Thus saith the Lord GOD; Behold, I am against the shepherds; and I will require my flock at their hand, and cause them to cease from feeding the flock; neither shall the shepherds feed themselves any more; for I will deliver my flock from their mouth, that they may not be meat for them. For thus saith the Lord GOD; Behold, I, even I, will both search my sheep, and seek them out. As a shepherd seeketh out his flock in the day that he is among his sheep that are scattered; so will I seek out my sheep, and will deliver them out of all places where they have been scattered in the cloudy and dark day. And I will bring them out from the people, and gather them from the countries, and will bring them to their own land, and feed them upon the mountains of Israel by the rivers, and in all the inhabited places of the country. I will feed them in a good pasture, and upon the high mountains of Israel shall their fold be: there shall they lie in a good fold, and in a fat pasture shall they feed upon the mountains of Israel. I will feed my flock, and I will cause them to lie down, saith the Lord God. I will seek that which was lost, and bring again that which was driven away, and will bind up that which was broken, and will strengthen that which was sick: but I will destroy the fat and the strong; I will feed them with judgment. And as for you, O my flock, thus saith the Lord God; Behold, I judge between cattle and cattle, between the rams and the he goats. Seemeth it a small thing unto you to have eaten up the good pasture, but ye must tread down with your feet the residue of your pastures? and to have drunk of the deep waters, but ye must foul the residue with your feet? And as for my flock, they eat that which ye have trodden with your feet; and they drink that which ye have fouled with your feet. Therefore thus saith the Lord God unto them; Behold, I, even I, will judge between the fat cattle and between the lean cattle. Because ye have thrust with side and with shoulder, and pushed all the diseased with your horns, till ye have scattered them abroad; Therefore will I save my flock, and they shall no more be a prey; and I will judge between cattle and cattle. And I will set up one shepherd over them, and he shall feed them, even my servant David; he shall feed them, and he shall be their shepherd. And I the Lord will be their God, and my servant David a prince among them; I the Lord have spoken it. And I will make with them a covenant of peace, and will cause the evil beasts to cease out of the land: and they shall dwell safely in the wilderness, and sleep in the woods. And I will make them and the places round about my hill a blessing; and I will cause the shower to come down in his season; there shall be showers of blessing. And the tree of the field shall yield her fruit, and the earth shall yield her increase, and they shall be safe in their land, and shall know that I am the Lord, when I have broken the bands of their yoke, and delivered them out of the hand of those that served themselves of them. And they shall no more be a prey to the heathen, neither shall the beast of the land devour them; but they shall dwell safely, and none shall make them afraid. And I will raise up for them a plant of renown, and they shall be no more consumed with hunger in the land, neither bear the shame of the heathen any more. Thus shall they know that I the LORD their God am with them, and that they, even the house of Israel, are my people, saith the Lord GOD. And ye my flock, the flock of my pasture, are men, and I am your God, saith the Lord GOD.

—EZEKIEL 34

This passage reminds the church that God is very attentive to the care and protection given to His people. God knows the condition of His sheep and has seen their brokenness, discouragement, and wounds. God knows that we need shepherds; therefore, He will save His flock so that they are no longer preyed upon, neglected, or abused. Evidently, God is serious about these affairs. Some people might respond, "But Pastor, I really don't know yet if I'm a sheep or if I'm a goat. Pastor, I'm confused. Sometimes I feel like a sheep, sometimes I don't. How do I determine this?"

In the Gospel of Matthew chapter 25, Jesus reveals that on the last day He is going to gather His sheep to His right hand, and the goats to the left. In this passage, the goats are not even aware that they are not sheep.

Matthew 25:31–32 says:

When the Son of man shall come in his glory, and all the holy angels with him, then shall he sit upon the throne of his glory: And before him shall be gathered all nations: and he shall separate them one from another, as a shepherd divideth his sheep from the goats.

In the past, I have met people who persist in trying to help their shepherd tell the difference between sheep and goats. The truth is that the shepherds always know the difference between the goats and the sheep, because the goats are always stubborn and do not follow the shepherd's voice. Most often I leave it to God to distinguish and separate the one from the other. The Lord is an expert at drawing the line and has promised to divide them like a shepherd divides the sheep from the goats:

> And he shall set the sheep on his right hand, but the goats on the left. Then shall the King say unto them on his right hand, Come, ye blessed of my Father, inherit the kingdom prepared for you from the foundation of the world: For I was an hungred, and ye gave me meat: I was thirsty, and ye gave me drink: I was a stranger, and ye took me in: Naked, and ye clothed me: I was sick, and ye visited me: I was in prison, and ye came unto me. Then shall the righteous answer him, saying, Lord, when saw we thee an hungred, and fed thee? or thirsty, and gave thee drink? When saw we thee a stranger, and took thee in? or naked, and clothed thee? Or when saw we thee sick, or in prison, and came unto thee? And the King shall answer and say unto them, Verily I say unto you, Inasmuch as ye have done it unto one of the least of these my brethren, ye have done it unto me. Then shall he say also unto them on the left hand, Depart from me, ye cursed, into everlasting fire, prepared for the devil and his angels: For I was an hungred, and ye gave me no meat: I was thirsty, and ye gave me no drink: I was a stranger, and ye took me not in: naked, and ye clothed me not: sick, and in prison, and ye visited me not. Then shall they also answer him, saying, Lord, when saw we thee an hungred, or athirst, or a stranger, or naked, or sick, or in prison, and did not minister unto thee?
>
> —MATTHEW 25:33-44

In this passage, the Lord is concerned with those who profess to believe in God but have forgotten the importance of caring for one another. The church must be aware of this and careful to teach that true followers of Christ are vigilant to the needs of others. True sheep exercise good vision and are able to notice when others are lacking. Many in the body of Christ claim to have entered the sheep door and belong to God but fail, as Jesus said, to provide for "the least of these my brethren" that belong to God's sheepfold. The followers of Christ are taught to see the sick and make their way to visit them. They become involved with feeding the hungry. They see the thirsty and give them something to drink. They see the heart of people who are in prison and have compassion and visit them. They clothe the naked.

Sheep can see the stranger and the foreigner and remember them—but goats do not see anything. They are just looking out for themselves and any possible junk food or tasty morsels of gossip to feast upon. True sheep are attentive to the needs of others: they find genuine means to meet the needs of others. Goats, however, never see anything but what serves their own self-centered existence.

I hope you now have a better understanding of the Sheep Gate and its present state of disrepair. To repair this gate, the body of Christ needs men and women who are willing to shoulder the weight of this responsibility and accept the serious burden of caring for the sheep. When will true servants of God willingly stand to take charge of caring for God's sheep? The Lord expects true servants to say, "Lord, I want to be part of repairing the Sheep Gate." The Sheep Gate has fallen and all the sheep have gone astray, each one after his own desire. According to what the Bible says, they are scattered everywhere—but God will raise up men who have the heart of David, who will shepherd His people with integrity and with skillful hands. Let us begin to repair the Sheep Gate.

PRAYER APPLICATION

Lord! Help the Christian church to restore the Sheep Gate. In every church, allow Christian leaders to restore the Sheep Gate so that Your house is a place where sheep are safe, protected, and properly cared for. Lord Jesus, I purpose to help shepherd every single one of your sheep with a sincere heart, always strengthening the weak, feeding the hungry, quenching the thirst of the thirsty, visiting the sick, healing the broken-hearted, comforting the afflicted, clothing the naked, gathering in the scattered, protecting the vulnerable from vicious wolves and other predators, and binding the wounded. Lord, I will purpose to restore the Sheep Gate so that Your glory fills the temple.

2

THE FISH GATE

> *Now after this he built a wall without the city of David, on the west side of Gihon, in the valley, even to the entering in at the fish gate, and compassed about Ophel, and raised it up a very great height, and put captains of war in all the fenced cities of Judah.*
>
> —2 CHRONICLES 33:14

This chapter on the Fish Gate focuses on the local church's charge to take on the awesome responsibility of reaching out to seek and save souls that are yet lost. The Bible often describes the unsaved and unbelieving as fish that must be caught in the nets for God's kingdom. Many sectors within the body of Christ are totally unacquainted with outreach ministry, forsaking to evangelize effectively by reaching the unsaved. In recent years more and more local churches have become self-absorbed, reclusive, and isolated, choosing rather to withdraw into their own shell-like denominations and play "church" antics. The spiritual apathy and indifference of failing to obey the call to "seek the lost" and "preach the gospel" to all peoples destroys the church from within. When the body of Christ begins to seriously seek and save the lost, the church will experience an authentic, genuine revival that is consistent with a healthy Christ-centered church.

The second gate mentioned in Nehemiah's restoration effort was the Fish Gate. A broken Fish Gate results from despising God's call to become successful fishers of men. The church of Jesus Christ must gather strength to restore the Fish Gate so that believers begin to win over those who are still outside the city walls.

> But the fish gate did the sons of Hassenaah build, who also laid the beams thereof, and set up the doors thereof, the locks thereof, and the bars thereof.
>
> —NEHEMIAH 3:3

The Fish Gate holds much significance by the priority given to it in the Book of Nehemiah. Second only to the Sheep Gate, the Fish Gate was erected. Church leaders should note the importance of God's care for His sheep and God's great love and concern for a lost and sinful world that still remains distant from God's salvation and love. Little else is more significant in God's heart than reaching the unsaved and lost. The heart of God is not divorced from those who remain yet distant from His salvation plan.

As the Fish Gate is restored, the church needs to recognize that each believer is God's special instrument for reaching the multitude of lost souls. They are reconciled and won over through strategic evangelism. A fundamental reason for the existence of every church is fishing and winning the lost for Christ. Leaders can hardly call a gathering of believers a legitimate "church" unless the members dedicate serious effort and time to winning the lost for Christ. The great commission to preach the gospel was given as a mandate to all believers in Christ. This charge should be understood and embraced by the church as its highest duty.

Who best to reach the lost than the objects of God's mercy that have already experienced His forgiveness and unconditional love? The church as a body is the best candidate to deliver the message of God's love and forgiveness. Each believer must be equipped to impart with all sure expression the matter concerning God's message of salvation.

Many of today's churches need to renew their commitment to reaching out to those that are lost. Restoring the Fish Gate helps the church understand the responsibility they have before God in participating with the winning of souls. Every church needs to train and efficiently equip believers in the work of reaching out and saving the lost. Carrying the burden of lost souls and effectively reaching the unsaved must be renewed amidst a self-serving and self-gratifying generation that thinks only of themselves.

For some churches, the Fish Gate represents a problem because it involves bringing unfamiliar and different people inside our fellowship comfort zones. At the Fish Gate, leaders transform the church from an "exclusive membership" to an "inclusive membership" where all are invited to come and find peace with God through repentance. The message given on Calvary's cross involves making provision for all men to seek and find forgiveness of sin and rest for their souls. The Fish Gate restoration includes purposefully seeking the most undeserving and telling them that they are actually the objects of God's true love and extreme sacrifice.

> For the Son of man is come to seek and to save that which was lost.
>
> —Luke 19:10

As the church begins restoring the Fish Gate, the members have an opportunity to revitalize and strengthen an important aspect of preparing each saint for the work of ministry. Evangelism outreach programs and missions should become an integral part of every local church curriculum. Many churches have forgotten the importance of a functional Fish Gate. Failure to restore the Fish Gate only leads the church to become self-absorbed, self-centered, and self-serving.

A church that fails to restore the Fish Gate becomes withdrawn from their community and ultimately become sterile, obsolete, and irrelevant. When a church begins to focus inwardly on their own needs, activities, and services, the ministry becomes a cloistered social club for members to seclude themselves in bubble-like fashion. When the Fish Gate is broken it creates a dysfunctional church and a breeding ground for members to become selfish, arrogant, religious Pharisees.

As leaders repair the Fish Gate, the church will learn the importance of taking every step necessary to assure effective outreach to the lost. God's servants must tap into the fury of heaven's host who are arduously working so that no one may perish, but that all might have everlasting life. A Spirit-filled life will lead the church to witness to others concerning God's saving grace.

The Fish Gate reminds the church of God's central message found in Scripture: the redemption and salvation of all who are lost. The sacrificial death of Christ upon the cross is the invaluable price paid toward God's greatest purchase—lost humanity. The extent and value of God's love toward a lost, forbidden world is clearly validated and confirmed by the price paid at Calvary's cross:

> For God so loved the world that He gave His only begotten Son, that whoever believes in Him should not perish but have everlasting life.
>
> —JOHN 3:16, NKJV

God the Father paid the greatest price for sinful, fallen man. No other object in Scripture has more value to God than a lost soul. This lost world evokes God's deepest passion and greatest gift of love. When Christ was sent to hang and die on Calvary's cross it was God's payment and ransom for every single lost soul.

Every church must devote serious effort and mark out a definitive role for itself in God's work of redemption to save the unsaved. The ruins of a broken Fish Gate are seen whenever a local church has neglected or despised the lost, forgotten the forsaken, and ignored the unsaved. Whereas many believe that redeeming lost man is God's most recent revelation in Scripture through the cross of Calvary, the contrary is true. From the beginning of time, God prepared a Lamb that was slain for the purpose of gathering in all the lost so that they might know and experience His salvation:

> And all that dwell upon the earth shall worship him, whose names are not written in the book of life of the Lamb slain from the foundation of the world.
>
> —Revelation 13:8

In this passage the Bible informs us that from the beginning of Creation the sacrificial Lamb was slain to provide an atoning sacrifice for the salvation of all those who had fallen short of God's glory. The church's primary function should be to proclaim effectively the gospel (the "good message") of Jesus Christ at all times to all people everywhere.

God made every effort to reach the lost, including recruiting men who could understand the difficulty of such a task. When Christ came seeking for such recruits He chose fishermen to make it clear that those following Him would be actively engaged in fishing for men.

> And he saith unto them, Follow me, and I will make you fishers of men.
>
> —Matthew 4:19

In order for the local church effectively to restore the Fish Gate, it will require the same tenacity and drive learned by those in the fishing trade. A ministerial team cannot attribute a functioning Fish Gate to good fortune. To restore the Fish Gate to good functioning order, God's people must develop the character and discipline needed in those who have made fishing their trade.

The calling to the first four fishermen Jesus selected was no coincidence. Peter, James, Andrew, and John all had the perseverance and stubbornness to accomplish whatever task was at hand. The commitment to withstand harsh elements and conditions speaks volumes about the fierce character required by those who take up fishing. The men chosen by Christ near the Sea of Galilee were weather-torn and beaten, but they continued to achieve their daily toil.

Every fishing colony of the world can readily attest to the crude and observable harsh reality of a tough life for those involved with, and surrounding, the fish trade. Rarely do fish just show up and jump into the net. Rather, many factors such as timing and precision are essential to succeed. Those in a fishing colony are acquainted with diligent efforts and responsibilities to the point that life itself becomes consumed with the discipline of catching fish.

Many of the Lord's first apostolic followers were fishermen who knew all too well that life requires putting forth great effort and endurance to become successful. Day after day, these men undertook the fatiguing labor of performing their task without surrender. More than just wishful thinking, these men knew that to fulfill their vocation they would need to prepare supplies and resources to succeed and make their day prosperous.

Any true fisherman must be prepared to study tides; forecast weather conditions; gather, repair, cast, and drag nets; battle storms; watch the phases of the moon; tie knots; dock their vessels; spend long nights working; and stay awake for days on end. Every fisherman must perfect his skills to accomplish this feat. Fishing takes more then an average person to withstand the weariness of each expedition, especially for those who preach the gospel.

The Fish Gate can only be repaired through the patience and perseverance of those willing to spend long hours, investing time and resources into fulfilling the Great Commission. Every true Fish Gate repair must be accompanied by the desire to patiently wait for the fish to bite on the bait. If believers become restless in reaching out and quickly lose patience in evangelism, the church will never become good fishers of men.

Rarely does evangelism show quick results in preaching the gospel. Believers must learn to wait. Often preaching the gospel means being taken by great storms that rise without notice. Nonetheless, the repairs needed at the Fish Gate require great courage and strength to contend against the elements outside the believer's control. Many times these acts of God require courage that is rarely seen in the body of Christ today.

So much has been said and taught about a "hidden life in Christ" that few Christians understand the necessity of reaching out to others. Every church must establish a plan to restore the Fish Gate by reaching out and concerning themselves with catching the lost for Christ. Many churches are so involved in their own activities that they forget the lost. They have made other preparations, such as sitting around waiting for the Lord's imminent return. Leaders must cease focusing on themselves and begin to place more emphasis on reaching those who are still outside the church walls. This is another reason the Lord chose a group of ordinary, unsophisticated men with whom to entrust the gospel news. Even though they were not a highly educated group, the twelve disciples understood the significance of working hard to achieve God's purpose.

Many times Jesus spoke in parables concerning the kingdom of God, equating salvation with a process of casting a large net into the sea and gathering every kind of fish:

> Again, the kingdom of heaven is like unto a net, that was cast into the sea, and gathered of every kind: Which, when it was full, they drew to shore, and sat down, and gathered the good into vessels, but cast the bad away.
>
> —MATTHEW 13:47–48

Another factor in the process of repairing the Fish Gate involves the aspect of reaching out to those who might be different from us. Many times the irreparable state of the Fish Gate is due to elements or factions within the church that would rather keep those "other kinds" far removed. Many times our unwillingness to reach out and share our faith to spread the gospel message is due to matters of prejudice or bias against another social class, cultural group, or ethnicity. No greater barrier or interference for restoring the Fish Gate exists than preconceived, prejudicial notions concerning other groups. In order for the church to successfully repair the Fish Gate, the leaders must first heal every heart in their assembly that carries any virus of discrimination or bigotry. Any prejudice against others will tend to exclude rather then include. At the Fish Gate the church must be reminded continually that all have fallen short of the glory of God, and therefore the invitation is open for all to repent and come into the city of God. (See Romans 3:23.)

Regardless of familiarity or preferences, the church must immediately remove any partiality before they can experience a well-functioning Fish Gate. The church must proclaim loudly and in unison that the Lord of the harvest intends to make no exception of persons, but desires that all should come to repentance so that none would perish. The evidence for this is found in John's Book of Revelation, where all nations, tribes, and tongues are found before the throne of God worshiping and praising the Lamb of God (Rev. 7:9).

Over the past several centuries, the church has stated its exclusivity and partisan values, instead of sounding the alarm that God has promised to pour out His Spirit on all flesh without exception (Joel 2:28). As the people of God, believers should proclaim salvation to all and let God sort them out. Christians must realize that God's most sacred work is that of saving those who have not experienced His loving care and protection.

Restoring and repairing the Fish Gate involves a deep look at saving souls, which is otherwise known as evangelism. Every church assembly should teach its members how to evangelize effectively so that God's people are able to reach this lost world. The tools needed to facilitate evangelism must be perfected in every church. Evangelism is the proclaiming of the gospel to those who have yet to taste God's saving grace. The word *evangelism* comes from the Greek word *euangelos*, which means "bringing good news." There are many methods available to reach out to those who still have not come to Christ. One method of evangelizing is as follows:

> ➤ Share the good news of the gospel to every man and woman.
>
> ➤ Pray for repentance and receive God's forgiveness through Jesus Christ.
>
> ➤ Confess out loud, believing in your heart, that Jesus is Lord and Savior, that He was crucified and shed His blood for the forgiveness of sin and that on the third day He rose from the dead to sit at the right hand of God's throne.
>
> ➤ Read and obey God's Word, and serve Jesus in the fellowship of His church.

This description includes more than confessing Christ to obtain forgiveness of sin. In addition to saving people from hell or saving them from their personal problems or life's casualties, the church must include a definition of evangelism that includes telling people to join and faithfully serve in the body of Christ until He returns. Many present-day churches believe that evangelism is a gift or talent to be exercised solely by the church evangelist or missionary, but Jesus commanded all of His followers to go into the world preaching the gospel to every creature:

> And he said unto them, Go ye into all the world, and preach the gospel to every creature.
>
> —MARK 16:15

Throughout Scripture, fish symbolize those who are yet to be caught in God's net. At the Fish Gate, the church sees what has been commonly revealed by God's heart toward the lost who still remain outside the protection and provision of His embrace. The Fish Gate helps believers understand that those who find themselves outside the city walls are the objects of God's concern and longing. For this reason, the church must seek the Lord prayerfully in evangelism so that believers do not resort to contriving mere carnal methods of reaching out with superficial entertainment and performance. The church has not been called to entertain the lost or fabricate social events to compete with worldly forms of recreation. Evangelism is the process by which the church conveys the gospel message in a compelling and relevant manner to bring others to the saving knowledge and grace of the Lord Jesus Christ, according to God's redemption plan. Leaders must be careful never to use church resources and budgets on outreach events that merely entertain rather than proclaim God's message. The church is reminded in Scripture that flesh gives birth to flesh and Spirit gives birth to Spirit, so leaders in the body of Christ must assure themselves to be led by God's Spirit and wisdom each time they participate in fishing for the lost. If evangelism methods fail to produce repentance in the hearts of those being reached, then the church must change direction and begin to seek fruits of repentance as evidence that they are on the right track. The church has not been called to entertain the masses but to proclaim the gospel.

Various evangelistic functions and outreach events have little promise of truly winning souls if the message of the gospel is watered down and looks more like a worldly concert or skating exhibition. The church needs to proclaim skillfully and proficiently the gospel message that all must turn and repent so they might have everlasting life. As the church begins to proclaim God's salvation plan, the lost must clearly understand that it is not a suggestion for man to repent but a commandment of God.

When God's people become apathetic regarding the work of evangelism, a major aspect of the church's vitality and growth is closed down. Unfortunately, for many congregations, the joy of newborn babes is just a thing of the past; it is no longer experienced. Sterility and barrenness in the church fellowship are a curse, and God has not given these as a promise to His church. The promise of God is that His people would be a fruitful vine with much offspring.

The process of birthing new babes into the kingdom of God brings renewed exhilaration and excitement into the church family. As believers bring souls to Christ, each person who attains a born-again experience becomes the renewed strength and hope of the whole spiritual family. God desires to have many sons and daughters come into glory, and the church has been entrusted with this awesome task of reaching a lost world.

The apostle Paul recognized that, once reconciled with God by Jesus Christ, it is the church that is given the work of reconciling all men back to God:

> And all things are of God, who hath reconciled us to himself by Jesus Christ, and hath given to us the ministry of reconciliation... that God was in Christ, reconciling the world unto himself, not imputing their trespasses unto them; and hath committed unto us the word of reconciliation.
>
> —2 Corinthians 5:18–19

The ministry of reconciliation involves bringing the whole world back unto God, and this daunting task has been committed to the church. While many churches pray and fast so that God might save the world, God in turn has entrusted that project to the church. The broken Fish Gate is apparent when the church pews are embarrassingly vacant and starving for fresh, new believers. As worldly factions continue to bait their hooks to fish for the souls of the men, women, and children of this generation, the church has become ill suited to cast its nets to a hurting world. The repairing of the Fish Gate teaches the body of Christ the importance of having fresh bait as part of their fishing tackle, so that all can come and quench their hunger with the relevance of the gospel message.

The Fish Gate requires the church to begin shaping all efforts for the promulgation of the gospel. Since the beginning of time, godly men and women were able to keep a fresh perspective to reach their own generation. Today, the church has rendered itself unable to cast its nets into the vast oceans of humanity that are lost without hope and without God to recover the precious lives that are still awaiting the incredible experience of God's forgiveness.

Many within the body of Christ today live in total disregard of the truth that stands behind the Fish Gate. So many churches have grown more and more distant from God and have forgotten that God stands as a broken father who longs for the prompt return home of all His wayward children. As a true father, God faithfully awaits the return of His prodigal children so that He can totally restore their eternal fellowship with Him through Christ. Few events can bring greater joy to a father like the repentance and return of a lost child.

The Gospel of Luke chapter 15 reveals a compelling demonstration of God's compassionate heart toward the lost. In this parable of the prodigal son, Jesus offers a stark contradiction to the sectarian, self-righteous religious systems of man that portray God as an angry and unforgiving tyrant. Apparently, the spiritual leaders in Jerusalem lost sight of and were totally unacquainted with the extent of God's mercy and love. Those at the forefront of spiritual climates should never allow the love of God, as an everlasting and eternal Father, to be suppressed or hidden behind the cloaks of religious zeal. We have no right to conceal the loving nature and heart of God from those who are farthest away. It is our responsibility, as the church, to represent accurately God's heart. We are to establish among God's people a spiritual climate that welcomes restoration, reconciliation, and redemption.

A close examination of this parable will reveal God's compassionate heart as a father who truly longs for the warm embrace and safe return of those who yet remain distant and lost. The father's countenance is never spiteful nor does he portray any critical, judgmental, or angry retaliation to vindicate his son's prodigal living. On the contrary, the father saw him while he was yet a great distance away and compassionately ran toward his lost son to embrace and kiss him with a welcome that was emotionally charged:

And he arose, and came to his father. But when he was yet a great way off, his father saw him, and had compassion, and ran, and fell on his neck, and kissed him.

—LUKE 15:20

This Biblical account shows us a vivid portrait of God's true sentiment toward those homeward bound. The father quickly runs toward this unworthy and lost son with great anticipation to welcome his safe return. The father's eagerness to forgive his son is seen by his prompt willingness to throw a party and celebrate his son's long-awaited return. This incredible reception displays the father's desire to restore his son's full honor and dignity. The jubilant manner in which this repented prodigal is received is consistent with God's heart concerning sinners who return to the Father. The father's orders to prepare the fatted calf in this passage correlate with the festivities and excitement felt in heaven by our heavenly Father as each sinner returns, seeking repentance before God. The angels of God in heaven likewise prepare a gourmet banquet each time a sinner repents and turns back toward heaven. Both of the following verses precede Jesus' parable of the prodigal son.

I say unto you, that likewise joy shall be in heaven over one sinner that repenteth, more than over ninety and nine just persons, which need no repentance.

—LUKE 15:7

Likewise, I say unto you, there is joy in the presence of the angels of God over one sinner that repenteth.

—LUKE 15:10

While God's heart toward the lost sinner is shown explicitly in these passages, we need to realize that many churches hold a contrary sentiment. Rather than anticipating the joyful return of the lost sinner, they stand as the prodigal son's older brother. This older brother thought it distasteful to celebrate the cause of his brother's return from fallen grace. He adamantly refused to enter into the home and chose rather to forego any participation with his father's feast in welcoming the prodigal son. The older brother was unable to identify with the father's sentiment and became totally alienated from his lost brother's return. The older brother stayed outside, demanding that his father focus upon his firstborn's personal achievements and accomplishments.

Jesus purposefully added the older brother's anguished resentment in this parable to emphasize the common attitudes of those who often see themselves as more deserving of God's favor. Sadly enough, many in the body of Christ show similar egotistical and eccentric attitudes in the church. God calls the church to lay down their lives for those in need. The continual personal desire for more and more in the body of Christ can lead us to forget the needs of those who remain lost. Many in the body of Christ have forgotten God's heart and choose to focus upon the pleading for more in their own cause.

I believe that restoring the ancient Fish Gate entreats believers to listen for God's heart, which is calling us to reach out, make merry, and be glad for every one of our brothers that were dead and are now alive. The church must be prepared to celebrate the restoration and forgiveness of those who were once lost and are now found. The older brother was caught up in his own world of self-righteous works and did not even realize the legitimate cause for joy.

> Now his elder son was in the field: and as he came and drew nigh to the house, he heard musick and dancing. And he called one of the servants, and asked what these things meant. And he said unto him, Thy brother is come; and thy father hath killed the fatted calf, because he hath received him safe and sound. And he was angry, and would not go in: therefore came his father out, and intreated him.
>
> —LUKE 15:25–28

The older brother's reaction seems so bizarre in light of his father's real sentiment. How the elder brother became so hardened seems very unusual. Normally an older brother would not respond with such angry indignation. His refusal to participate caused the father to go out and plead with him to understand the significance of what was occurring. I believe the restoration at the Fish Gate will also serve to mediate and entreat others within the body of Christ to enter in the house to celebrate the return of all the lost.

Many times the church becomes a place where people are taught to focus on their own virtues and self-righteous merits. This attitude usually causes the church to alienate themselves from God's heart which cries out with true longing for the lost. This parable addresses God's desire that the church begin to pay better attention to those who are returning in godly repentance. Many churches have become blinded by their own personal ambition and self-seeking aspirations that totally prevent them from ministering to those who are making their way back home. A restored Fish Gate stands as a monument that there is much work for the church to accomplish in making room to celebrate and rejoice the return of every lost prodigal son or daughter.

Many times, those who are lost feel rejected or ostracized by the church as unworthy to participate in salvation. When the church postures itself as a self-righteous entity, and is unable to relate with the cause of the brokenhearted and outcast sinner it has failed as a church. As leaders begin to restore the Fish Gate each church must position itself as a lighthouse bringing lost ships into a safe harbor. Every person that is tossed to and fro by the storms of life needs to see the Christian church as a welcoming safe haven that is joyfully expecting and receiving those who need calm. The following words spoken by Jesus must ring out loudly and resonate clearly from every church hall in the world:

> Come unto me, all ye that labour and are heavy laden, and I will give you rest.
>
> —MATTHEW 11:28

> All that the Father giveth me shall come to me; and him that cometh to me I will in no wise cast out.
>
> —JOHN 6:37

> In the last day, that great day of the feast, Jesus stood and cried, saying, If any man thirst, let him come unto me, and drink.
>
> —JOHN 7:37

The Fish Gate stands to assure that every local church renew an authentic heart for the lost. Many times believers suffer in their inability to walk as Jesus walked. One of the most significant accounts relating to God's desire to reach out to the lost is found in the Gospel of John chapter 4, beginning with verse 9. After reading this passage of Scripture, the church will begin to perceive the Fish Gate from a totally new perspective. God's true desire is to seek and save that which is lost.

In no uncertain terms, the Samaritan woman represents a person totally unqualified and unworthy of God's attention and salvation. She is fetching water at the well in the heat of the day, a time when all other women in the community have already gone home. This may indicate her rejection by, or even her excommunication from, the community due to her immoral and wayward lifestyle. The Samaritan woman understood all too well the realities of rejection and was ready to accept more denunciation from Jesus. She thought He would classify her as being unfit and absolutely unworthy of being spoken to by any pious Jew.

> Then saith the woman of Samaria unto him, How is it that thou, being a Jew, askest drink of me, which am a woman of Samaria? for the Jews have no dealings with the Samaritans.
>
> —JOHN 4:9

Seeing that Jesus was a Jew, she quickly voiced her surprise that He would ask her for a drink. Jesus attempted to convey the reality of

God's message to her that salvation is a gift of God given freely to all those who would believe. This Samaritan woman, like many unbelievers, held the preconceived notion that God's forgiveness was too costly and based on one's ability to purchase with righteous living. She did not understand that fellowship with God is free because it has already been paid for with Christ's costly blood.

The gospel of Jesus Christ proclaims the good news that salvation is costly, but that the price has already been paid for through Christ's sacrifice upon the cross of Calvary. The forgiveness of sin is a free gift of God for all who come and believe upon His Son. Jesus continued telling the Samaritan woman that if she knew the gift of God, she would not hesitate in asking for and receiving the living waters of eternal salvation:

> Jesus answered and said unto her, If thou knewest the gift of God, and who it is that saith to thee, Give me to drink; thou wouldest have asked of him, and he would have given thee living water.
>
> —JOHN 4:10

In this remarkable divine appointment Jesus makes it well-known that God intends to make no exception of persons; all are invited to turn to God and quench their thirst through Him. When Jesus reached out to this woman, He was destroying every preconceived social, ethnic, religious, and cultural prejudice that could possibly stand to prevent her from coming to God's grace. The Fish Gate reveals that God's people should remove any partiality, bigotry, or bias that stands in the way of reaching the lost. Socially and religiously, the church tends to discriminate by judging who is worthy or not to come and experience God's forgiveness and salvation.

For every pretense and purpose, the Samaritan woman represented an embarrassment and anathema to respectful, pious Jewish citizens. Her life's past record of having five former husbands, and presently pursuing an adulterous affair, made further for a terrible reputation and rejection in the village community where she lived. The request for water that Jesus sought from this outcast and socially distraught woman went totally against the social and religious norm of His day. Her response indicates total futility and hopelessness, thinking that Jesus would not want to deal with her problems since He had nothing with which to draw water from the deep well:

> The woman saith unto him, Sir, thou hast nothing to draw with, and the well is deep: from whence then hast thou that living water?
>
> —JOHN 4:11

The Samaritan woman's statements indicate a subtle yet deep inner despair of hopelessness over life's problems; she has no answers to address her plight. In other words, she was questioning Jesus' ability to solve her problems. Everything in her life seemed like a huge impossibility, a bottomless pit with no way out.

From the record of this awesome encounter, the church can learn more and more about how to respond as Jesus did. He would never permit anything to interfere with this sinful woman's opportunity to accept the free gift of God. All her problems with sin and the incredible accumulation of years of guilt and wrongdoing were no match for this loving Savior's ability to save. Jesus stood prepared to forgive and erase her entire past, canceling all outstanding debt. No other message deserves a more precise and accurate delivery than the message and reality of God's redemption and forgiveness. Jesus was willing to forego this woman's preconceived errors regarding thoughts of unworthiness and convoluted theological misunderstandings. Jesus did not permit any obstacle or stumbling block to interfere with her capacity to come to God. Jesus continued to say that He is still the answer, and that God is seeking worshipers such as her to enter into fellowship with Him.

> But whosoever drinketh of the water that I shall give him shall
> never thirst; but the water that I shall give him shall be in him
> a well of water springing up into everlasting life.
> —JOHN 4:14

The remainder of this biblical account reveals that the Samaritan woman finally welcomed Jesus' offer and immediately began to reach out to others living in her community. Somehow this woman was finally able to receive the message of God's love, and her decision to receive Christ opened the way for many more people. The Bible confirms that as she returned to the village and testified about Jesus, many men from the village came looking for this Christ to hear more of His message.

The Fish Gate serves to remind the church to reach out and readily welcome others to participate in coming to Christ. Regardless of people's present state, and despite the depth of their sinful condition, God desires all His followers to reach out to the lost. The Fish Gate tells the church that Jesus stands ready, willing, and able to forgive even the "chiefest of sinners." Through Jesus, God has made provision and invites the most unworthy, unfit, and disgraceful men to repent and begin enjoying the fellowship of God's embrace.

The motivation to preach to others will come as a direct result of experiencing God's forgiveness. In Psalm 51, King David acknowledges that upon receiving forgiveness and total restoration, he would then teach sinners and they would convert back to God.

> Restore unto me the joy of thy salvation; and uphold me with
> thy free spirit. Then will I teach transgressors thy ways; and
> sinners shall be converted unto thee.
> —PSALM 51:12–13

Without properly restoring the Fish Gate, a church may continue to project a distorted view of God's message and lead many to think they are unworthy to participate because of their sinful state. Unless the

Fish Gate is restored, those who are presently suffering from rejection, guilt, and condemnation will never understand that God has already made provision for their salvation and forgiveness. The unwelcoming sentiment of many believers must be readdressed in the Christian church. Christians, above all peoples, must recognize that Christ, the Lamb of God, was slain for all to come and receive forgiveness.

Upon repairing the Fish Gate, every church will begin to proclaim with an honest and loud voice that Christ was sent not to condemn the world, but that through Him the world might be saved. For many years, Christians have committed the mistake of preaching and teaching condemnation much louder than their proclamation of God's love and forgiveness through Christ. This error causes sinners to perceive God's condemnation above His forgiveness. This is a travesty because it causes sinners to run *from* God's love instead of running *to* God's love. The message that the church should proclaim with all certainty and clarity is found in the following passage, where God sends His Son not to condemn the world but that the world through Him might be saved:

> For God sent not his Son into the world to condemn the world;
> but that the world through him might be saved.
> —JOHN 3:17

The Bible clearly shows that God intends for every Jew and Gentile from every nation, tribe, and tongue to be saved, and that they are all invited to come to Christ and receive the forgiveness of sin with the assurance of eternal life. When the Fish Gate is restored, the church can begin reaching out to the lost so that Christ can save them regardless of their present state. The Fish Gate tells the whole world that God intends all to come and be saved. The Lord does not discriminate or distinguish people by their physical, racial, ethnic, social, political, religious, doctrinal, denominational, sexual, cultural, financial, or generational state. All can turn to Christ for forgiveness and salvation. The Fish Gate tells the whole world that salvation is extended to the lost and that all can return home to a God who opens the door into His eternal kingdom.

This may seem unrealistic, but the ability to prevail as the church of Jesus Christ against the gates of hell will require the true restoration of the Fish Gate. Anything that would prevent others from coming to Christ's forgiveness must be eliminated so that God's ultimate desire may become a reality. God desires no man to perish but for all to repent and have eternal life. Believers are not called as a church to prevent others from coming into God's city, but to go out into the highways and hedges, and compel them to come in, so that God's house may be filled.

PRAYER APPLICATION

Lord! Help every Christian church restore the Fish Gate by teaching believers that Christ first called us to be "fishers of men." I pray to begin proclaiming the gospel of Jesus Christ so that the message of God's love and forgiveness is able to reach every person under heaven. Lord Jesus, take away all my bias, prejudice, and spiritual pride so that I can begin to reach out to others regardless of their sinful state or condition. I know that You do not desire for any person to perish, but that all should come to repentance and have eternal life. Holy Spirit, fill me so that I can become a bold and effective witness of God's love and truth to all peoples everywhere. From this day forward, I purpose to rebuild the Fish Gate in my church community so that many souls can be won for the kingdom of God.

that are intended to abide without alteration forever.

The Old Gate teaches leaders to discover, define, and preserve God's timeless, unchanging, immutable truths that do not lapse for all eternity. At the Old Gate, the church learns not to despise things only because they are old. The Old Gate gives the church the ability to understand that God intended some things to never change and last forever. There are certain aspects of God's design and creation, particularly in matters involving His church and kingdom, which God intended to always remain.

At the Old Gate, the local church is to witness how God intended to preserve a reflection of His immutable counsel and boundaries toward those things that are everlasting. God intended to offer all believers a confirmation and a complete illustration of the essential, irreplaceable truths that are the foundations of the Christian faith.

Many church leaders love to get rid of old things in order to usher in new, innovative things. These leaders may have a serious problem with the truth behind the Old Gate. At the Old Gate, church leaders should learn not to be quick to throw out or despise something as worthless just because it has been around for a long time.

As God's people, the church is obligated to discover and define those divine truths and kingdom principles that have existed since the beginning of time. God desires His eternal truths never to be moved or replaced by anything new. Church leaders must make sure that the immutable things of God keep their rightful place. Whether in a family, a local church, or a community, Christians need to understand that God has determined that certain things need to remain unshakable.

The old adage "different strokes for different folks" is not true at the Old Gate. At the Old Gate, every believer conforms to the ancient truths that always need to be present in the lives of everyone—those of yesteryear, those alive today, and those who will be living one thousand years from now. The reparations of the Old Gate require the church to begin acquiring and learning those truths that are to never change.

As reparations of the Old Gate move forward, the church must seek to discern the heart of God as spoken through His prophets.

Throughout Scripture, the people of God are instructed repeatedly to seek and walk upon the old paths where the good ways will provide pleasant rest for their souls:

> Thus says the LORD: "Stand in the ways and see, And ask for the old paths, where the good way is, And walk in it; Then you will find rest for your souls.
> —JEREMIAH 6:16, NKJV

God's instruction for the reparation of the Old Gate is to stand out in the middle of the ways and ask for the ancient paths—where the good way is. When this path is found, the church will find the refreshing oasis for their souls. The Word of God provides the answers for the weary soul. The mystery behind a rested soul is solved by asking and finding the ancient and old paths. The church needs to seek those foundational truths that are embedded in God's character that will never change but remain steadfast for believers to embrace each and every day.

Many may attest that the Christian church has suffered much loss from its inability to keep up with the times. However, there is far more evidence of destruction in the church's membership due to the church's inability to hold firmly to the old paths. In today's churches, part of the problem in restoring the Old Gate is that few are seeking for the ancient paths. The old paths that are intended to preserve the church from generation to generation are obscure or totally hidden. On the other hand, most church members have hastened with swift agility to trample underfoot those truths that have been firmly established from generation to generation.

The Old Gate is broken in every local church that exchanges biblical truth for modern replacements that burden the souls of believers with fanfare and elaborate religious demonstrations. When the church truly repairs the Old Gate, they will begin to seek and hold on to the ancient paths that bring peace to believers' hearts. Every assembly that gathers must begin to seek God in prayer, asking for a stronger leadership that is willing to lead believers in seeking the ancient paths and holding on to the old truths of God's Word.

The ancient principles of God's wisdom are like precious jewels that adorn the church with imperishable splendor and glory. As believers learn to embrace the ancient paths of God's instruction, they will enjoy rest from vain religious practice. The church must cease embracing newly found hopes in superficial half-truths that have no substance or weight of authority. Believers need answers that have stood the test of time in order to deal with the anxieties of our modern culture.

The contemporary church has suffered the effects of replacing the Old Gate with a new and improved Modern Gate. Even among the youth, the church has allowed the Old Gate principles of chaste abstinence and godly courtship to be redefined by "new and improved" dating concepts. The modern church has replaced God's truth with modern dating schemes. Many modern church leaders justify their actions by asserting modern ways of thinking. Many say, "We live in a new age, and today's young Christians need to be more in tune with the tolerance of modern culture to see if our children are compatible with each other. We can't continue forcing our children into antiquated concepts such as virginity until marriage."

Today the world is seeing that the ancient path of abstinence has become the road less traveled by Christian youth in the Christian church. This is the reason that the church's divorce rate is no different from the secular world. There is no longer peace and rest to the souls of our married couples in the Christian church who have forsaken the old paths of abstinence. When I first became a Christian and heard the ancient paths as found in Scripture regarding abstinence, I thought, *This is out of this world. This cannot be for today.* After a short while, I learned the fear of the Lord and decided to take that ancient path of abstinence until marriage. I can attest that not having premarital relations with my betrothed truly allowed me to find rest for my soul. The rest bestowed upon a Christian marriage by abiding within the boundaries of this God-honoring ancient truth allows Christian offspring to enjoy peace in their homes through a closely knit family unit.

Many ancient truths allow the believer to lay solid foundations in building their lives. The Christian family and church can use ancient boundaries to build up safe family structures that will endure adversity and conflict. Regardless of what the modern culture offers, the church needs to advocate on behalf of those ancient ways of life that were set by godly men long ago—those boundaries and landmarks that God has given to the church to safeguard its people from the erosions of modern times. God promised His people that if they learn to walk in those ancient paths, He will guarantee their rest from the ordinary toils and burdens that befall others. As children of a holy and royal line, we must learn to hold fast and embrace the confines of godly instruction for all time.

While the church begins to rejoice in a God that makes all things new, they must understand that there are specific truths that have no variation or shadow of turning. God truly intends to keep certain things unmodified and unaltered that are established from the beginning of the world. As God's people, the church is instructed to earnestly seek and ask for the ancient paths that are good. The Old Gate instructs every generation, from great-grandfathers to great-grandchildren, to find and discern those truths that are to be passed down from generation to generation.

Leaders must not allow a new generation to despise and trample the precious morsels of a previous generation. The voice heard in today's Christian youth rallies are as follows: "I'm not doing what great-grandpa the preacher did!" There is great blessing and favor upon the church's forefathers due to their faithfulness. Today's leaders must admonish their youth not to depart from yesterday's counsel, but to follow closely the godly counsel of old. The blessings that were given by church founders and forefathers should continue to be passed down from one generation to the next.

The restoring of the Old Gate allows the church to see the old biblical truths as blessings. These truths must never be altered to take a new form or a more innovative design. Any desire to alter or replace God's timeless truths will only serve to destroy the Christian heritage. The inheritance that God has laid up for His children is steadfast and unchanging. Any attempt to modify or adjust the Christian life or walk would otherwise contaminate and severely pollute the enduring and lasting truths that are much too significant. The following verse in the Gospel of Matthew shows one aspect of what God has left for all posterity:

> Heaven and earth shall pass away, but my words shall not pass away.
>
> —MATTHEW 24:35

The supporters of a more modern Christianity desire to renovate the gospel to reflect a newer trend in line with today's immoral climate. These modern marvels state that the Bible has become unreliable because it is much too old. These wayward modern activists desire to throw out the Bible because they think the writings have become much too antiquated for their style. Their preference is to alter God's Word and make it fit a more contemporary audience.

This erroneous request for updated versions of God's Word has very sinister motives. Like a stream that erodes a riverbank, the wickedness of these people desires to water down the force and strength of God's Word inch by inch to accommodate their sinful desires. What a travesty to water down the Bible and reduce each epistle by removing the instructions that address the ills of a degenerate and immoral modern culture. Those who are prone to modify God's truth by substituting modern philosophical and contemporary dissertation will obliterate the Old Gate. At the Old Gate believers learn and come away with an understanding that Christ, the Word made flesh, is the same yesterday, today, and forever (see Heb. 13:8). There is "no variableness, neither shadow of turning" of His ways or of His wisdom (James 1:17).

Time and again, God admonishes with strong words of rebuke the people who desire to reject or stumble out of His ancient paths:

> And they said, "That is hopeless! So we will walk according to our own plans, and we will every one obey the dictates of his

evil heart." Therefore thus says the LORD: "Ask now among the Gentiles, Who has heard such things? The virgin of Israel has done a very horrible thing. Will a man leave the snow water of Lebanon, Which comes from the rock of the field? Will the cold flowing waters be forsaken for strange waters? "Because My people have forgotten Me, They have burned incense to worthless idols. And they have caused themselves to stumble in their ways, From the ancient paths, To walk in pathways and not on a highway, To make their land desolate and a per-petual hissing; Everyone who passes by it will be astonished And shake his head. I will scatter them as with an east wind before the enemy; I will show them the back and not the face In the day of their calamity."

—JEREMIAH 18:12–17, NKJV

God expects His people to stay the course and continue traveling the path prepared and established as a highway for the church. No church member should stumble in their ways or fall away from God's ancient paths, unless they desire God's rejection and ultimately find themselves in an embarrassing wilderness before all to witness.

The restoration of God's local church must include believers' earnest efforts to find God's ways and wholeheartedly embrace these ancient paths. Every ancient truth is a hallmark that brings the blessings and favor of God upon the Christian's life. There are certain ways of living that carry God's promised protection and provision to keep all His children from evil. These ancient promises carry sufficient power to visit each generation with God's continued blessing and favor. The Bible promises God's faithfulness for a thousand generations to those who keep and love His ways:

Know therefore that the LORD thy God, he is God, the faithful God, which keepeth covenant and mercy with them that love him and keep his commandments to a thousand generations.

—DEUTERONOMY 7:9

For many, maintaining themselves on ancient routes is a difficult process. In order to prevent continual loss and destruction believers must make efforts to seek and safeguard ancient pathways. The adversary knows how to plunder God's people by leading them away from God's firmly established order and well-grounded eternal truths. When a church forsakes the rebuilding of the Old Gate and rejects the ancient ways of God, they stand to inherit utter chaos and confusion. Church leaders must teach their students that the ways of God exist, are proven, and are relevant for all generations to embrace and welcome. An old proverb states wisely, "That which is true is not new because it has been under the sun far too long and has proven and shown its veracity."

With each new generation that passes, pastors continue to witness a heartbreaking trend: the exodus of Christians from the ancient paths of the Lord. When Christian leaders fail to restore the Old Gate, young believers begin to consider the Bible irrelevant and seek to resolve contemporary problems with any new form of religious practice such as New Age, yoga, or Wicca. This amazing exchange from Christ to false religions has become North America's favorite pastime. The church has suffered greatly in North America because of Christian leaders who have failed to minister God's ancient truths in a relevant and powerful manner. False religions continue to seduce many Christians to exchange biblically based truths for new teachings that are contrary to God's Word. Any spiritual teaching that encourages a Christian to cover up ancient pathways and forsake the old boundaries that are established in God's Word should be immediately discarded.

The generation of the sixties was the most hostile and defiant generation, setting new records in the removal of the ancient boundaries. That generation decided to experiment and rebel by diving in to new forms of love and peace. They paved new roads of free sex and psychedelic drugs that only caused more confusion and destruction, ruining lives with each boundary that was moved. This hippie generation did more to destroy future generations by removing ancient boundaries and challenging the establishment that kept us for so many generations. They forsook many divine parameters that were laid out by God for our protection. By foolishly sowing rebellion in every form of the establishment, the sixties culture created a harvest of corrupt fruit that lives on to this day in the Christian church.

The sixties' hippie movement is characterized by rebellion, rejection, and repugnance for any semblance of order or uniformity, especially for anything old or before their time. This apparent disgust and rebellion for established pathways has been deeply embedded in every form of our modern daily expression. There is a steadfast mockery of whatever lasts too long, almost as if the world cannot sincerely expect for things to last.

God's Word has stern admonitions that God's people are not to remove ancient landmarks set by our fathers:

> Do not remove the ancient landmark, Nor enter the fields of the fatherless.
>
> —PROVERBS 23:10, NKJV

> Do not remove the ancient landmark Which your fathers have set.
>
> —PROVERBS 22:28, NKJV

This should not be difficult to understand. Do not remove those landmarks or borders that have been set from old by your fathers. Upon restoring the Old Gate, the church will begin to experience the blessings of honoring, respecting, and adhering to those ancient landmarks by giving deference to the boundaries set by holy men of long ago. This principle of honoring ancient boundaries can restore the inheritance laid up for those who fear the Lord. By preserving the clear demarcations of godly instruction and principles, believers are essentially receiving the breadth of our blessing and inheritance as God intended for His people.

In Deuteronomy 19, clear instruction is given that God's people are not to remove certain landmarks that men of old have set for inheritance purposes:

> You shall not remove your neighbor's landmark, which the men of old have set, in your inheritance which you will inherit in the land that the LORD your God is giving you to possess.
> —DEUTERONOMY 19:14, NKJV

What are these ancient landmarks? Where can the next generation see these well-defined places in the church? Does the church offer clearly defined boundaries that preserve the inheritance of a good land that swells with milk and honey? Or have modern church leaders provided poorly lit boundaries and ill-defined demarcations, filled with confusion, drought, and withered desolation? How will tomorrow's Christian believer know what marks to follow and what limits to place in their unfettered paths? Will this generation leave clearly marked indications of God's ancient paths so that the following generation might inherit the blessings that were intended by God? The leaders who have enough courage to restore the Old Gate will soon hear the following words out of the mouths of every member in their church:

> The lines have fallen to me in pleasant places; Yes, I have a good inheritance.
> —PSALM 16:6, NKJV

God wants to make sure that no one is deprived of their God-given inheritance. But there is much more depth that goes into understanding these divine proclamations of truths in order to prevent us from forsaking our spiritual inheritance.

The restoration of the Old Gate involves learning not to reduce, increase, alter, modify, or change the limits of the boundaries set by God in His infinite wisdom. Every single boundary is set by God and can be found in His Word. As a legacy that passes down from generation to generation, the church needs to safely guard our precious spiritual inheritance and possessions.

The church should yearn for the deep presence of God's ancient truth. Leaders should set the foundations of that which is pure, undefiled, and true. Many times, church members desire to replace quickly the solid and unmovable for that which is emotional and shallow. The church leaders should resist modern, carnal antics that replace the character of a holy God for the giftedness of unstable men. In the name of convenience, too many Christian leaders have followed the way of the world and become a generation that has exchanged the solid nourishing foods of our God for synthetic fast foods that fail to sustain and nourish a healthy spiritual life. Many are unwilling to take their seat at the Lord's table and feast on true spiritual food. The present-day spiritual diet of an average believer is something more akin to eating processed chicken nuggets, which many feast on and consider a good meal. These by-products provide poor nutrition to the body, and yet many believers are willing to pay the price.

When believers exchange their old ways for modern ways, they run the risk of losing their inheritance and the peace that God intended for their afflicted souls. If the Old Gate is not fully restored, the church will continue to be plundered and its membership will continue suffering from deception and the loss of the many blessings God has ordained.

The modern culture in which the church presently exists automatically presumes that anything old is no good and requires immediate replacement solely because of its age. The church has not trained believers to reflect and consider whether or not it remains useful or beneficial. At once the believer thinks, "Is it old?" If the answer is yes, then out it goes! If leaders are not careful, they might find themselves despising and disposing of many great treasures of God's truths that are intended to shower the church with rich blessings. Church leaders must understand that certain old truths must be restored and preserved so that the enemy can no longer access their loved ones or possessions.

When the church restores the Old Gate, believers will begin to embrace the ancient ways of an all-knowing, almighty, omnipotent, and everlasting God. The church cannot expect God's blessings to come when they continually show reluctance to preserve and walk in His ways. While the church demands blessing and prosperity, they must realize that the promise of blessing will come in the degree that they are willing to meditate upon and obey God's Word.

We cannot expect to see God's favor and blessing until we stop pursuing selfish desires that run contrary to God's ways. The church needs to acknowledge that God's design is best and their journey will prosper if they purpose to seek and keep alive divine truths with accurate precision and perseverance. Restoring the Old Gate requires an honest admission and acknowledgment that God was faithful to carefully set borders and boundaries to protect and prosper His people.

The Old Gate reminds the church that God has set limits and restrictions that are good. The purpose of these boundaries is to shape Christians in the way God designed them to live for their own benefit. When this generation begins to lift up Jesus and His standards, all men will be drawn to God. The church will no longer be scorned into disrepute, but all will see that God's design is best.

Certainly, God has laid out the parameters He intended for the church to keep and to abide in. In order to attain an abundant life in Christ, the church must uphold these divine, ancient boundaries and not disregard them as outdated.

All of God's creation gives evidence that within His divine design all things are a blessing. Likewise, outside of this order every created thing can only expect chaos and confusion. Scientists have stated that if the sun were to move just one degree closer to the earth, the earth and all its inhabitants would burn. If the sun were to rebel against God's ordained placement, as many believers have decided to rebel, the end result would be destruction. In the same manner, within God's design believers can begin to enjoy that which is within God's ordained goodness. Moving away from those ancient boundaries will cause destruction. The constant chaos and confusion experienced by many believers today is caused by severe rebellion of God's instruction and divine placement.

From the beginning of man's existence, God has constantly warned His people to preserve His boundaries without adding or taking any away. God's ways are perfect and anyone who alters them will be in danger of inheriting all the plagues and curses found in the Bible:

If any man shall add unto these things, God shall add unto him the plagues that are written in this book: And if any man shall take away from the words of the book of this prophecy, God shall take away his part out of the book of life, and out of the holy city, and from the things which are written in this book.
—REVELATION 22:18–19

It is a very serious offense to interfere with the limits and boundaries of God's instruction. The Lord has ordained very accurate instruction to preserve our existence upon the earth, and He has given His Word with the very purpose to bless and keep His church. Listing every single ancient truth and boundary would be too much to include in this book, for that God has given us the Bible. All the dilemmas facing mankind can be resolved by seeking God's Word. It is sufficient for now to note that the old pathways and ancient boundaries of truth do exist in God's Word and the church must pursue them with all deliberate passion. The church has a duty to follow these ancient paths and inform others that God's ways are perfect and His design is everlasting. This generation of church leaders should not continue to despise godly instruction given to them through God's faithfulness and mercy.

Occasionally some rise up and desire to replace godly boundaries by saying something to the effect of, "You know this thing has been set here for too long; let's change it." These simpletons think they can change what God has already established. They come with all manner of manipulation using smoke, mirrors, whistles, and horns to shake things up at every opportunity to force new concepts, adjustments, and standards exchanging the Old Gate with a contemporary edition. To this the church must respond, "Thank you very much, but leave the Old Gate where it is." The church's obligation is to inform these "grand innovators" that the church does not need any novelties; those who have restored the Old Gate are content with the time-honored truths of God's Word.

The church must render their worship to the Ancient of Days. They are determined by the grace of God to keep His ways and resist anyone who might attempt to force upon them any modern concepts that preclude God's divine grace. Many times these "ground-breaking prophets" will appear under the guise of progress or improvement, and try to exchange the historical, proven landmarks for new fads and fashions in serving the Lord.

For several generations people have justified departing from ancient, godly truths by saying that the church needs to be more culturally sensitive and tolerant. Secular proponents advise the church to walk in the light of social science and empirical evidence to better understand the needs of the Christian believer. Many falsely suggest that God's Word is obsolete and impractical in modern culture.

When the Old Gate is restored in the church, the believers will understand that the body of Christ is better served by walking in the light of God's ancient counsel rather than in the dimly lit vision of modern morality. New theories that focus on man's basic needs as grounds for establishing truth only serve to diminish godly standards of decency and order. Regardless of the many modern technologies that entice unbelievers, the Christian church must guard against any invitation to replace tried and true principles of godly behavior and conduct.

In these modern times, church leaders have chosen to ignore the Holy Spirit's conviction and cater to the present-day cultural philosophy of social tolerance. Evangelism has turned into a marketing scheme of filling so-called "seeker-friendly" churches that have most often chosen not to confront or address sin or anything else that is remotely controversial in the lives of their followers. The modern church has sold its birthright by agreeing not to speak on any topic that addresses sin or denying of one's self. By allowing the church to fill up with secular humanism and worldly concepts, today's church leaders have turned the house of God into social clubs and fellowship halls that resemble more of what the world has to offer. The church should reflect much more than a wholesome gathering of good people. Every church should stand as an entity of God-fearing believers preparing to hear God's voice and give Jesus their best for His.

There was a time when the presence of God and His eternal Word were sufficient to further the work of God's kingdom. Why do church leaders prefer to appease the appetites of human sensationalism thereby structuring their church programs, instead of serving the heart of God? Church leaders must begin to acknowledge that God has given them a far better selection of divine wisdom to impart, which has been around since the beginning of time.

How does social science and humanistic (man-centered) philosophy affect the church, other than to breed real problems? What can human wit give to those who have been endowed with the Spirit of truth and grace? The promise of God that truth can set the believer free has been replaced by another gospel, which measures success by running after the newest fad of this world, asking what are the ultimate fashions, performances, or styles?

The church's progress should be furthered in the knowledge of Christ. Every believer should have a deeper understanding of what Christ intended to leave them. Their daily Christian walk should not be determined or measured by the latest styles or fashions, because these will only serve to hinder the task of building the kingdom of God.

The Old Gate is the place where believers learn to embrace the Ancient of Days and preserve His timeless words. The only assurance of overcoming the evil of this day is by equipping the saints with the sound doctrine found in God's unchanging Word. As long as the church continues to falter before the continual accusation of modern culture, we have no hope to overcome.

Church leaders must stop adhering to the false charge that the Christian church has failed to keep up with the times. Christian churches that give in to this godless chatter will never prevail as a fortified city. Christian believers must cease to feel guilty and embarrassed for holding on to "yesterday's truth." The Christian church should be known as the body that preserves truth, rather than the group that destroys the foundations set by a mighty God. Church leaders should wholeheartedly embrace the task of promoting and strongly advocating for God's truth regardless of the fact that it is ancient wisdom.

The Old Gate confirms that foundational truths, when accurately preserved and established, render the church undefeatable. Every church that sells its birthright for modern morsels will be rendered defenseless and unable to contend against those who seek its destruction. To give up the foundations will cause the church to walk in darkness like those who despise God's Word. When the foundations are gone, the church stands to lose insight, perspective, and understanding, thus ultimately walking in utter darkness.

> They know not, neither will they understand; they walk on in darkness: all the foundations of the earth are out of course.
> —PSALM 82:5

The Old Gate is our only hope to push back darkness because this gate was designed to show the world that apart from God's eternal truth the church can do nothing. Apart from God, the church has nothing. Without Him, nothing beneficial for the cause of Christ can happen. In Him we live; in Him we move; and in Him we have our being. Christ is our portion, He is our cup, and He is our inheritance—He is our everything.

The church must not concern itself with the latest methodology or postmodern practice. As the winds of modern doctrines blow, threatening to disrupt everything from Sunday school programs to church growth methods, the church may consider it a great blessing to stand with a solid, unmovable foundation in the midst of quickly evolving contemporary times. Nonetheless, regardless of the church's ability to grasp new styles and restructure modern formats of worship, Christian believers must place a renewed, heightened emphasis on those things that anchor our faith and ground us in God's unchanging truth.

The body of Christ often sees the frenzy of new ideas as a twenty-first century phenomenon. The Bible gives stark historical evidence that the church has always protected and preserved God's time-tested truths against insurgents who prefer to embrace the latest and most recent notions. The Bible recounts the custom of certain Greek philosophers who loved to sit around and contemplate all that was new. Many Christians today can be characterized in this light:

> And they took him and brought him to the Areopagus, saying, "May we know what this new doctrine is of which you speak? For you are bringing some strange things to our ears. Therefore we want to know what these things mean." For all the Athenians and the foreigners who were there spent their time in nothing else but either to tell or to hear some new thing.
>
> —ACTS 17:19–21, NKJV

Modern Christian philosophers and foreigners may ask themselves, *What's new in Christianity today? What is the latest fad and most up-to-date move of God's Spirit?* Fresh new teachings and the latest revelations can be of great use and show spectacular promise, but the church should not forget to ground themselves in Christ and the ancient truths provided in God's Word. Pundits of modern mania should realize that time-tested treasure is better than the hopeful desire of newly found nuggets.

The church should walk in sound wisdom by recognizing that while the world is seeking something new, God has given each believer the insight to know what Solomon learned a long time ago:

> The thing that hath been, it is that which shall be; and that which is done is that which shall be done: and there is no new thing under the sun.
>
> —ECCLESIASTES 1:9

Every Christian should resist new movements that promise the latest and the greatest. The Bible warns that the last days will be characterized by people following after the new trend and the latest truths. This modern mania is going to lead to the deception of many Christians that have been trained mentally to follow after the latest teaching and doctrine. The Bible says that in the last days, many will be enticed by people saying, "Run here and run there after the latest anointing and teaching":

Then if anyone says to you, "Look, here is the Christ!" or, "Look, He is there!" do not believe it.

—MARK 13:21, NKJV

The church needs to realize that God's provision has been here since the beginning of time. God's truths are in the foundation of what has always been. Believers should not be moved to despise the sound teaching of old. The apostle Paul forewarns his young disciple Timothy to be careful because the time would come when some would no longer endure sound doctrine and begin turning their ears from truth to follow after fables:

> For the time will come when they will not endure sound doctrine; but after their own lusts shall they heap to themselves teachers, having itching ears; And they shall turn away their ears from the truth, and shall be turned unto fables.
>
> —2 TIMOTHY 4:3–4

The time has come where this passage of Scripture has been fulfilled many times over. Many church pastors have succumbed to the whim of those who no longer endure sound doctrine. Everything but the Word of God is being preached from Christian pulpits around the world. Today, the majority of young girls would rather forsake the biblical instruction to seek godly counsel from older Christian women. Instead, young Christian girls seek advice from other immature peers who are following after unwise choices. The older women have more to offer by way of counsel, according to time-tested practices that carry much more weight of wisdom. Young girls deciding to follow biblical counsel would walk away with untold riches and priceless treasure. If young girls would purpose to spend one afternoon learning the counsel and advice from older women, they would avoid many dreadful tears and heartaches.

Even young men would benefit if they sat with someone with a little gray hair every now and then. They would do well to sit and learn from the wisdom of their elders. Many of the problems in the body of Christ would be avoided if Christians were willing to obey Scripture and spend some time with the elderly, cherishing and honoring them. Young people today would save themselves a lot of trouble if they would do this.

There is ancient wisdom, ancient purity, and ancient holiness that the church can tap into and find boundless provisions of God's glory. There is no replacement for absolute obedience to the counsel of long ago. At the Old Gate, there is character and faithfulness that will never change regardless of our most fascinating fantasies of progress. As church leaders continue to progress toward maturity, they must seek the new outpouring of God's provision, but never despise or undermine what they have already received and has been established from long ago. Each day God promises new mercies to His people, but never did He intend for the church to replace the irreplaceable.

When Paul wrote to Timothy in 2 Timothy 3:1–14, he warned Timothy to know that the last days would be dangerous because men would be lovers of themselves, embracing all sorts of wrong attitudes and behavior. In the midst of these perilous times, Paul advises Timothy to be steadfast and unmoved. Paul was reminding Timothy to continue in what was well established and taught in the Word of God. These instructions came to warn Timothy that as time continued, the body of Christ would face horrible imposters and men whose wickedness would increase toward every form of evil:

> But evil men and seducers shall wax worse and worse, deceiving, and being deceived.
>
> —2 TIMOTHY 3:13

The reason many will be deceived is because men will take on the appearance of godliness. An imposter is someone who is fake, but looks like the real thing. In these verses, Paul told his young apprentice that the solution to this counterfeit dilemma was to remain steadfast and continue in the things that he already knew to be clearly established in God's Word:

> But you must continue in the things which you have learned
> and been assured of, knowing from whom you have learned
> them, and that from childhood you have known the Holy
> Scriptures, which are able to make you wise for salvation
> through faith which is in Christ Jesus.
> —2 TIMOTHY 3:14–15, NKJV

These words were written to clearly warn the church that those who will be safeguarded in the last days will be those who repair the Old Gate by digging their heels into God's Word and continuing to walk steadfastly without wavering to the right or to the left. As each church restores the Old Gate, they shall cease to be tossed to and fro by every wind of doctrine and slight of men, who with cunning craftiness lie in wait to deceive those willing to follow their folly.

With each new day, believers will be exposed more and more to the latest trends and fads within the Christian faith. For this reason the church must do all it can to stand on the truth of God's Word to continue extending the same legacy to the next generation. Above all else, church members need to establish themselves in God's timeless truths more than anything new and modern. The church does not need to continue seeking that which is impressive, because that will not keep believers in the day of their tribulation. Instead of letting these words fall on deaf ears or hardened hearts, the church must begin to pray to restore the Old Gate.

PRAYER APPLICATION

God, help the Christian church to restore the Old Gate. I pray that every church begins to value the ancient truths of Your Word and instruction so that every life, family, and group will begin to reflect the wisdom of Your timeless truth. Lord, instruct us in the ways of old, let the church stand, see, and ask for the old paths where the good way is for their life. Jesus, I purpose to transform the way I think. I want to change my mind, change my heart, and change my will so I can finally conform to Your image. From this day forward, I will usher in what You have established of old for me.

4

THE VALLEY GATE

And there came a man of God, and spake unto the king of Israel, and said, Thus saith the LORD, Because the Syrians have said, The LORD is God of the hills, but he is not God of the valleys, therefore will I deliver all this great multitude into thine hand, and ye shall know that I am the LORD.

—1 KINGS 20:28

This chapter focuses on restoring the Valley Gate. Here the church learns to follow God wherever He will lead, even if that means through sufferings and trials. The Valley Gate is the place where every believer can count suffering as joy, especially when they fall into various trials, knowing that the testing of their faith produces patience.

The Valley Gate symbolizes to the church that God never fails, even though believers experience all kinds of trials and adversities. Restoring the Valley Gate involves the church teaching believers to continue to trust God during these times of trials and tribulations. The church must embrace suffering and not run from it. God has chosen valleys to be the hidden pathways to blessing and increase. Every believer must know that God designed valleys of suffering and tears to help bring depth and maturity into the body of Christ.

Many churches promise their believers only mountaintop experiences and prosperity, but fail to prepare Christians for the valleys of life. Restoring the Valley Gate includes showing the church how they stand to inherit vast riches and glory if they learn to trust God as He perfects them through the valley of affliction. As we restore the Valley Gate, the church can begin to trust God as He leads them through needed valleys of adversity. If the Valley Gate remains broken in the church, Christians will continue to react in immature, superficial, uncommitted, and confused manners that will lead others to question and doubt God's faithfulness.

A broken Valley Gate is evident when Christians falter and stumble when they experience hardship and trials. Instead of enduring these valleys as God's perfect plan to the next mountaintop victory, many Christians seek after a pain-free existence, thus forsaking their walk with God and pursuing other avenues. The problem with despising the valley is that it is God's design for perfecting the saints.

The fourth gate to be mentioned in Nehemiah's restoration effort was the Valley Gate:

> Hanun and the inhabitants of Zanoah repaired the Valley Gate. They built it, hung its doors with its bolts and bars, and repaired a thousand cubits of the wall as far as the Refuse Gate.
>
> —NEHEMIAH 3:13, NKJV

Without a Valley Gate, the Refuse Gate need not exist. This is because it is in the valley where all the garbage for the Refuse Gate surfaces and is exposed. During times of testing and trials, God is able to reveal and dispose of that which hinders our Christian walk.

With all the present-day aberrations taught in Christian circles, the church needs to work on restoring the Valley Gate so that it is in good working order. The Valley Gate is where believers see that God is able to take them through the valleys of their Christian walk to determine what is truly in their heart. The Valley Gate reminds God's people that problems and trials merely reveal our true character. During times of great difficulties and affliction, that which is in man comes out as soon as the believer hits the Valley Gate trail.

Here is a short anecdote for each believer to meditate upon:

> One day, they are walking along and they are happy and have no problems. Then, God allows them to experience a bump in the road. This bump makes their inward character spill out. Their inward character was not produced by the bump. Their inward character was already there—the bump simply revealed and surfaced the substance. Maybe they had the notion that their insides were created by their problems. But it is not so—what is inside, and the problems that God allows to bump against them, only manifest their true character, and many times our true character is awfully embarrassing.

The Lord knows that each believer needs to deal with the things that exist in our innermost being. The Valley Gate is the best place to show Christians what has really developed inside. Living the mountaintop experiences is no doubt exciting, but the mountaintops are seldom good and fertile ground to produce a godly harvest. Usually a valley is more fertile for producing a fruitful harvest. The Valley Gate tells the church to brace itself for brokenness and to understand that downward spirals in life are where God allows the believer to flourish in His power. The Christian leader must discern that valleys are the appropriate place for believers to find fertile soil for their lives. With the fertile ground of God's valleys, the church is able to replenish their storehouses with abundant grace.

God has made the valleys in our lives indispensable because they provide opportunities for growth and maturity. The Christian journey has no better setting to develop and grow godly fruit than the fertile valleys in God's design. Farmers rarely cultivate their harvest or fruit trees at the top of a mountain. Most of the succulent fruit crops grow in the valley. That is where Christians can stand to harvest the fruits that bring the most pleasure to God's heart. When believers fail to repair the Valley Gate, the devil is able to divert their steps for continual plunder. At this gate, God reminds the church that each valley in the Christian walk is prepared and designed to bring much harvest of glory to the King.

Here are a few observations about valleys: Christians do not like valleys. They prefer mountaintops. Christians enjoy revivals. Church members are often inclined to ask their pastors for revival. Every time believers say, "Pastor, why can't we just have a good time all the time?" The response should be, "Well, God wants fruit, and parties do not produce fruit. Fruit is cultivated by walking with God through deep valleys." God wants godly character, and character is produced through suffering. If churches are full of people who are unwilling to experience suffering, then believers will never develop character sufficient to see the glory of God. The life of Jesus provides believers with a great example of how enduring God-ordained valleys enables a person to attain godly character.

> Not only so, but we also rejoice in our sufferings, because we know that suffering produces perseverance; perseverance, character; and character, hope.
> —ROMANS 5:3–4, NIV

The character of Christ will never be perfected in the church until Christians understand that trials are God-ordained avenues and the workbench of God's grace. The promises in the Bible consistently show that God has stored much provision in the valleys of trials where believers fear to tread. The psalmist was able to see plenty of grain covering the valleys, and this served to bring much joy and singing into his life:

> The pastures are clothed with flocks; the valleys also are cov-
> ered over with corn; they shout for joy, they also sing.
>
> —PSALM 65:13

When the church begins to repair the Valley Gate, the world will begin to distinguish Christians as those who are able to "count it all joy" (James 1:2) when God allows them to experience trials in their lives. When Christians are able to perceive hardships as the preparation needed to fill their lives with God's strength and provision, then they will endure adversity with great expectation for a great harvest. The valley provides the body of Christ with a means to mature and grow deeper in their Christian walk and experience.

The modern church has many immature, superficial, and shallow believers who are unwilling to bear with the God-ordained valleys of their lives. Today's average believer is willing to walk every high place with God, but is totally unwilling to endure the depth of trials with Christ. As the church moves to repair the Valley Gate, the dark and gloomy moments of life will be seen as opportunities for a vast increase in grain for future situations. As every new believer learns to endure each trial, they will see suffering as justified and necessary to attaining God's plan. God does not rejoice in Christian suffering, but He allows this painful process so that it might produce joy and dancing in a time to come.

The Bible shows the psalmist recognizing the valleys as a place to replenish and quench his thirst. In Psalm 104 God tells us that He sends springs into the valleys to quench the thirst of every beast of the field and to quench the thirst of the wild donkeys:

> He sends the springs into the valleys, They flow among the hills. They give drink to every beast of the field; The wild don-
> keys quench their thirst.
>
> —PSALM 104:10–11, NKJV

Notice that God does not promise springs at the mountaintop, and that the quenching of thirst takes place in the valleys. When believers are able to grasp this, they can walk in all assurance with God, knowing that the valley is a place for renewal and refreshment. God's promise to take believers into valleys where springs flow will greatly encourage most believers.

Many scriptures illustrate God's promise that rivers of grace and blessing will begin to flow in the seasons of a trial. The following verse is one such scripture where God promises to open abundant pools and springs in the wilderness and dry land:

> I will open rivers in high places, and fountains in the midst of the valleys: I will make the wilderness a pool of water, and the dry land springs of water. I will plant in the wilderness the cedar, the shittah tree, and the myrtle, and the oil tree; I will set in the desert the fir tree, and the pine, and the box tree together: That they may see, and know, and consider, and understand together, that the hand of the LORD hath done this, and the Holy One of Israel hath created it.
> —ISAIAH 41:18–20

Each Christian should learn to expect that their spiritual journey in Christ will be filled with difficult valley experiences where God will manifest His abundant, merciful grace and faithful provision. Believers should not be surprised that the race set before them is filled with valley-like experiences that God expects them to traverse. If trials, adversity, and affliction continue to come as a surprise to God's people, the Valley Gate has not been repaired. However, when the church restores the Valley Gate they no longer consider it strange to face trials and tribulation. Instead of being surprised, Christians begin to learn that their provision of joy and gladness awaits them in the valleys of their suffering. The following admonition of the apostle Peter addresses this reality:

> Beloved, do not think it strange concerning the fiery trial which is to try you, as though some strange thing happened to you; but rejoice to the extent that you partake of Christ's

sufferings, that when His glory is revealed, you may also be glad with exceeding joy.

—1 PETER 4:12–13, NKJV

Many Christians incessantly quote Scripture passages of triumph and victory. I have always said that when God promises to take the church from victory to victory, and from triumph to triumph, they must realize that what stands between one victory and the next is always a battle. Failing to realize this is insanely impossible; the believer cannot expect to get to the next mountaintop unless they go through the next valley. So next time the Christian believer hears God promise to take them to another glorious mountaintop, they must expect and get ready for a tremendous journey through some valley. The time has come for Christians to understand that between one mountaintop and the next lays a valley.

As God leads each believer through a valley, they grow and develop the needed maturity that plays a significant part in strengthening them for future endeavors. Each valley that a believer travels helps them develop strength and godly character. As each church member learns to persevere through valleys, each valley becomes a lesson teaching unforgettable realities of Christian growth and maturity. Without valleys, there can be no growth in character.

When Christians fear valley experiences, the church becomes filled with superficial and frail believers. Without a valley, there is no proof of our true stature, measure, and strength in Christ. Without valleys, the church has no way of knowing what strength is available to them as they prepare for the next battle. God expects the church to increase in strength. With each new adversity, believers are to be able to show forth their true strength. The strength of the church and the depth of each believer is determined by the valleys they have endured through various kinds of fiery trials and affliction that have tested them.

If thou faint in the day of adversity, thy strength is small.

—PROVERBS 24:10

In the second chapter of the Song of Solomon, Christ is introduced as the "lily of the valleys." This figure of speech clearly depicts the inherent beauty of Christ to gracefully endure suffering. Every member of the body of Christ is also called to endure hardship in a graceful manner that bears witness to Christ's beauty and character, which is being formed in the inner man. The Song of Solomon is filled with significant parallels that portray suffering as an opportunity to reflect more and more of Christ's character and fragrance. Therefore, believers should consider each spiritual valley as an opportunity to pick up those lilies of the valleys as they endure various trials. Believers cannot expect to gather a bouquet of lilies at the mountaintop. While many Christians run from these valley experiences, others find them to be a chance to grow closer to Christ.

The valley represents the great shadows of the Christian walk. The Valley Gate calls for a restoration in endurance through trials. When the real darkness and reality of having to go through valleys sets in, the church must understand they need to make the best of their experience. As soon as the church restores this understanding in their membership, believers will not be caught by surprise when they find themselves in the midst of fiery affliction.

As church leaders rightly restore the Valley Gate, they will see fewer Christians throwing in the towel of surrender. Their flocks will cease to shout words such as, "I quit!" or, "That's it. I give up!" When pastors hear such despair from members who are facing various trials and affliction, they know that it is time for immediate restoration of the Valley Gate. Many preachers have promised a gospel of mountaintop victories, but seldom teach their congregations the realties of trusting God as He leads His people through the valley. This cheap gospel has spawned many immature believers within the body of Christ who have forsaken the church during periods of trial and testing. This is totally contrary to the early Christian followers who wore their suffering and affliction as a badge of honor.

After Jesus' resurrection, hardship and suffering became ordinary for those who decided to deny themselves and follow the man of sorrows. Ever since church leaders began teaching and preaching a gospel with no suffering, the world has seen the present-day church reduced to a brittle army of frail sorts. The false promise of continual and absolute spiritual bliss made by these soapbox preachers has increased the enlistment of Christian soldiers into God's army solely on the basis of receiving the fringe benefits.

One of the secrets church leaders can learn about the valleys in the Christian walk is that dark shadows usually cover the terrain, which prevents the believer from seeing clearly. On the other hand, the sun shines bright at the mountaintop allowing the believer to see clearly for miles. A believer's ability to see what is before him affords him the assurance that he or she is on the right track. In addition, up at the mountaintop a believer can hear the familiar sounds coming from the direction of the path they desire. The opposite is true down in a valley where sounds are faint, distant, and distorted causing travelers not to hear accurately words of instruction. The lack of clear vision and unreliability of echoed sounds in the valley often cause a person to get lost and discouraged.

In the valley, believers have to remember what they saw and heard during their mountaintop travels in order to base their reliance on what they know is true and right. There is no doubt that Christians are not able to see anything in the valley because everything becomes obscure, gloomy, and shadowy. A believer can only rely upon what they remember of the mountaintop, and if they do not remember, they are in big trouble. This reality should motivate believers to memorize God's instructions. In Philippians we are told to cling to whatever is true:

> Finally, brothers, whatever is true, whatever is noble, whatever is right, whatever is pure, whatever is lovely, whatever

is admirable—if anything is excellent or praiseworthy—think about such things.

—PHILIPPIANS 4:8, NIV

Every true, noble, right, pure, lovely, admirable, excellent, and praiseworthy thing will help a believer as they travel through each valley. If the church learns to embrace all things that are true and right at the mountaintop, then they can accurately continue their course in the midst of their valley and not get lost. They will have an assurance that they are going the right way. There is nothing more satisfying than hearing a Christian confess, "I'm going the right direction even though times are hard!" Regardless of the depth of the valley, Christians should always be able to profess, "I remember and know what is true." When believers forget what they have seen while at the mountaintop, and they don't remember what they have heard, they can easily become confused and get lost.

In the first chapter of the Gospel of John, the Bible recounts the day John the Baptist was on a spiritual mountaintop during the height of his ministry. This day would be the culmination and highlight of John the Baptist's ministry. No other event in this man's life would surpass the moment he announced that Christ is the answer to humanity, the Lamb of God who takes away the sin of the world:

The next day John saw Jesus coming toward him, and said, "Behold! The Lamb of God who takes away the sin of the world! This is He of whom I said, 'After me comes a Man who is preferred before me, for He was before me.' I did not know Him; but that He should be revealed to Israel, therefore I came baptizing with water." And John bore witness, saying, "I saw the Spirit descending from heaven like a dove, and He remained upon Him. I did not know Him, but He who sent me to baptize with water said to me, 'Upon whom you see the Spirit descending, and remaining on Him, this is He who baptizes with the Holy Spirit.' And I have seen and testified that this is the Son of God."

—JOHN 1:29–34, NKJV

This was the most glorious event that could happen in the life of John the Baptist. He was victorious. He confessed and proclaimed, "This is the Messiah." This was the climax of John's spiritual experience and the opportunity to fix his eyes on the fulfillment of his ministry as he introduced the Messiah to the world.

Every believer can attest that there are days in the Christian experience when they clearly see and proclaim the truths of God with courage, assurance, and boldness. Every member of the church can look back at days that were like John's, in which they were able to discern good from evil, right from wrong, and dark from light. There are those days when the believer finds his way easily and his sight does not fail him; those times when he clearly sees God's anointed, can tap into God's purpose, and can courageously testify and proclaim God's truth. When other people around John the Baptist were seeing a plain and ordinary Jewish man, John the Baptist was seeing the Savior of the world.

But what happens when God permits a believer to travel through a valley? Immediately their vision becomes blurred and obscured so they cannot see as clearly as before, and their witness becomes a little disoriented. When it was John the Baptist's turn to be led by God into a terrible valley, he required the assistance of others to remind him what he had already seen and known during his spiritual experience at the mountaintop. God was able to preserve a snapshot of John's valley in the Gospel of Matthew chapter 11, at a time when John the Baptist could not see or hear so clearly:

> Now it came to pass, when Jesus finished commanding His twelve disciples, that He departed from there to teach and to preach in their cities. And when John had heard in prison about the works of Christ, he sent two of his disciples and said to Him, "Are You the Coming One, or do we look for another?"
>
> —MATTHEW 11:1–3, NKJV

Is this not a valley? Is this not a time to remember and not to see? This is a time to walk in what you *know*, rather than what you *see*. This was the time for John's valley experience. When God permitted him to travel down the dark crevices of life, he found himself in prison and asking, *I wonder if it was that way. I wonder if I saw clearly. I wonder if I know what I should know.* So he sent two disciples to Jesus to ask Him, and Jesus answered him and said, "Go and tell John the things which you hear and see" (Matt. 11:4, NKJV).

Sometimes, when you are down in the valley, it is good to reach out to those who can see and hear more clearly because they are on the mountaintops. Asking others is a great help, especially those who can go and get a hold of Christ. From the valley, you can call out to them, "Hey! What do you see up there? Am I walking correctly? Are you sure?"

That is what John the Baptist was doing when he sent two people to the mountaintop. The voice of Jesus came back and said, "Go and tell John the things which you *hear* and *see*: The blind see and the lame walk; the lepers are cleansed and the deaf hear; the dead are raised up and the poor have the gospel preached to them" (Matt. 11:4–5, NKJV, emphasis added).

If believers are to overcome and prevail as true Christians they need to understand two things: 1. Always hold on to and remember what they have seen, and 2. Never forget what they have heard. Those Christians who fail to remember what they have seen and fail to hear what they have heard while on the mountaintop are sure to falter and go astray. In essence, God designed the Valley Gate to teach believers that He desires for them to walk by faith and not by sight.

> For we walk by faith, not by sight.
> —2 CORINTHIANS 5:7, NKJV

The Valley Gate speaks of developing maturity in Christians so that they never lose heart but continue in absolute commitment to their walk with the Lord in every situation. Believers need to follow King

David's example of remembering God's faithfulness as they traveled through each difficult valley experience. Psalm 13 is a classic reminder for God's people, as they traverse difficult times, to meditate on God's past faithfulness and goodness. During these times Christians may think, *Lord, I remember my experience in past difficulties and no one is going to tell me different. No one can convince me of what I know regarding your goodness and what my eyes have seen in the past concerning your faithfulness.*

> How long wilt thou forget me, O LORD? for ever? how long wilt thou hide thy face from me? How long shall I take counsel in my soul, having sorrow in my heart daily? how long shall mine enemy be exalted over me? Consider and hear me, O LORD my God: lighten mine eyes, lest I sleep the sleep of death; Lest mine enemy say, I have prevailed against him; and those that trouble me rejoice when I am moved. But I have trusted in thy mercy; my heart shall rejoice in thy salvation. I will sing unto the LORD, because he hath dealt bountifully with me.
>
> —PSALM 13:1–6

In the middle of King David's darkest hour, he reminds himself that God has always been faithful to care for him in the past. His words, "I will sing unto the Lord because he hath dealt bountifully with me," would sustain David as he pressed forward up the next mountain range. David remembered God's track record. He never forgot that God was with him and promised to never leave him nor forsake him. David would look back on the Lord's past faithfulness and see how He who never sleeps nor slumbers would always take good care of him. David remembered when he was up in the mountains from whence came his help. Every time David looked into the future and saw the dark gloom of suffering and anguish, he relied and trusted upon what he already knew—God is in control: *But Lord, I remember my past victories. I saw when You saved me with Your mighty arm.*

David purposed to sing to the God of his salvation because He had always dealt bountifully with him. David knew that God was always taking care of him and would continue to do so even when he could not see God's hand. Instead of continuing to lament and grieve in sad despair, David decided to sing and rejoice. His heart broke out in spontaneous song because as far back as He could remember God had always been there for him. David knew that God always fought all his battles. God had always been victorious and He stood faithful to deliver David from all his fears.

Restoring the Valley Gate is possible when a believer experiences the oppression of a deep, dark valley and begins to question the Lord, asking, "Where are you, Lord? Why have you forsaken me?" If the believer learns how to remember what they already know, and if they can know what they saw and heard, they are going to go through that valley with no problems. The Valley Gate shouts out God's desire to use men who tread valleys like King David. That is what God wants, so that when they are in the midst of a valley, they begin to rejoice and sing songs of salvation.

In Psalm 23, when David was facing his greatest trials and afflictions, he continually spoke the affirmative proclamations that his faithful God was able to deliver him out of all his troubles:

> Yea, though I walk through the valley of the shadow of death,
> I will fear no evil: for thou art with me; thy rod and thy staff
> they comfort me.
>
> —PSALM 23:4

As churches begin to restore the Valley Gate, Christians will learn to be still and make affirmative proclamations of what they know concerning God's continual goodness and unceasing faithfulness. God desires a people who are willing to fearlessly advance amidst difficult valleys without fretting or giving way to their allegiance to God. As unexpected trials and valleys continue to come, the church must stand with all assurance that God is faithful to bring them completely through without harm.

As a personal testimony, I recall years ago, my first year as a lawyer, a gentleman complained that I had purposefully hurt his legal case. As a result, he filed a grievance with the review board. I thought, *Lord, why are You permitting this process? I have done nothing wrong, why did You allow this to come into my life?* I felt the Lord respond, "I need you to go through this valley, so that you might experience the suffering and anguish of being wrongfully accused, so that you might comfort others in similar situations." His answer was somewhat of a relief, and I thought to myself, *Okay, Lord, I'm willing to* go through *this valley as long as I know You are with me.*

Eventually, the grievance was dismissed. It was concluded that I had not committed any errors in my legal representation of this client. To this I replied, "Thank you, Lord. You truly are faithful to lead us through the valley!" I was able to understand that unless believers go through valleys, they are not going to be able to comfort others and testify of God's faithfulness in keeping them. Christians can only comfort others with the same comfort with which they have received and been comforted.

From time to time, Christians may find as they're entering a valley that they have the attitude of, "Lord, don't You see? I'm not going up. It looks like I'm going down." The Lord lovingly responds, "I need you to go through this valley." As believers learn to trust the Lord, He is able to lead them through valley experiences they would never have obtained on some mountaintop. These experiences will serve as a continual source of comfort for generations to come.

The mightiest manifestation of God's power and deliverance was witnessed through the lives of those willing to trust God in the most severe and tragic situations. In the Book of Daniel, three young men decided to experience the awesome faithfulness of God in the midst of a fiery furnace:

> Shadrach, Meshach, and Abed-nego answered and said to the king, "O Nebuchadnezzar, we have no need to answer you in this matter. If that is the case, our God whom we serve is

able to deliver us from the burning fiery furnace, and He will deliver us from your hand, O king. But if not, let it be known to you, O king, that we do not serve your gods, nor will we worship the gold image which you have set up."

—DANIEL 3:16, NKJV

God always responds with mighty acts of faithfulness when He takes His people through a valley experience. The unbelievers in this world always want to know, "Who is like the Lord our God who can answer prayer and deliver His people?" This is why God chooses to lead His people through valleys—because He is going to answer the question of who is Lord of lords. Through these trials and tribulations, God is able to manifest His power and might so that His glory is magnified. When people ask, "Who is the God who will deliver you?" Imagine the body of Christ filled with Christians that would answer like these three young men, "Our God whom we serve is able to deliver us from the burning fiery furnace, and he will deliver us out of thine hand, O king. *But if not…* we will not serve thy gods, nor worship the golden image which thou hast set up" (Daniel 3:17–18, emphasis added).

At the Valley Gate, the church learns that in good times and bad times God continues to be God. At the Valley Gate, the Christian "talk" turns to "walk." Christians are known for the words they speak, but valleys are a true opportunity for the world to witness God's power and faithfulness in His people like at no other time. When Christians decide that God continues to be their God regardless of the adverse conditions and circumstances they face, then the whole world shall see the glory of God. The Valley Gate is where the rubber meets the road. At the Valley Gate, the body of Christ learns that winners never quit and quitters never win. When spiritual leaders repair the Valley Gate, they will be able to separate the men from the boys. As church leaders repair the Valley Gate, they will be able to distinguish the sheep from the goats. A Christian that never endures the valleys will not be able to experience nor manifest the power and glory of God.

The presence of almighty God is made real as Christians travel through God-ordained valleys. During a believer's journey on a spiritual mountaintop, he can read a good Christian book or study the Bible and have a verse to read and proclaim out loud. Conversely, down in the valley, the believer must hold on to God's hand because he will not be able to see anything, nor can he feel any emotional strength. In the middle of certain valleys, a believer will no longer be able to see the map illustrations so they must hold on to the Master's hand.

The restorations at the Valley Gate will teach the church that valleys are not the kind of places to take up permanent residence. When God designed the Valley Gate He intended for all believers to know that valleys are made for "passing through." Believers are not to stay in valleys permanently; these are only to serve for a season. The believer's inner knowledge and confidence is that valleys serve the temporal purpose of filling our life with abundant springs of divine strength and godly refreshing. As the psalmist passed through bitter valleys, he acknowledged them as an opportunity to make them a spring and receive refreshing rain that would take him from strength to strength:

> Blessed is the man whose strength is in You, Whose heart is set on pilgrimage. As they pass through the Valley of Baca, They make it a spring; The rain also covers it with pools. They go from strength to strength; Each one appears before God in Zion.
>
> —Psalm 84:5– 7, NKJV

This verse is a beautiful expression of God's purpose for leading those whose hearts are set on a pilgrimage through the valleys. *Valley of Baca* is translated the "valley of tears," a place for testing and trials. Through this valley of tears God desires to transform His people and bring them to a place where they can renew their strength and replenish their wells with pools. Believers can trust God for sufficient rain to cover the parched ground with pools of water everywhere. Mourning will be turned into dancing; weeping into gladness. Believers can expect their present tears to produce future springs as a result of their willingness to journey steadfastly through these God-ordained valleys. What a surprise to see today's famines as the possibility of ushering in tomorrow's feast! Those valleys that God allows in a believer's life will always become the continued source of refreshing for God's people in their future. The psalmist writes that those whose confidence is in the Lord will go forth from strength to strength by turning the valley of tears into a wellspring of blessing. That means you are certain to grow stronger now that you have walked through the depth and struggles of this pilgrimage.

Personal trainers will tell you that muscles require being broken down before they can be rebuilt and regenerated. When Christians are broken and torn, their strength multiplies and the trial produces endurance of character. When you take Christ seriously, then God is able to say, *You have to go down into the valley. Let's go for a workout. Let's go for a little bit of blood, sweat, and tears where the exercise of godliness is perfected through brokenness.*

It is during these pilgrimages through the valleys of hardship that we can hear the still, small voice of Christ's teaching: "Blessed are they that mourn: for they shall be comforted" (Matt. 5:4). This is a promise from God when He brings mourning into your life or allows suffering to come your way. We can say, *Lord, I can't wait to see the springs. I can't wait to see the fountains. I can't wait to be comforted by you.*

During two decades in the local church, I have witnessed many believers who despise the existence of the Valley Gate. I have heard preachers and teachers say, "Knock it down," and, "Get it out of your life and out of the church! There are no valleys here." Any one of these statements can be seen as an attempt at pushing and tearing the Valley Gate down.

Many teach that in Christ there are no tears, no suffering. Many have replaced the Valley Gate for a new and improved Happy Gate. Many preachers have refused the Valley Gate in their church. They think it better to fashion a Glad Gate to appease the happy-go-lucky crowd of believers. This however, betrays Christ and the cross, and any thought of suffering for the cause of Christ. They are not advancing genuine faith. The Valley Gate needs to be rebuilt and set in place with its doors hung and its bolts and bars repaired. The Book of Acts shows us how confirming the souls of the disciples and exhorting them to continue in genuine faith was consistent with teaching the necessity of much tribulation in the path that leads into the kingdom of God:

> Confirming the souls of the disciples, and exhorting them to continue in the faith, and that we must through much tribulation enter into the kingdom of God.
>
> —ACTS 14:22

This chapter allows us to see why God designed the Valley Gate as an entrance to His beloved city. Let us put the Valley Gate back where it belongs. Let us remove that flimsy Happy Gate that is unable to keep God's people secure. It is the Valley Gate that must be restored and needs to be repaired and put back on its hinges.

The devil and his host have always led God's people to believe that they are going to be defeated if they go down into the valleys. The devil has intimidated believers into thinking that down in the valley they can only experience defeat. The devil believes his mocking threats can scare you from coming down to fight. For many, he has taken strategic possession of valleys making you believe that he is sure to win down there. In fact, the devil rarely ever attacks Christians when they are experiencing revival because we easily chase him out of our lives. We say, "Get thee behind me, Satan. I cast you out in Jesus' name."

Many times the devil will wait and send you an invitation to come into the valley so that he can ambush and ransack you. He tries to surround you and your mind. He thinks there is no possibility of victory for you when you travel through the valley. He thinks that Christians obtain more victories while they are on the mountaintops. Many Christians get back from a revival meeting or some kind of crusade feeling untouchable and invincible. The devil does not mess with you for two weeks after that. He waits patiently until you simmer down again. In those times of revival, your prayers seem to be answered quickly, and the devil does not attack you for a while. You pray in the spirit for hours. Your prayer life seems flawless. Your devotional time grows deeper.

We hear questions such as "Where did these people come from? What a blessing! They are just so nice." But in the valley, we hear things like "These people! Where did they come from? Not even worldly people behave like this." In the valleys, they say the same thing. When money is coming in by the loads, God gets the credit as the Provider. But in the valley, we are left asking, "What happened? How am I going to eat?"

I remember growing up as a Christian, every time I was on a revival I would go out and buy a new highlighter. I was ready. I was going to learn the Word of God. At those times, we are unmovable, unshakeable, and we are looking for the opportunity to glorify God and crush Satan. The devil, his temptations, his demons, and his evil spirits hold off their hellish attacks. Many of the temptations are withheld until the time of famine. The fiery darts of the enemy are held back because your shield of faith is able to block every attempt to smite you by the evil one. The devil attacks when he knows we are down in that valley because we are vulnerable, and not when we are at the height of revival. God reverses this deception by showing us His strength at the Valley Gate. God proves to us that He is not only the God of the mountains, but also the God of the valleys. He is able to usher in victory, proving that "no weapon formed against you shall prosper" (Isa. 54:17, NKJV). When the enemy comes in like a flood, God will lift up a standard against him to ward him off.

> And the servants of the king of Syria said unto him, Their gods are gods of the hills; therefore they were stronger than we; but let us fight against them in the plain, and surely we shall be stronger than they.
>
> —1 KINGS 20:23

90

The devil knows that he is not very likely to have many victories when everything is going great. He proclaims that he is not able to fight against us at that level. Yet, look at the confidence the devil has to be able to attack you in the valley. At the mountaintops, we are praying forgiveness for our brethren. We bestow blessing upon those who have offended us or hurt our feelings. The enemy is betting on a different outcome, and takes advantage of our vulnerability:

> And do this thing, Take the kings away, every man out of his place, and put captains in their rooms: And number thee an army, like the army that thou hast lost, horse for horse, and chariot for chariot: and we will fight against them in the plain, and surely we shall be stronger than they. And he hearkened unto their voice, and did so.
>
> —1 Kings 20:24–25

It is highly unusual to see the enemy so confident, unless he has witnessed previous battles. Apparently, there is a statistic that proves God's people do better in the hills then they do on the plain:

> And there came a man of God, and spake unto the king of Israel, and said, Thus saith the Lord, Because the Syrians have said, The Lord is God of the hills, but he is not God of the valleys, therefore will I deliver all this great multitude into thine hand, and ye shall know that I am the Lord.
>
> —1 Kings 20:28

Every Christian should highlight this verse in their Bibles and commit it to memory. You must know that your God fights with you on the mountaintops, gives you victory, and delivers your enemies into your hands—even in the valleys. God is willing to stand at your side and prove that He is the omnipotent Lord and God of the valleys. For too long, the church has been intimidated by the illusion that we cannot overcome in times of adversity. In fact, the church was birthed in adversity and shines the brightest when travailing through the deepest, darkest persecution. We can no longer believe that any experience that leads us into the valley means that God has forsaken us. The old adage that you surely must be in sin or in disfavor with God if you are experiencing a valley should not be taught. Going through valleys cannot be defined as losing favor with God.

The Valley Gate shows the church that their God is not only the God of the mountains, but also the God of the valleys. In the valleys, God will move with incredible strength on behalf of those who wait upon the Lord. Every great Christian has received personal witness and testimony that God has shown Himself the strongest in the midst of life's darkest valleys. In Psalm 23:5, the psalmist reveals that God's people should not worry as they travel through the valleys of life because God is faithful to prepare a banquet table before the presence of their enemies.

Understanding the Valley Gate principle helps believers withstand trials. They know that God will reward those willing to run down to the valley hoping to find a harvest of victory for the glory of God. As the church reflects on the battle between David and Goliath, believers will be reminded that even the young can take the opportunity to introduce the God of the valleys to their biggest enemy:

> And the Philistine said, I defy the armies of Israel this day; give me a man, that we may fight together.
>
> —1 SAMUEL 17:10

In the Bible, Goliath shouted defiantly, inviting one of Israel's many warriors to come down and engage in battle. His hellish threats intimidated Israel's army so that all the men of Israel fled from him, and were sore afraid. Goliath refused to go up into the mountain but remained in the valley, spewing all kinds of nightmarish provocations to demoralize and discourage his weary foes:

> And it came to pass, when the Philistine arose, and came, and drew nigh to meet David, that David hastened, and ran

toward the army to meet the Philistine.

—1 SAMUEL 17:48

I praise God for this young boy David who had many previous experiences traveling through the Valley Gate. He knew that the God of the valleys would never forsake him and would lead him only in triumph. Young David did not hesitate to fight the battles of the Lord. The very moment David heard the wickedly defiant voice in the valley, he ran to the king and requested an opportunity to defend God's honor. Despite the king's profound concern regarding David's young and frail stature, David was permitted to contend against the giant down in the valley. David took offense that Goliath would defy and disrespect the Lord's host. He took this opportunity to introduce his enemy to the God of the valleys. David quickly overcame Goliath in the valley and cut off his head.

In the difficult times of trials and testing, God reminds the church to be still and stand fast. Every church member must ultimately realize that God is able to bless them at all times. When believers are in the mountains God blesses them with dew that comes from heaven. When they are facing the depth of a valley, God is able to deliver them with springs of life. Every believer can expect an equivalent proportion of victory by the length of time they spend traveling down into difficult valleys. The height of their next victory will be in proportion to the valley they just traveled.

Many times, young believers do not understand the need for a Valley Gate in the Christian church. As young believers learn to trust God through valleys, they might find that trials and afflictions are too difficult, causing them to wonder, "What is this all about?" However, God is sovereign to guide them and direct them through any and all difficult situations. Soon the inexperienced believers will learn that in valleys God can teach His people how to prepare themselves for battle, teaching their hands to war, and their fingers to fight. Soon they will learn that God leads them always from glory to glory, from victory to victory, and from triumph to triumph. God has faithfully promised to lead His people to a land that is filled with valleys and hills:

> But the land, whither ye go to possess it, is a land of hills and valleys, and drinketh water of the rain of heaven.
>
> —DEUTERONOMY 11:11

Christians must rest assured in God's promise to lead His people to a promised land of hills and valleys that always has access to a great supply of rainwater from heaven. The Christian journey would be difficult if the hand of the Lord was not upon His people. For this reason, when doubt arises that God has forgotten His people, they should be reminded that God promised to take the church into the land where they would see hills and valleys. Christians should not be surprised about the valleys they face in the Christian life, knowing that following the valley they will find the provisions God has promised. The following passage reminds the church what God intended with the valleys:

> Therefore thou shalt keep the commandments of the LORD thy God, to walk in his ways, and to fear him. For the LORD thy God bringeth thee into a good land, a land of brooks of water, of fountains and depths that spring out of valleys and hills; A land of wheat, and barley, and vines, and fig trees, and pomegranates; a land of oil olive, and honey; A land wherein thou shalt eat bread without scarceness, thou shalt not lack any thing in it; a land whose stones are iron, and out of whose hills thou mayest dig brass. When thou hast eaten and art full, then thou shalt bless the LORD thy God for the good land which he hath given thee.
>
> —DEUTERONOMY 8:6–10

Finally, when a Christian looks at the Valley Gate from the human perspective they perceive a terrible terrain leading to lows and depths that are difficult to travel. However, when the valleys are seen from

God's vantage point they seem like heavenly mountains waiting to be filled with all of God's spiritual wealth and purpose. One of the pillars of the early Christian church was the apostle James who wrote the following words to Christian believers:

> My brethren, count it all joy when ye fall into divers temptations; Knowing this, that the trying of your faith worketh patience. But let patience have her perfect work, that ye may be perfect and entire, wanting nothing.
> —JAMES 1:2–4

The very first topic that the apostle James addresses to his large audience, the twelve tribes, was the issue of not losing heart when facing difficult trials. In fact, James writes that trials should not be considered negative or depressing. Instead, the sentiment that Christians should embrace when they are permitted to dive deeply into diverse dilemmas is joy. James encourages the brethren to count it all joy whenever trouble has come upon them. According to James, Christians should place valleys in the positive and joyous column of their spiritual bookkeeping, counting them as joy. In other words, joy is the sentiment that should pervade and accompany Christians during times of troubled valleys.

For the apostle James to focus upon this subject as a primary matter of his letter to the brethren indicates that trials and suffering are a very important aspect of the Christian life. James understood that every believer's life must be saturated with trials and difficulties in order to be established in God's plan. He further writes that the brethren should know that suffering is consistent with God working out character and faith in each believer. The very possibility of considering valleys as opportunities for joy is when Christians know that the trying of their faith is working a character that will be useful for God in some future endeavor. The one thing that can motivate each Christian to count it all joy (considering each valley as reason for joy to the maximum degree) is holding on to the knowledge that trials and suffering are not in vain. They serve the specific purpose of God testing and trying the believer's faith so as to perform or fulfill a specific plan in God's design.

As the church restores the Valley Gate, Christian leaders will find great opportunity to encourage others during difficult times of hardship and trials, to count every valley as a motive for joy. Recognizing the need to restore the Valley Gate in every Christian church will determine whether or not believers will ever attain the needed spiritual maturity and character to fulfill the design of God's call.

PRAYER APPLICATION

Father God! Help every Christian church to restore the Valley Gate. Lord Jesus, from this day forward I purpose to help my brothers and sisters to build and repair the Valley Gate so that as they pass through the valleys of trials, hardship, suffering, pain, heartache, affliction, and adversity they count it all joy and fear no evil, for You are with them. Lord I thank You for leading me to the rock that is higher than I so that I can add depth to my Christian walk and endure all other remaining valleys by trusting in Your faithful, sovereign plan and design for my life.

5

THE REFUSE GATE

> *Woe unto them that call evil good, and good evil; that put darkness for light, and light for darkness; that put bitter for sweet, and sweet for bitter!*
>
> —ISAIAH 5:20

This chapter on the Refuse Gate focuses on the aspect of the local church and their ministerial leadership to exercise discernment. The church's ability to develop a keen sense on deciphering between treasure and trash will ultimately determine whether the church is able to please God or not. In the restoration process, no other gate will cause more controversy or debate than the Refuse Gate. The necessity of the Refuse Gate is not the source of the controversy, but rather how the church decides to draw the line between what the church keeps as refined treasure and what the church disposes of as refuse.

To accomplish this task in human terms, the church must learn how to expel appropriately those things and persons that need to be discarded as trash. As church leaders approach the challenge of restoring the Refuse Gate, they are confronted with the reality that God is a holy God. He is not interested in marring the fellowship of His saints with impure, polluted, contaminated, unclean, and dirty objects. The character of God is blameless, clean, pure, and holy. In Nehemiah, the restoration efforts in old Jerusalem included the "dung gate."

> But the dung gate repaired Malchiah the son of Rechab, the ruler of part of Bethhaccerem; he built it, and set up the doors thereof, the locks thereof, and the bars thereof.
> —NEHEMIAH 3:14

At the Dung Gate, otherwise known as the Refuse Gate, church members begin to understand that God's desire is to remove all that corrupts and contaminates the surrounding premises of His dwelling. Those objects that subtract value from God's people are to be far removed from God's sanctuary. The church must understand that while God accepts the worst sinner, He has also decided to remove their sin as far as the East is from the West. Therefore, God, in His sovereign design, has purposefully included a gate for the purpose of ejecting specific content that can be defined as dung, refuse, or waste. Every believer should be aware of the need to restore this gate and become trained experts at performing all duties related to a functional Refuse Gate.

The word *refuse* suggests unworthiness of acceptance. In ordinary conversational language people will hear, "I refuse to do this or that," which is the common usage of the word. Refuse means to "not accept." The following words further describe the concept of refuse: decline, defy, deny, discard, discharge, dump, waste, garbage, trash, pass up, reject, resist, scrap, turn away, and turn down.

In the restoration of the Refuse Gate, the body of Christ is compelled to take responsibility for itemizing and characterizing those things that God adamantly refuses and to remove them far from their midst. As the church restores the Refuse Gate, they must acknowledge that certain conduct and behavior is not welcomed and will by no means be accepted by God. Thus, the church is instructed to put them away.

The church must acknowledge that we live in an age where people have become more tolerant. Most people dislike characterizing anything as bad, evil, or trash. Regardless of the fact that people have become accustomed to collecting and hoarding trash, God is not interested in the accumulation of useless junk. At the Refuse Gate, the church has the opportunity to restore a timeless practice that God never intended to cease—throwing out trash.

The presence of a Refuse Gate in ancient Jerusalem is a monument to the fact that God's people are expected to constantly remove certain things from their midst. While the task of discarding refuse seems a little unusual or bizarre for church settings, the restoration of the Refuse Gate requires the church to develop skills of discernment to protect believers from pandemic. During this process of discernment, the church learns to rid the house of God from all forms of grotesque, rotten, and spoiled trash.

There is no doubt that, when improperly performed, restoring the Refuse Gate can turn into an occasion for some to commit severe abuse and negligent maltreatment. For this reason, some people would rather dispose of the Refuse Gate altogether so as to avoid future abuse or harm. This travesty is true and applies in many other disciplines. For example, the fact that some medical doctors often commit malpractice on their patients does not serve as sufficient grounds to eliminate all doctors from practicing medicine. In the same fashion, God entrusted the Refuse Gate to mature, responsible believers that are able to discern God's heart and manifest a true concern for the general welfare of God's people.

The concept behind the Refuse Gate should not surprise anyone, for this is a common practice and everyday responsibility. In fact, people normally set up trash bins in multiple places, such as inside and outside their homes, at work, in restrooms, under their desks, in their cars, in restaurants, and in offices. Practically everywhere people go they understand the customary purpose and activity of trash bins. In communities all over the world, waste removal is a daily reality.

What do people find when they visit a trash bin? If they were to inspect the items in a wastebasket, people would rarely find anything useful. A wastebasket is usually filled with dirty, filthy stuff that requires immediate removal. Few people question whether a soiled diaper or a dirty napkin that has recently been used to blow someone's nose should be thrown out. It would be very strange for anyone at church to preserve such smelly and filthy items. The reality of refuse is that, if permitted to lie around too long, it becomes unbearably odorous and potentially harmful.

Rarely does anyone question when dirty items are thrown out, or seldom does anyone retrieve dirty things once they have been thrown out. As previously stated, another description for the Refuse Gate is the Dung Gate. The word *dung* means "excrement, or that which is shameful, corrupt, or has decayed." While Christians in modern times have never seen a dung gate, nor are they familiar with the dung gate's use, God's people in ancient Jerusalem were quite accustomed to this gate. All of Jerusalem's people were familiar with the Dung Gate and its purpose of expelling, disposing, eliminating, and removing all those things that failed to promote the general welfare of Jerusalem's inhabitants. The general litmus test developed by the leaders in Jerusalem was to discard anything that upon smelling provoked nausea. Whether a dead dog, decaying horse, animal spoil, manure, or human dung, the inhabitants of Jerusalem were well trained to exercise discernment and eradicate the refuse and waste found lying within the city walls.

Before proceeding into the various aspects and benefits of restoring the Refuse Gate, it is important to acknowledge the existence of biblical mandates to the church to remove those individuals or persons that have become "persona non grata," or those who are no longer welcomed because of serious sin and trespass. Removal is not a common practice within many Christian churches of our day. The Bible gives the church divine instruction on how and when to remove the ungodly from their fellowship.

This chapter on restoration of the Refuse Gate is not intended to serve as an in-depth study of the methods and practices of removing the undesirables. It is sufficient for this book to say that restoring the Refuse Gate is a necessary part of restoring God's glory to the church. The following words are often utilized to explain the process of removing a person from fellowship because of unrepentant sin: discipline, excommunication, banishment, shunning, dismissal, removal, disfellowship, or expulsion. In other words, the removal will include a spiritual censure, which is used to deprive or suspend membership in a fellowship community due to continued improper conduct. These words literally mean "to place out of communion" or "remove from fellowship."

We will never know how many Christian fellowships and church assemblies the devil has been able to destroy and divide by the failure of church leaders to remove the wicked from their midst in a timely manner. Regardless of how it is called or approached, the Refuse Gate can be restored by discerning what elements to remove from the fellowship of the body of Christ. These are elements that no longer promote the general welfare of the body; they do not bring honor to God and His Word, which is customarily encouraged in the service of God's worship.

While many may question this practice of removing that which is defined as refuse or dung, the church must realize that God teaches the necessity of this process. In the biblical account of Genesis, God removed the first man and woman from the garden, where they enjoyed fellowship in God's presence, because of their sin:

> Therefore the LORD God sent him forth from the garden of Eden, to till the ground from whence he was taken. So he drove out the man; and he placed at the east of the garden of Eden Cherubims, and a flaming sword which turned every way, to keep the way of the tree of life.
>
> —GENESIS 3:23–24

Both Adam and Eve were removed from the garden and driven away, thus becoming exiled from the place where they had enjoyed incredible fellowship with God. Even though God made future provision for their restoration, it was necessary to be removed from that place which they previously enjoyed until they would be restored. While the process of removing people from fellowship is very painful, it is also very necessary to preserve authenticity and genuineness of worship.

Since the very beginning, God has required the removal of anyone from the fellowship who purposefully rebels and continues in disobedience. This removal from fellowship serves the purpose of protecting the best interests of His people. The church needs to understand that God has chosen expulsion as a process to preserve the integrity of His honor and holiness, while protecting His people from harmful elements. In each case, God will use this removal process to deal with perpetrators who have seriously violated His honor.

The following verses at the beginning of the Bible also show the shame and anguish experienced by those who suffered excommunication. Those who at one time enjoyed fellowship with God but continue to commit heinous acts of treason against God and His people can end up suffering separation and rejection:

> Behold, thou hast driven me out this day from the face of the earth; and from thy face shall I be hid; and I shall be a fugitive and a vagabond in the earth; and it shall come to pass, that every one that findeth me shall slay me.
> —GENESIS 4:14

This manner of dealing with serious sin is never unjust or unmerciful. Since the beginning of time, the angels who enjoyed fellowship with God and later became disloyal and treacherous were cast down from heaven. The church must not close their eyes to the realties of God's continual removal of the wicked from His presence.

> And the great dragon was cast out, that old serpent, called the
> Devil, and Satan, which deceiveth the whole world: he was cast
> out into the earth, and his angels were cast out with him.
>
> —REVELATION 12:9

The Bible account of God's highly entrusted archangel, Lucifer, shows that he once enjoyed close fellowship with God. Lucifer was heavenly ordained as the seal of perfection—until he acted out in pride. Lucifer, together with one-third of the angels, rebelled against God and was kicked out of heaven. He now inhabits this worldly sphere. (See Isa. 14:12–14; Ezek. 28:12–17; Luke 10:18; Rev. 12:3–4; 20:2.)

This process of removing the wicked and ungodly from church fellowship is no ordinary or trivial matter. As a pastor, I often struggle with the responsibility I have in this regard. The purposeful separation of the wicked from the fellowship of God's people is to avoid further damage and loss by those whose conscience has become seared. These individuals no longer respond or adhere to godly instruction, admonishing, exhortation, and correction.

We see from the apostle Paul's instruction in Philippians 3:18, church leaders should have their eyes fill with tears when they speak about those who have become enemies of the cross of Christ. Their pursuit of shameful acts, which betray and dishonor the body of Christ, has doomed them to the fate of eternal misery as they side with earthly things instead of following the call of Christ and His church.

To avoid the errors of religious legalism the church should always seek to achieve total redemption, restoration, and genuine reconciliation of those who have dishonored or betrayed the confidence of the body of Christ. In the past, some church leaders have caused irreparable harm to believers by utilizing church discipline to further carnal interests. Church leaders must always approach this removal process by erring on the side of mercy and grace. They must always be careful not to remove a fly from a brother's forehead with a hatchet.

Thinking in these terms is hard for the church pastorate. They usually prefer to forego the actual removing of a church member until removal is inevitable because greater damage will occur if the removal is further delayed. In the past, when pastors have not followed the dictates of God's Word in these matters, the failure to remove the ungodly has caused much worse hurt and problems for the body of Christ. Often times, pastors do not like to think that removal is an option when dealing with church members and families. Some Christian churches and ministry leaders have failed to understand the importance of obeying God's Word of removing the ungodly from their midst.

The church needs to understand the incredible importance of the Refuse Gate and the role it plays in preserving the integrity of the church's makeup and character. The church is commissioned to act with all seriousness and responsibility to assure that leaders are able to discern between those in the house of God that are destroying the church life or fellowship and those who contribute to the church's authentic growth and development.

At the beginning of my pastoral ministry, I was approached by a person who questioned the veracity of removing persons from church fellowship. Using the biblical text found in the Gospel of Mark, this Christian brother fervently insisted that church was to tolerate the wicked because Jesus had come for the sick and not the healthy:

> When Jesus heard it, he saith unto them, They that are whole have no need of the physician, but they that are sick: I came not to call the righteous, but sinners to repentance.
> —MARK 2:17

The individual continued questioning whether removal of persons from fellowship was correct in the light of the foregoing passage. The man continued to state adamantly that churches are to serve like infirmaries or hospitals where the sick receive help for spiritual disease.

Fortunately, my father had been a medical doctor for many years, and I was well acquainted with the policies and procedures of hospital management. I was able to share that I agreed with his hospital analogy, but that even hospitals refuse to allow their sick patients to roam the corridors, recklessly infecting others. Patients that come to a hospital are not welcomed to wander aimlessly through the infirmary halls without adherence to strict guidelines and specific treatment. Hospitals pay strict attention to avoiding the spread of contagious ailments. In the most severe cases, hospitals even quarantine patients so as to prevent the widespread epidemic or pandemic of serious disease.

Jesus did come for those who are sick, with the specific purpose to make them whole. Through this exchange, I was able to see that many in the world believe erroneously that the Christian church is the place for the ungodly to roam. They randomly infect unsuspecting believers that come into inadvertent contact with their serious contagious infections and spiritual ailments. I finished by telling this man that each person attending the church as a sick patient must attend in the same light as a patient does a hospital. Those who refuse to abide by the specifications of their needed care in the church are not welcomed to start a pandemic of contagious sin, rebellious attitudes, or continual disobedience in other believers.

The body of Christ has failed to develop discernment in this area for many years. Many times, Christian leaders distort these lines so that this area remains foggy and unclear. For this reason, the Bible has many verses (especially in the New Testament) that address the need for incredible judgment and discernment in dealing with this aspect of protecting the fellowship of the saints. The removing of the ungodly and unruly people from church fellowship prevents the church from becoming a place where sinful attitudes prevail and people feel free to persist in unrepented wickedness. There is an awful tendency to think that Christ's plan of redemption and grace for the church has abolished the activity at the Refuse Gate—discarding that which is rubbish. Jesus teaches the church to follow carefully the instruction in the Gospel of Matthew chapter 18:

> Moreover if thy brother shall trespass against thee, go and tell him his fault between thee and him alone: if he shall hear thee, thou hast gained thy brother. But if he will not hear thee, then take with thee one or two more, that in the mouth of two or three witnesses every word may be established. And if he shall neglect to hear them, tell it unto the church: but if he neglect to hear the church, let him be unto thee as an heathen man and a publican.
>
> —MATTHEW 18:15–17

Jesus set out some basic steps to follow when a brother in the believing community acts like an unbeliever and refuses to turn from his ungodliness. The first step is to talk to the sinner in private. If there is no change, then the situation is discussed in front of two or three brethren, and if he persists in disobedience, then the situation is told to the local church gathering. If the person does not turn from his sin, then he is to be treated as what he is: someone whose actions show them to not be a part of the group.

Those who refuse to repair the Refuse Gate, claiming that it is not a New Testament truth, must revisit the Lord's specific instructions. The early church leaders followed in Christ's example by teaching and following the very words taught by Christ. As church leaders continue to read the New Testament they will find the apostle Paul's letters to the churches included the same teachings. The apostle Paul made removal of the ungodly very clear to the Corinthian church as he instructed them not to associate with immoral people that called themselves brethren. The biblical instruction is not about those who are immoral in the outside world, but about those who supposedly believe and are partaking with church fellowship but continue to live in their sin. Paul warned them not to even eat with such a person.

> I wrote unto you in an epistle not to company with fornicators: Yet not altogether with the fornicators of this world, or with the covetous, or extortioners, or with idolaters; for then

must ye needs go out of the world. But now I have written unto you not to keep company, if any man that is called a brother be a fornicator, or covetous, or an idolater, or a railer, or a drunkard, or an extortioner; with such an one no not to eat. For what have I to do to judge them also that are without? do not ye judge them that are within? But them that are without God judgeth. Therefore put away from among yourselves that wicked person.

—1 Corinthians 5:9–13

While the purpose at the Refuse Gate is not to make enemies, the Bible is clear that the banned brethren need to understand the seriousness of their disobedience and rebellion. Separation is meant to send the message that the gravity of their sin is enormous, and removal lets them know that the consequences are getting high because of how far they have wandered from God's pleasure.

And if any man obey not our word by this epistle, note that man, and have no company with him, that he may be ashamed. Yet count him not as an enemy, but admonish him as a brother.

—2 Thessalonians 3:14–15

The removal also allows everyone else in the fellowship to be forewarned so that they are not enticed to follow en route. The Refuse Gate is an opportunity to distance the wicked and perverted from those who remain in fellowship. The refusal to obey Christ is a very harmful and dangerous matter. When the church refuses to remove those who claim to be Christians but whose actions cannot be considered consistent with honoring Christ or His name, they bring much confusion and hurt to the body of Christ. The apostle Paul's instruction to his beloved disciple Timothy was to remove himself far from those who had an appearance of godliness but were actually denying Christ's work of sanctification.

> This know also, that in the last days perilous times shall come. For men shall be lovers of their own selves, covetous, boasters, proud, blasphemers, disobedient to parents, unthankful, unholy, Without natural affection, trucebreakers, false accusers, incontinent, fierce, despisers of those that are good, Traitors, heady, highminded, lovers of pleasures more than lovers of God; Having a form of godliness, but denying the power thereof: from such turn away.
>
> —2 TIMOTHY 3:1–5

For Timothy to receive these instructions as a young leader seems awkward. His spiritual father and leader was instructing him to turn away from those who apparently need God the most, but Paul knew that these men were wicked reprobates, no longer walking in the fear of God. In the same chapter, Paul writes that these men were "ever learning, and never able to come to the knowledge of the truth" (v. 7). By resisting the revealed truth of Christ they preferred to pursue earthly achievements, due to their corrupt minds being reprobate concerning the faith. Paul's concern was that Timothy would understand that certain men will not proceed any further and their folly shall be manifest unto all men because they lack a true heart toward the things of God.

Paul constantly watched for those who needed to be marked out and avoided because of their intentional and ungodly offenses against the cause of Christ. The church is to follow the biblical instruction to watch out for those in the Christian church that do not serve our Lord Jesus Christ but their own belly; who always lead astray the heart of the simple with deceptive words and fair speech.

> Now I beseech you, brethren, mark them which cause divisions and offences contrary to the doctrine which ye have learned; and avoid them. For they that are such serve not our Lord Jesus Christ, but their own belly; and by good words and fair speeches deceive the hearts of the simple.
>
> —ROMANS 16:17–18

> If there come any unto you, and bring not this doctrine, receive
> him not into your house, neither bid him God speed.
>
> —2 JOHN 1:10

The remainder of this chapter on restoring the Refuse Gate deals with the specific instructions found in God's Word concerning the church's need to grow in spiritual discernment. With regard to discernment, the church needs to learn that God intends believers to be separated from those who customarily fellowship at church yet are vile and lukewarm. These individuals are neither hot nor cold, and they will ultimately stand to be vomited from the body of Christ. (See Revelation 3:16.)

As previously stated, all of Jerusalem's people were familiar with the Dung Gate and its purpose of expelling, disposing, eliminating, and removing anything found within the city gates that caused nausea. We must learn the biblical references to situations that are applicable to the body of Christ today. Christ's sentiment in several passages reveals aspects of God's heart to which the church must finally adhere. The church has a responsibility to exercise discernment and follow all biblical instruction. For example, the following passage in Revelation states that Christ will expel and vomit from His body all those whose remain lukewarm:

> I know thy works, that thou art neither cold nor hot: I would
> thou wert cold or hot. So then because thou art lukewarm, and
> neither cold nor hot, I will spue thee out of my mouth.
>
> —REVELATION 3:15–16

I would tender the suggestion that the Refuse Gate can begin greasing its hinges for those in the body of Christ who continue their lukewarm attitudes and indifference to the cause of their Lord. The Bible reveals that "lukewarmness" is sure to produce nausea and vomiting in the body of Christ. The purpose of this biblical passage is to warn the lukewarm believers that they stand to be expelled from God's innermost being lest they address this matter of being neither hot nor cold.

In ancient Jerusalem, scent also served as an indicator of whether or not an item from the city should be expelled. Smelly matters were sure to be gathered and removed from the city limits. God provided that the church was to remove such refuse from their midst. On the other hand, while God encourages believers to remove smelly items, He readily welcomes things saturated with His aroma and fragrance.

As the church restores the Refuse Gate, God desires to bring them to the place where they are able to discern that which is useful and good from that which is useless and bad. Imagine if God wanted to expel or throw out things that are wholesome. In this case, God would have changed the named of the Refuse Gate to the Good Gate. The church is reminded at the Refuse Gate that God wants to keep what is good and remove that which destroys and brings evil into His city. To allow a wretched odor to prevail in the body of Christ would cause outsiders to disdain God's presence and hold their noses. For this reason, the Refuse Gate requires serious discernment and godly wisdom so that God's sanctuary is not profaned among the nations as a trash heap.

The fact that many in the church have opted not to restore the Refuse Gate is evident from the amount of garbage that lies within the church gates. Many churches have a reputation in their community of gathering in the most wicked and ungodly people in town. Every crooked businessman, thief, and dishonest citizen packs the Sunday worship service week after week with no accountability of their wicked actions. No wonder some would rather not participate in their community churches. They prefer to avoid hypocritical worship with known scoundrels and charlatans.

The flow of trash at the Refuse Gate has been severely misdirected due to many years of church leaders refusing to guard the temple for Christ's honor. Under the guise of love, mercy, and grace, the contemporary church has been hard-pressed to repel the inward flow of dung and garbage that fills church pews. The church is constantly driven to accept and erroneously approve what we otherwise would never accept in any other community fellowship. The church is continually offered the opportunity to welcome trash from outside the city, and safeguard it within its walls.

Clarification is required in this instance. I am not addressing wayward sinners that have yet to repent and experience the cleansing tide of Jesus' precious blood, to which the arms of God's invitation remain steadfastly open. The filth and trash that I refer to in this chapter are those people who are constantly welcomed back into fellowship despite the fact that they continue as dogs returning to their own vomit. They are like pigs that have been washed and then turn to their wallowing in the mire.

The church must finally realize the dire necessity of properly directing the flow of garbage outside the church instead of into its innermost secret chambers. The church has no obligation to accommodate in their Christian fellowship and agape feasts those that do not desire to be made clean and who promote lifestyles that are inconsistent with the welfare of God's people. Many of those in need of immediate removal from church circles are Christian leaders who bring reproach to the name of Christ because of their wicked actions and behavior.

The common practice now is for people to bring their garbage and leftovers to the church. Prior to discovering the Refuse Gate, as a pastor I was faced with the necessity of inviting believers to leave their spiritual trash outside the church, not inside. The church will begin to move in a great revival the day that the Dung Gate is restored. The Dung Gate restoration will encourage believers to realize that the church is not a junkyard or trash pile. Rather, the Lord intended His church to be a place of glory, reverence, honor, love, and respect for the things of God. Soon, believers will invite others to remove their ungodly, defiled garments and cast them into the sea of forgetfulness. When news regarding the restoration of the Refuse Gate travels around town, the world will see that the church is finally conducting God's legitimate business, and it will gain respect and reverence.

Not permitting trash to accumulate inside the Christian church will be revolutionary. When believers cease permitting the accumulation of ungodly attitudes and actions in their houses of worship, then the world shall see the glory of God shining bright. Certain believers feel it is necessary to cling to their ungodly heritage and perpetuate their defiling nature by contaminating as many in their reach as possible. If the church continues to welcome impenitent sinners to feel at liberty to heap their trash within the church, then there is no hope of providing a plague-free environment for other families and friends.

Somewhere along the line, the church has lost its ability to decipher between that which is good and that which is unbecoming. Every employer and existing social order has the ability to determine whether a person is welcomed or whether they qualify as unaccepted; a "persona non grata." Apparently, present-day Christian leaders have forgotten the task of protecting the interest and welfare of their church members. Every time a pastor, teacher, prophet, evangelist, or apostle ignores and fails to address the wicked, heinous, depraved, and sinister characters that fill their church pews, services, crusades, and events, they enable them to conspire to plunder believers and their families.

The church is to assist people in their desire to walk with God for His glory. Every member and participant in a Christian church must understand that church gatherings are for the purpose of promoting and maintaining the integrity of God's design and purpose. For many, the church has erroneously become a form of religious entertainment or social gathering whose attendance does not require serious reflection or participation. The apostle Paul contended with those under his care, reminding them that he intended to present them to God as a chaste virgin without spot, stain, or blemish:

> For I am jealous over you with godly jealousy: for I have espoused you to one husband, that I may present you as a chaste virgin to Christ.
>
> —2 CORINTHIANS 11:2

Many Christian leaders have lost the notion that believers can aspire to represent Christ's victory by showing forth the fruits of

God's cleansing power through Christ's sacrifice on the cross. While few believers are trained to walk in the power of God's redemption, there is ample evidence that God intended to cleanse every stain permanently so that the church could abide without blemish.

There is no doubt that sanctification can become a powerful witness in this world—when the church decides to restore the Refuse Gate. If the church's purpose is to pursue carnal aspirations and worldly corruption, no human barrier would keep them from that perversion. However, because the church has been called to live for God, they should restore the Refuse Gate and eliminate any obstacle that thwarts the achievement of their ultimate purpose. The Refuse Gate helps the church understand that the heart of God is to deliver Christian communities from those elements that are inconsistent with their purpose as participants in the church of the living God.

The spirit of discernment plays a great part in restoring the Refuse Gate back to good and working order. When discernment is not present or properly exercised, the Refuse Gate lies broken, thus the church is not able to distinguish good from bad. When the Refuse Gate is not functioning adequately, the church suffers catastrophically from people that have no ability to discern right from wrong. When the church is unable to classify something as clean or unclean, it loses its ability to exercise the function the Lord entrusted to it, and they are not able to carry out their calling.

There are villages in the world where people worship cows. In these villages, the people take cow dung from the pastures and put it upon the walls inside their homes as an act of honor. After a while, the residents of these homes lose all judgment and sensibility to the horrendous odor emanating from their walls. At the Refuse Gate, the church is required to discern that which is wholesome from that which is rotten. A similar illustration comes from workers in the produce business, whose work consists of looking around and finding rotten or decomposed items within the packaged produce. There is little difficulty in indicating which fruit container is rotten because the foul scent immediately reveals the source. In the same manner, similar signs are sure to appear in a church when rot begins to plague the congregation. The Refuse Gate helps the church understand the importance of learning the God-given commandment to discern between the precious and the vile. God promises that if His people accept this challenge to delve into the work of discernment, then victory, deliverance, and redemption will cause the church to be invincible:

> Therefore thus saith the LORD, If thou return, then will I bring thee again, and thou shalt stand before me: and if thou take forth the precious from the vile, thou shalt be as my mouth: let them return unto thee; but return not thou unto them. And I will make thee unto this people a fenced brasen wall: and they shall fight against thee, but they shall not prevail against thee: for I am with thee to save thee and to deliver thee, saith the LORD. And I will deliver thee out of the hand of the wicked, and I will redeem thee out of the hand of the terrible.
>
> —JEREMIAH 15:19–21

Behind this passage lies the answer to the frailty and diminishing power of the church's influence in today's world. As the church grows less willing to make the distinction between what is precious to God and what is vile, they shall see the deterioration of their walls and the continued plunder of their riches. The church's legacy as God's people is dependent on a functioning Refuse Gate, fulfilling what God intended for His people.

Church leadership should now be able to understand why the church has become such a flimsy, defenseless, and vulnerable house of straw. If the church is able to achieve its God-given task of removing the precious from the vile, then the Lord promises His church to be a strong fortress to contend against. God will make His people seem as a fortified bronze wall. In this work of separation, God promises that when the enemies fight against the church, they shall not prevail. When the church begins to remove the precious from the vile, they will inherit the benefits of overcoming and standing victoriously. The enemies that continue to plunder the church through worldliness and unfettered, insatiable lust shall be destroyed. It is an awesome thought to imagine the church becoming a mighty, secure fortress—a fenced, brazen, and fortified wall—solely from the willingness of leadership to separate the vile from the precious.

The Christian church is God's refuge and sanctuary crying out and proclaiming the offer of God's salvation to all those who have been wading in the mud. In restoring the Refuse Gate, however, believers need to be careful not to throw out the baby with the bathwater. The obligation to restore the Refuse Gate does not exempt the body of Christ from fulfilling its call to continue encouraging, forgiving, comforting, exhorting, and strengthening the weary, the feeble, and those who by virtue of their weakness require more and more of God's grace and mercy to overcome.

The deep, cleansing power of God's Word and His fellowship are for those who desire to walk in godly purity. Above all others, Christians should be cognizant that God is willing, as an expert cleanser, to purify the worst of blemishes produced by selfish sin and worldly lust. The Refuse Gate calls the people of God to humbly discern trash from treasure. Apparently, there are serious problems in Christian circles because churches are filled with corrupt, useless objects and trash. These human trash deposits are unprofitable. Having no value, they continually pollute, defile, and contemptuously parade their wicked rebellion without shame or remorse within the courts of God's sanctuary.

This divine concept to redeem the clean from the dirty at the Refuse Gate is not foreign to Scripture. God has always invited His people to settle accounts and turn the infested, wretched, sin-stained garments into bright, clean, pure, and white coverings:

> Come now, and let us reason together, saith the LORD: though your sins be as scarlet, they shall be as white as snow; though they be red like crimson, they shall be as wool.
>
> —ISAIAH 1:18

Throughout Scripture God commands His people to exchange their filth for His purity. In other words, out with the dirty and in with the clean. This invitation shows God's willingness to cleanse all those who desire to be numbered among His ranks. The church has forgotten to include this announcement and reality in their sermons and service. Church leaders must decide to walk in the bold proclamation of truth that establishes clear parameters between what is good and what is bad. If the church continues embracing mediocrity as their standard of conduct, church leaders can only expect a flimsy wall to safeguard the greatest of our assemblies.

If the Refuse Gate is not functioning, believers will find even the simplest task difficult; like telling the difference between good friends and godly friends. God has clearly promised victory for those who have the capacity to distinguish and separate the good from the bad. The Refuse Gate is a reminder for God's people to keep track of and faithfully continue removing unclean objects far from God's dwelling. If the church can begin doing this work, it can reasonably expect a mighty and godly army to arise. Once again, the church will become an unstoppable force, never again to be deceived and plundered. The promise of God stands calling His people to start cleaning house so that He can faithfully pour out His blessings without measure. Once God feels that He can move in a holy, pure, and clean camp, the church can expect innumerable victories and deliverance.

When the Refuse Gate has fallen, a healthy, vibrant church becomes filled with dirty vessels unfit for God's use. God refuses to pour out His provision for the world into unclean vessels. God has chosen to avoid the use of corrupt vessels to manifest His glory. The endless provisions of His grace and mercy are reserved for vessels of honor that have cleansed themselves. Many attend church for years and call themselves vessels of God, but do not realize that God desires vessels that are washed and free from any blemish.

When the leaders of God's church continue to allow the unrepentant sinner to remain in our midst, the church loses credibility and becomes a disservice to the best interests of others in the body of Christ. The apostle Paul writes to Timothy regarding this issue of drawing the distinction between becoming a vessel of honor and remaining as a vessel of dishonor. The only method believers should follow to become an appointed vessel of honor so that the church can prevail is purging themselves from ungodly people and things:

> But in a great house there are not only vessels of gold and of silver, but also of wood and of earth; and some to honour, and some to dishonour. If a man therefore purge himself from these, he shall be a vessel unto honour, sanctified, and meet for the master's use, and prepared unto every good work.
>
> —2 Timothy 2:20–21

In the same manner, when the church purges the assembly of all types of evil, it will be able to serve as a vessel of honor, sanctified for the Master's use, and prepared unto every good work.

Safeguarding the health and welfare of individual family members takes place every day in every home. The same concept applies to the church family, where the welfare and health of the church is safeguarded and protected. The church must also realize that the bigger their agape feast, the larger the pile of trash that is produced. Each time a family celebrates a feast in their home, they end up with bags upon bags of garbage. Likewise, when the church experiences revival meetings, the leadership must stand ready to discern the difference between what stays in the house and what elements are potentially hazardous if not immediately disposed of.

For example, if the church has an outreach event, concert, or prison ministry where many are invited to come to Jesus, it does not mean that the church should become the favorite hangout for those people to come and conduct their wicked business as usual. Christian youth groups should not be offered as an opportunity for vandalism, rebellion, or graffiti (albeit Bible verses) on church walls. When the church reaches out to the lost, it should not be an invitation to the ungodly to ransack the church with their misfit behavior and malicious conduct.

The church loses enormous credibility when the wicked view it as a place to take advantage of and further their ungodly enterprises. Outreach does not mean that the church needs to integrate and welcome those who desire to continue in their nefarious behavior.

These types of situations have become the reason why people do not desire to attend Christian gatherings or church assemblies anymore. The general public and media constantly disparage the Christian church as the den of thieves, warning that church circles have become treacherous places where criminals, such as thieves, pedophiles, molesters, and other deceptive practitioners, have taken harbor. Recently the Christian church was involved in various scandals; some involved the church harboring ministers accused of molesting young children and others who have been accused of dubious financial mismanagement. These scandals have tarnished the church beyond recognition.

The riveting accusations launched at the church time and again are proof that we have failed to purge the willfully wicked from our midst. Failure to repair the Refuse Gate causes the scent of corruption to emanate from the church, infecting the entire Christian community to the point that many refuse the fellowship of Christian believers. The noticeable stench in Christian circles accounts for the epidemic of negative views of Christ's sanctuary, which causes many to stay away. The majority of unbelievers marvel in amazement at how quickly church leadership is willing to continue conducting God's business by sweeping immoralities and improprieties under the proverbial "ecclesiastical carpet." Matters such as these cause the church to lose integrity, and negatively impact the cause of Christ in this ever-changing culture.

While it is true that God makes incredible sacrifice to capture the unholy and unclean, the church needs to acknowledge that God also takes serious issue and offense with pigs that enjoy wallowing in their mud. For those who perceive that the restoration of the Refuse Gate is a problematic accomplishment, I would like to suggest that not repairing the gate causes God's judgment to come upon the church. One thing church leaders will find totally amazing is that those who take issue against the Refuse Gate are usually the first to promote a congregational dung fest where all their faithful devotion and commitment is placed upon priorities that serve other interests instead of pleasing the heart of God.

God has given His only Son Jesus Christ so that He might sanctify a people to walk before His presence in cleanliness. Every Christian knows that without holiness, no one will see the Lord. Everyone is required to go through a process of purification and cleansing. The purification laws in the Old Testament show types and shadows that attest to God's standard of cleanliness. There were mandatory purification rites for every instrument and article in service to God in His sanctuary. While many churches no longer implement traditional purification rites, they cannot assume that God now intends to use dirty utensils. The very purpose of Christ giving Himself for the church was to wash and present the church to Himself as a glorious church, not having spot or wrinkle or any such thing; but that it should be holy and without blemish. Without resorting to religious legalism or false holiness, the church should promote and foster a desire in Christian hearts to remove any stain that smears or smudges the character of Christ's bride. Any other motive for holiness will discolor the Christian fabric so that blemishes are seen more often than not. The blood of Jesus has sufficient cleansing power to wash sins and whiten garments more than any other strong soap or detergent, so that the church can live a pure life reflecting the glory of God's countenance.

While others take great displeasure, personal offense, or surprise in the call for restoring the Refuse Gate, many acknowledge that this remains the reflection of God's heart. When the church exercises the godly instruction to dispose of that which is corrupt, they will begin to experience fresh revival that leads believers to a complete restoration of godly worship in the sanctuary.

In order to ensure against possible mistakes and future hurts, many would forego the reparation of the Refuse Gate. The reluctance to follow God's mandate to remove the ungodly and corrupt from the house of worship causes the pendulum to shift to a dangerous, unhealthy extreme.

Here, none are removed, despite their harmful practices or behavior.

Any church that intends to restore the Refuse Gate shall surely run the risk of being called legalistic, hyperreligious, cultic, pseudosanctified, pharisaical, or out of touch with reality. Despite the negative consequences and criticism, a wholesome church must boldly confront Christians, holding them accountable for their improper and ungodly acts that hurt the cause of Christ.

Many believers will be astonished because they have never heard of such a concept as the Refuse Gate. Even though some claim to have been raised in Christian families, they have never witnessed a Refuse Gate in action. How is it possible? This concept, which requires the church to use discernment in confronting and dealing with the ungodly and the perverse in the church fellowship, will revolutionize Christianity forever. As Christian leaders begin to usher the ungodly out through the dung gates of Christian churches, keeping in step with biblical instruction and obligation, many shameless, impenitent, so-called "Christians" will turn their backs and weep bitterly. They will claim that the church leaders are coldhearted and insensitive.

The activity at the Dung Gate should not be considered as unsympathetic or uncaring. Those that find themselves removed from Christian fellowship will begin to consider that maybe God desires true repentance and not prolonged disobedience or rebellion. The Dung Gate helps the ungodly deliberate their actions that are not acceptable to God or His people.

In every church, God requires Christian leaders to adhere to His mandate to draw the line between what is pleasing to the Lord and what is not. The church should not continue relegating this responsibility or postponing it to the next generation lest they fail to define right and wrong accurately:

> Woe unto them that call evil good, and good evil; that put darkness for light, and light for darkness; that put bitter for sweet, and sweet for bitter!
>
> —ISAIAH 5:20

Church leaders cannot sanction ungodly living in those who regularly attend the Christian fellowship. God expects His leaders to follow in stride, understanding the difference between good and evil so that they can accurately judge matters of right and wrong according to His Word. All church leaders are required to address matters in believers' lives in the same manner as Christ would when He comes in His kingdom. The separation of sheep and goats is a reality in God's kingdom. The Dung Gate helps church leaders confront those who are walking like goats. As the ungodly are refused fellowship or gathering with the Lord's sheep they can seek repentance and restoration.

The will of God was never to make His church the breeding place and resting ground for sin, rebellion, and disobedience. God's people are constantly reminded in the Word to put away evil from their hearts. God has a strict charge that His people put evil away from His sight. Scripture confirms that as God's people agree to put the ungodly things away, He is willing to stand in their defense. Regardless of the sin that befalls the body of Christ, God is always willing to change and fully cleanse His people from unrighteousness. God is able to take those buried in a dunghill and gloriously lift them out so they can take their place of honor, sitting with leaders among His people:

> He raiseth up the poor out of the dust, and lifteth up the beggar from the dunghill, to set them among princes, and to make them inherit the throne of glory.
>
> —1 SAMUEL 2:8

God desires to raise the ungodly and wayward. He wants to remove them from the plague of their infirmities so that they are no longer immersed in the dunghill of filth and rebellion. Those that ultimately find themselves exiting out through the Dung Gate are encouraged to call upon the name of the Lord so that they might find repentance. When they repent and confess, then they may be restored into Christian fellowship.

The power of God is visible in my testimony: God found me in the sewer of a spiritual wasteland, cleansed me, and sat me as a leader among His people. This redemption process is complete and perfect so that believers need not wander back into the sewer. Once a believer has been cleansed he must put away his evil doings as a gesture of love and gratefulness to the Lord. God desires all His people to cease doing evil and make themselves clean before His eyes:

> Wash yourselves, make yourselves clean; Put away the evil of your doings from before My eyes. Cease to do evil.
> —ISAIAH 1:16, NKJV

The church must obey God's instruction by putting away the evil of their doings from before His eyes and removing themselves from that which is defiled. The Lord has given specific instruction to make the church clean by putting the wicked out from among the fellowship. The apostle Paul's first letter to the Corinthians addressed the church's need to disassociate from those who persisted in wicked behavior:

> But now I have written unto you not to keep company, if any man that is called a brother be a fornicator, or covetous, or an idolater, or a railer, or a drunkard, or an extortioner; with such an one no not to eat…Therefore put away from among yourselves that wicked person.
> —1 CORINTHIANS 5:11, 13

By spurning its duty, the modern-day church has purposely disobeyed the specific instructions of God's Word. It has decided instead to utterly cast out the Refuse Gate because it is too pragmatic. When the Refuse Gate is missing or fallen, the unforgiving, fornicator, covetous, idolater, railer, drunkard, extortioner, and adulterer continue in Christian fellowship without repentance or remorse. Those permitted to continue in fellowship even while outwardly pursuing ungodly acts are in danger of becoming harmful reprobates to the body of Christ. The church was never intended to spawn apostates who continue to enjoy full access to church worship halls and continue in fellowship with the body of Christ, as they perfect their wickedness. The Refuse Gate requires exposing and confronting the apparent wickedness and filth in the lives of every believer to ensure a genuine Christlike devotion in every church.

At the Refuse Gate, those having their conscience seared with a hot iron, who continually speak lies in hypocrisy and no longer have sensibility to the spirit of God for repentance, must be marked out and removed from the church. Church leaders must begin to discern and exact the measure or standard of godly conduct and character in the midst of their church congregations in order to preserve a godly lineage. When the Refuse Gate is missing, the church begins to reproduce and spawn believers that are full of religiosity and hypocrisy. The failure to obey God's Word in this regard will only cause the continual rising up of ungodly believers who later have the potential of becoming ungodly leaders.

It is sinister to allow the ungodly to continue aspiring and attaining Christian teachings such as doctorates in theology and masters in divinity and biblical studies. Every graduation, award, recognition, diploma, or certificate advanced to a man of ungodly character is an endorsement that will be used against the body of Christ to harm hundreds of thousands of families. I was recently told of a specific case where a woman was attending her husband's pastoral ordination and graduation from a particular denominational seminary. During the graduation ceremony, she was overcome with strong emotional sentiment and tears. The head chancellor noticed her display of emotion and approached her afterward. He told the woman that her sentiment of joy was appropriate in the light of her husband's accomplishment of fulfilling all the seminary requirements. As the bishop continued to congratulate and comfort the seminarian's wife, she interrupted and told him that she was not shedding tears of joy over her husband's accomplishment, but of great sadness and grief. The wife told the head chancellor that had his institution really known her husband they would never have ordained him nor awarded him a diploma. The wife continued clarifying that the university had failed in scrutinizing the person they were endorsing and graduating. She added that her husband was a terrible example of the Christian faith. Finally the woman said, "If it were up to me I would never have permitted my husband to graduate and finalize his biblical studies because he lives none of the Word of God that he has allegedly been taught."

Many times, church leaders desire to engage in all sorts of instructional, educational, and intellectual practices of the Christian faith without realizing that Christ has given the church a different charge. The Refuse Gate warns the church against rewarding and graduating those who have openly contradicted the teachings of Christ by living immoral lives, failing to uphold and maintain the requisite testimony of Christ's character. Many churches have Bible institutes and offer degrees in biblical studies. They open their registrations to thousands who should not step foot into church halls of learning due to their reprobate character and ill reputation. When church leaders fail to exercise discernment at the Refuse Gate, they run the risk of reproducing an ungodly kind.

Jesus also gave this warning to the church leaders of His day when He stood before the hypocrites and stated the following words:

> Woe unto you, scribes and Pharisees, hypocrites! for ye compass sea and land to make one proselyte, and when he is made, ye make him twofold more the child of hell than yourselves.
> —MATTHEW 23:15

Who would have thought it possible for the church to win over a soul, train him up in Christian sanctuaries, and then when they finished discipling him they find he has become twice the child of hell than the leadership who mentored him. Any invitation extended for others to participate in church fellowship without the welcomed scrutiny of a life that pleases the Lord is nothing more than an incubator of hell. Church leaders must be careful not to provide an environment that foments or nurtures that which is contrary to the building up of the Lord's church. The broken Refuse Gate permits the church to breed children of hell that later devour and subvert God's people.

Jesus also instructed that His people are like salt, and when they lose their flavor, they are no longer good for anything but to be thrown out and trampled underfoot by men:

> You are the salt of the earth; but if the salt loses its flavor, how shall it be seasoned? It is then good for nothing but to be thrown out and trampled underfoot by men.
>
> —MATTHEW 5:13, NKJV

If believers are the salt of the earth yet no longer have their flavor, Jesus said they are good for nothing except to be thrown out and trampled underfoot by men. This means that men will trample the ungodly Christian witness underfoot as useless because they are no longer able to prevent corruption. The purpose of the Refuse to Gate is to prevent the festering of rot and decay so that they do not corrode the church. Surely, God deserves a church that reflects the wholesomeness of His sovereign work and redemption at the cross of Calvary:

> Woe unto thee, O Jerusalem! wilt thou not be made clean?
>
> —JEREMIAH 13:27

God must stand amazed that after all He has done to make provisions for His people's cleansing, His church continues to be marred by abominations and persistent rebellion. Believers that undermine the precious price that Christ paid to cleanse sin through His blood are a travesty. As a teenager, I felt very conscientious of the price paid for the forgiveness of my sin. I prayed, *Lord, I messed up again. I'm sorry. I'm using more of Your blood—the blood that was beat out of Your body—I need a bit more for the forgiveness of my sins.*

As the people of God, we must begin placing significant value on the price of cleansing. The price paid for believer's washing at the cross of Calvary cannot be considered a common thing to be trodden under believer's feet any longer. When Christians consider the weighty significance of the sacrifice that cancelled their debt, they will not run irresponsibly toward sin any longer. The transaction of forgiveness must become something valuable as we acknowledge from whence comes our cleansing—from nothing but the blood of Jesus. The church must communicate the reality of the blows and scourging given to Christ on the day He gave His life. The believer must affirm that every time they confess their sins, God is just and faithful to forgive and cleanse them from all unrighteousness. Even though the blood of Christ will never run dry, believers should avoid trampling the blood of Christ under their feet as ordinary. Much more than the blood of goats and lambs, their cleansing is derived from the blood-purchased sacrifice of God's only begotten Son who was crucified on Calvary.

In the church, there is so much cleansing taking place that there needs to be a Refuse Gate to avoid widespread contamination and infection. The Refuse Gate must serve as the system whereby church leaders can process the removal of filth from all the cleansing that is taking place. Between the garbage heap on Earth and the heavenly city, the Lord has chosen the church to serve as a place for His holiness to abide. God delights in those who aim at cleanliness and whose true desire is to attain the full measure of holiness and purity God's grace can provide. God's people must become saturated in the aroma of Christ by accepting God's call to a holy and pure life. The church's quest for truth leads believers to an admission that God's heartfelt desire is to produce a sanctified people. These people have washed themselves and are willing to live the remainder of their lives as proof that God's manifested power and grace can make one clean. There is no doubt that Scripture is full of God's continual instruction commanding His people to wash everything: hands, feet, garments, mouths, eyes, hearts, sons, daughters, dwellings, families, thoughts, actions, and deeds. The specific details in God's continual and explicit instruction prove that God longs for this to become a reality for each person that is a part of His family, especially leaders who stand at the forefront of using His name.

Those who think that the Refuse Gate is solely for the overtly wicked and depraved will be greatly surprised when they learn that the Dung Gate is also an opportunity for those who are walking in righteousness. As the church learns the particular workings of the Refuse Gate, they will discover that many times a believer's own righteousness and strength can be counted as "dung" and must be removed and immediately disposed of through the Refuse Gate. God instructs His people in the Old Testament that all people are unclean and all their righteous acts are as filthy rags of unrighteousness before the Lord:

> But we are all as an unclean thing, and all our righteousnesses are as filthy rags; and we all do fade as a leaf; and our iniquities, like the wind, have taken us away.
>
> —Isaiah 64:6

The "filthy rags" were, in Isaiah's time, the dirty menstrual cloths used by Jewish women during their monthly menstrual cycle. A Jewish woman during this time was considered unclean and was quarantined from her family and friends so that they would not run the risk of being contaminated by the blood of her menstruation. Relating this to today, every believer should be careful not to contaminate God's church with their own acts of self-righteousness. They should instead give way for God's righteousness to prevail. The apostle Paul clearly understood this aspect of the Refuse Gate as seen in the following passage written to the Philippians:

> Yea doubtless, and I count all things but loss for the excellency of the knowledge of Christ Jesus my Lord: for whom I have suffered the loss of all things, and do count them but dung, that I may win Christ
>
> —Philippians 3:8

Paul wanted to remove anything in his life or curriculum vitae that might hinder the work of God's righteousness. Once the church determines to count something as dung there is only one place to take it, the Refuse Gate. The Refuse Gate is the perfect place to discard anything that might interfere with the church's work or relationship with Christ.

As long as the Refuse Gate is in good working order, church leaders can teach their members where the trash belongs. When my children were two and three years old, they did not know the difference between good and evil. So my wife and I taught them what was good and what was bad. Now that the children know the difference between right and wrong, they are able to choose and embrace that which is good and beneficial for their lives.

Through the grace of God, there is ample washing and cleansing. In the natural, people spend time taking care of their outer man and physical body, but many times our spiritual bodies are left unclean. God's expectation for the church to become a clean, holy, and purified place of worship is well warranted.

Many times, people keep their spiritual closets full of smelly trash with the curious intention and desire to preserve the trash forever. The following is an illustration of this attitude:

> A wife recently told of her experience when she attempted to successfully conclude her spring-cleaning on a particular weekend. She came across a plastic bag with a very peculiar stench that was lying in her closet. She asked her husband, "Honey, do you know what this is?" "Oh, yes," he responded, "these are my tennis shoes from when I was in the sixth grade."

The Refuse Gate requires gatekeepers to live an open, transparent life of godliness, thus avoiding the proverbial custom to continue as whitewashed tombs—clean on the outside, but filled with dead men's bones and rot on the inside. The purpose of the Refuse Gate is not to exercise some form of pharisaical religious ritual to hurt sinners with excommunication. The proper use of the Refuse Gate is to put out those gathering within the body of Christ who, after many admonitions, exhortations, and stern corrections, refuse to repent. These people continue to act in ways that are willfully disobedient and openly rebellious, causing serious problems to the general welfare of the church.

At a minimum, the church should preserve the integrity of the body of Christ with the same zeal and diligence that other organizations use to protect the welfare of their institutions. One recent example of a secular organization implementing this concept is the well-known People for the Ethical Treatment of Animals (P.E.T.A.). This organization fired one of their top models, Naomi Campbell, for continuing to wear fur in a fashion show. Her actions totally contradicted her previous commitment as a spokesperson for the P.E.T.A. anti-fur campaign. In the same manner, Christians should defend the integrity of the body of Christ by removing so-called "Christians" who persist in dishonoring and disgracing the church. Restoring the Refuse Gate requires Christian leaders to take some course of action to remove those who hold themselves out as "Christian" but constantly engage in behavior that contradicts their claim. Generally, those who continue to engage in conduct that purposefully dishonors the name of Christ showing no remorse or repentance may require removal before they harm someone.

To safeguard against throwing out a "diamond in the rough," Christian leaders must first follow the biblical instruction to give every believer an opportunity for repentance. Every believer should have access to godly correction, counseling, admonishing, and encouragement, which are all very important to redeeming, restoring, and reconciling those who have fallen. Nonetheless, believers who remain impenitent and persist in disobedience and rebellion are prime candidates for removal through the Refuse Gate.

To properly exercise the function of the Refuse Gate, church leadership must be willing to open their lives as godly examples and public standards of genuine integrity. The church should be reminded that their aim is to honor God by portraying holy and reverent conduct in the place of worship. This is so the world may have proof that God is able to keep in godliness, strength, and wisdom those whom the world once called ungodly and weak:

But God hath chosen the foolish things of the world to confound the wise; and God hath chosen the weak things of the
world to confound the things which are mighty.

—1 CORINTHIANS 1:27

The church must not forget that God demands godliness from those
who have become His offspring and lineage. God's working power in
the blood of Christ cries out for a standard of godliness that honors
Christ rather than reproaches the name of God. There is ample time
for repentance and godly sorrow to motivate believers to walk in
the purity and grace of God's strength. The Refuse Gate should not
serve as a witchhunt to judge, condemn, mock, humiliate, ridicule, or
criticize weak believers. The Refuse Gate claims the removal of those
that continue to act out in ungodly arrogance and depraved immoral
insurrection against God's Word and the sanctity of His fellowship.
Jesus taught His followers that the process of requiring others to come
clean includes cleansing oneself first:

And why do you look at the speck in your brother's eye, but
do not consider the plank in your own eye? Or how can you
say to your brother, 'Let me remove the speck from your eye';
and look, a plank is in your own eye? Hypocrite! First remove
the plank from your own eye, and then you will see clearly to
remove the speck out of your brother's eye.

—MATTHEW 7:3–5, NKJV

Jesus instructed His disciples to first remove the log from their own
eye and then move on to address the life of the community. At the
Refuse Gate, no one is exempt or above the rules, as every believer
is called to accountability and right living in Christ. When church
leadership attempt to ask others to remove the specks from their eyes,
they better make sure they have removed the plank from their own
eye first. Failing to do this will serve only as a hypocritical stumbling
block and hindrance to those they are called to minister to. When
Christ imparted this truth, He did not intend to stop His followers

from removing that which was no good from others' lives. Rather, Christ intended for leaders to first remove those things in their lives that are wrong, and then to request others to conduct themselves after the same godly example.

Christ's clear instruction for followers to address problems that blur their vision has now become every Christian's excuse for neither the removing of the plank nor the speck. The travesty of not following Christ's teaching in this area has caused many believers to have their vision blocked from seeing how to walk in God's divine purpose. Many leaders are unwilling to obey the first part of Christ's instruction and therefore they never get to the second part of helping others remove their speck. If the church is able to restore the Refuse Gate, the Holy Spirit will lead believers to God's grace. This is so all believers might live holy lives for Christ, even in the midst of a perverse, corrupt, and wicked generation.

PRAYER APPLICATION

Father God! Help the Christian church to restore the Refuse Gate. Lord, all believers need the gift of discernment so that they may be able to distinguish between the holy and the unholy, good and bad, right and wrong, light and darkness, so as to remove from their midst those things which are unfit for Your presence. Jesus, give all Your saints the courage to dispose anything in the church's midst that is contrary to the welfare and best interest of the body of Christ. Not that Christians have already attained perfection Lord, but I thank You for the full work of redemption, restoration, and reconciliation that permits believers to faithfully press toward the goal for the prize of the upward call of God in Christ Jesus.

6

THE FOUNTAIN GATE

O LORD, the hope of Israel, all that forsake thee shall be ashamed, and they that depart from me shall be written in the earth, because they have forsaken the LORD, the fountain of living waters.

—JEREMIAH 17:13

This chapter focuses on restoring the Fountain Gate. Here at the Fountain Gate believers will be challenged to seek God, and only God, for all their needs and provisions. As believers make every effort to meet their needs and obtain all their provisions they should look to God as the only true source and fountain. Every time a Christian attempts to meet their needs outside of God, they will suffer great derision and loss. Every Christian church that permits a broken Fountain Gate profanes the name of God, who is able to provide all things.

Failure to restore the Fountain Gate turns the Christian church into a mockery. Believers begin to choose alternative provisions and phony substitutes for God's true provision and faithful sustenance.

Restoring the Fountain Gate in the church is important because it establishes that Christians should never allow themselves to be misled into seeking after empty promises in other fountains. The necessity of repairing the Fountain Gate must not be overlooked. This restoration allows the church to establish insightful wisdom and understanding for those interested in rebuilding a fortified church for God's people. The restoration efforts in the Book of Nehemiah lead to this gate in verse fifteen called the Fountain Gate:

> Shallun the son of Col-Hozeh, leader of the district of Mizpah, repaired the Fountain Gate; he built it, covered it, hung its doors with its bolts and bars, and repaired the wall of the Pool of Shelah by the King's Garden, as far as the stairs that go down from the City of David.
> —NEHEMIAH 3:15, NKJV

The Fountain Gate is the fifth gate to be repaired in the restoration efforts of the ancient Jerusalem city. In everyday life, people tend to drift in the direction of where their needs are being met. Many are strongly influenced to walk toward the place where they can find the resources that continue meeting their needs. People tend to schedule or program their lives around the places or things that are able to provide their needs. Many great cities were formed and populated based on the provision of nearby resources. Their ability to attract people was based on their capacity to provide work or other resources such as commerce, trading, or employment.

Failing to restore the Fountain Gate in the Christian church causes the Lord's people to seek resources outside of the church. When the Fountain Gate is repaired, people begin to seek God as the true source and origin of all their needs. A fallen Fountain Gate is evident when the church begins to lose members who disassociate themselves to follow after wayward paths. These people are seeking satisfaction or fulfillment in other things or places. When the Fountain Gate is in ill repair, believers are led astray to seek other streams as the source to supply their needs.

When a church continues to exist with a broken Fountain Gate, Christians tend to instill in the hearts of other Christians—both young and old—the idea that God cannot meet or supply their needs, thus insinuating that they must turn aside in search of another fountain. Unfortunately, many decisions are often made according to the availability of resources. As a result, many of God's people tend to swerve out of God's will in order to accommodate the influence of their new-found source of provision.

At the Fountain Gate, the church is required to impart the understanding that God is the only true, authentic, and ultimate source of all we will ever need or desire in this world. In the modern church, the Fountain Gate is utterly cast down and destroyed every time a believer chooses to forsake seeking or waiting upon God. When a Christian begins to seek elsewhere to find someone, something, or somewhere to satisfy and supply their innermost longing or needs, God is regarded as unfaithful.

The church has suffered great loss due to those who continually look for and claim to have discovered their provisions outside and away from God. When church members forsake the restoration of the Fountain Gate, the hearts and minds of God's people are led to explore far from the fountain of all true provision. Those who forsake this restoration process in their church and in the lives of their flock will ultimately deceive only themselves and end up paying a hefty price for foregoing God's wellspring of provision.

This chapter on the Fountain Gate will help many Christians who presently hold on to the prevalent misconception that believers should forsake God and go elsewhere to meet their needs and quench their thirst. The Fountain Gate is restored when God's people not only discover that God is the only true source to meet all their needs, but also that in pursuing Him the believer can satisfy all their hunger, thirst, and longing.

The word *fountain* is defined as "the source, origin, or beginning from which a thing proceeds or is supplied." Restoring the Fountain Gate requires the church to depend solely upon God as the eternal source and supply of all things needed. It is clearly evident that many believers attending the Christian church have lost sight of this truth. Right now, there are many churches that lie without the Fountain Gate in its rightful place. The broken Fountain Gate has allowed many Christian families to suffer loss and continual plunder because they have been lead to believe that there are other sources for provision and truth outside of God. When believers are led to question the true origins of all things, they are exposed to severe attack and deception by the enemy.

At the Fountain Gate, all believers will learn that God is the only sufficient source of all their provision and supply. As believers, Christians are expected to know that all things come from God and God alone. When believers fail to establish this truth in their lives, and their hopes or expectations are defined by a different source of truth, then they will begin to suffer all kinds of evil.

As efforts are made to restore the Fountain Gate, Christians will begin to learn that God's children will never be able to exhaust the storehouse of God's boundless provision. Many times Christians fail to recognize the vast wealth of God's riches that is laid up for those who wait upon the Lord. In the restoration of the Fountain Gate, every Christian is called to acknowledge, repent, and confess the many times they have disregarded the reality of God's faithful provision. Only God knows the losses suffered by the body of Christ for not believing and waiting upon His faithful promise to generously provide all things. Christians have turned away, and subsequently place their expectations for the supply of all good things upon someone or something other than God. Restoring the Fountain Gate can only take place when the church realizes that all too often believers are wrongly led to seek the meeting of their needs in a source or fountain far from God's storehouse.

More often than not, God's people are deceived into thinking that their problems are better solved or answered by something other than God. As the church begins to restore the Fountain Gate, Christians must learn that only God is able to thoroughly quench all thirst with the good and perfect measure of His wellspring. When believers realize that God is the source of every good and perfect gift, they will never thirst again. The Bible confirms for the church time and again that every good and perfect gift comes solely from one place:

> Every good gift and every perfect gift is from above, and cometh down from the Father of lights, with whom is no variableness, neither shadow of turning.
>
> —JAMES 1:17

Regardless of the motivation that causes believers to seek elsewhere, and despite their looking for answers in someone or something else, the Christian church must realize that they all too often have misled others in forsaking the best origin and source for all good things. Each time God's people forego seeking Him for their provision the result is the same: they end up with great loss, disillusionment, deception, heartbreak, and despair.

Once the Fountain Gate is restored, rebuilt, and put back in place, the church will learn to boldly exhort their members to wait and never again forsake God, knowing that He alone is able to truly provide all their needs. The Fountain Gate instructs the church that God alone is the overflowing origin of all their wants, desires, dreams, and hopes. Every promise of God's faithful provision for the believer takes place and is being constantly fulfilled in, by, and through Christ. Hopefully, through the restoration of the Fountain Gate, the church will learn never to consider any other source to meet their needs other than God Himself.

As natural men and women with a fallen nature, believers are generally accustomed to revert to their past reaction of considering another alternative other than God as a means to meet their needs. As soon as a believer faces a problem, they seek immediately for answers in other places. God's sheep always think they can find provisions in other pastures, even if those pastures are not so green. At the Fountain Gate, God reveals to His children that He is the only One who can meet their every continual need. God is the One who will meet every need a Christian may have, and as long as they seek Him for their requests they will never lack any good thing.

Christians that forget God's faithfulness to provide, and who choose to forsake *Jehovah-Jireh*, which means, "the Lord will provide," can only experience false hope and desolate destruction from all other venues of provision. There is ample evidence that once believers decide to forsake God's provision and choose another source to meet their needs, they suffer continually—being plundered and robbed, remaining in absolute desolation. The Word of God continually reminds God's people that He demands them to seek Him and Him alone for the abundant supply of all things. In Jeremiah 2:12, God's sentiment is clearly portrayed as He rebukes those who have forsaken Him as the faithful source of their provision:

> Be astonished, O ye heavens, at this, and be horribly afraid, be ye very desolate, saith the LORD. For my people have committed two evils; they have forsaken me the fountain of living waters, and hewed them out cisterns, broken cisterns, that can hold no water.
>
> —JEREMIAH 2:12–13

If Christian leaders were to describe the state of the families that attend their church today, they would have to admit that their condition is one of utter ruin. The word *desolation* means "a state of devastation, ruin, wretchedness, and misery." Desolation is the cause and consequence of forsaking God—the Fountain of living waters—and seeking for provisions elsewhere. If the church desires to restore the desolate ruin in their families and church communities, they must turn their hearts back toward the true Fountain of living waters and seek to meet their necessities from God's hand and His hand alone.

As the Fountain Gate is restored, no longer will God's people hew out cisterns—broken cisterns—that hold no water:

The young lions roared upon him, and yelled, and they made his land waste: his cities are burned without inhabitant. Also the children of Noph and Tahapanes have broken the crown of thy head. Hast thou not procured this unto thyself, in that thou hast forsaken the LORD thy God, when he led thee by the way? And now what hast thou to do in the way of Egypt, to drink the waters of Sihor? or what hast thou to do in the way of Assyria, to drink the waters of the river? Thine own wickedness shall correct thee, and thy backslidings shall reprove thee: know therefore and see that it is an evil thing and bitter, that thou hast forsaken the LORD thy God, and that my fear is not in thee, saith the Lord GOD of hosts.

—JEREMIAH 2:15–19

The preceding scripture reveals that those of God's people who continued to forsake God as the source of their needs, ended up creating a wasteland out of His cities. Even God's habitation became of place of ruins as a result of God's people continually forsaking the Lord. The modern-day church blames every past Christian movement and former leaders instead of placing the blame where it belongs—on themselves. Those who claim to be God's people strive incessantly to supply their own needs outside of God's presence, to the point of repeatedly falling flat on their faces.

During these times of defeat, God asks this question, "Was not this all your doing?" Many times, the church consults with secular sources and worldly counsel to address their deficiencies instead of seeking God's face. Many believers incessantly go astray drinking from strange sources to satiate their thirst, instead of returning to God's river of life. Many times God warns His people that deviating to other sources of provision will eventually end in shameful embarrassment. The most effective instructors for correcting humans are pain and suffering caused by their own folly. This is why God says that their frequent backslidings and turnings will call their attention. As the church advances to restore the Fountain Gate, Christians will discover that there is an awful price to pay when they replace God as the ultimate choice for obtaining provision.

Careful attention must be given to the fact that forsaking God comes as a direct result of having lost the fear of the Lord. As Proverbs 9:10, reveals, "The fear of the LORD is the beginning of wisdom." A church without wisdom is destined to look elsewhere for answers and depend on anything and anyone but God.

Those in the household of faith who desire to restore the awful state of today's church must address the tendency of God's people to forego Him as the legitimate source for their supply. God desires every church that bears His name to repair the Fountain Gate. God desires everyone that forms part of His church to call upon Him and realize that He is sufficient to provide a limitless supply of all things. No plan outside of God shall serve to prosper God's people. In the past, every time that God's people have sought to prosper without Him, atrocious enemies that have easily devoured, destroyed, and ransacked them and their possessions have met them.

God admonishes His people for being quick to run to Egypt, asking, "What hast thou to do in the way of Egypt?" In the Bible, *Egypt* signifies worldly thinking, the systems of men, and carnal (natural) reasoning. God wonders why His children would go elsewhere—*Why try to resolve your problems with the answers of man? Why take the road to Assyria? Why go to Egypt to drink the waters of Sihor?*

God was curious as to why His people would resort to the Nile River where raw sewage and dirty water were the only provisions. The seduction to seek provision from an unclean source will plague our lives with disease and noxious waste. Every inclination to forego God as the Fountain of living waters will end up in absolute injury and total loss. God always assures His people that they can find refreshing, life-sustaining provision in His plan. The end result of a people looking for provisions away from God is a city that is burned and emptied of all their inhabitants.

When Christians remove their trust from God and pursue the confidence of mere men, they position themselves in a vulnerable situation. They most often end up suffering opposition and ridicule. The unforgettable lesson at the Fountain Gate is that God calls His people to learn from their terrible mistakes and resist the tendency to seek out provision from other sources.

The Fountain Gate teaches the church that they are not to run anywhere else for their provisions. God desires that His people would see this truth as more than an intellectual exercise of faith. Many people of faith fall apart in practical terms because they fail to practice what they claim to adamantly believe. Believers are not only to profess belief in God's truths; they must manifest assurance of the realities of what God has promised in His truth. The church must teach believers to turn from any temptation that invites them toward other merchants who promise to satiate their ever-wanting souls. The apostle Paul, in his letter to the Ephesians, reminded the early church that God is a powerful source able to do exceeding abundantly above all that believers can ask or think:

> Now unto him that is able to do exceeding abundantly above all that we ask or think, according to the power that worketh in us.
>
> —EPHESIANS 3:20

Once believers receive the revelation of God's truth, that He intends to adequately and abundantly provide for all those things that they ask or think, they will resist going astray to seek after false sources of provision. Those who place their trust in God's ability to provide will definitely see His faithfulness, mercy, and grace. Never again should the church return to a life that second-guesses the Lord's ability to help meet their needs according to His great power and riches in glory. In fact, believers who run towards other sources of provision because they perceive them as better or stronger will find that God takes offense because they did not seek Him:

> Woe to them that go down to Egypt for help; and stay on horses, and trust in chariots, because they are many; and in horsemen,

because they are very strong; but they look not unto the Holy
One of Israel, neither seek the LORD!

—ISAIAH 31:1

If the modern church restores the Fountain Gate, the restoration shall become the source of continuous victory. Never again would the adversary, the devil, defeat the church whose members place their hope steadfastly in the Lord's ability to provide all things according to His wisdom and goodness. Those who place their hope in the Lord shall never be put to shame. Each believer should be admonished to never expect to prosper or accomplish any feat outside of God's provision. May they never be so daring as to think they can obtain victory absent from God's wellspring. I truly hope the body of Christ learns that every perceived victory attained far from God's stream of blessing becomes a stench, an eyesore, and at best becomes their shame.

God has not given Christians the task of manipulating situations to carry out their own prosperity. True prosperity can only arrive when Christians are willing to wait for God to satiate their thirst and fulfill His promise to provide for all their needs according to His vast riches in glory. When the church is willing to become the humble recipient of God's infinite grace and mercy, then believers can participate and witness God's endless supply of blessing to be poured out in large measure to those who wait upon Him. The church must allow God to prosper them so that only God receives the glory of blessing and establishing them.

The world is tired of seeing churches seeking out their own prosperity. These believers end up losing their reputations and families, and repeatedly reap a sour harvest of rotten fruits. When the Fountain Gate is restored, God will give the church victories so that they can witness and testify that their achievements and prosperity have been established by God alone. The Lord desires to create abundant supply and provision for His people so the world will marvel and ponder how Christian believer's needs are met. God loves to perform wonders of grace so that others may observe His grandiose strength, power, and might:

> That they may see, and know, and consider, and understand together, that the hand of the LORD hath done this, and the Holy One of Israel hath created it.
>
> —ISAIAH 41:20

Every church must begin to restore the Fountain Gate, seeking only the Lord's supply so that the world may see, know, consider, and understand that the hand of the Lord hath met our needs. Upon entering into this right relationship of trusting God as an authentic and reliable source to meet their needs, the church shall experience provision that exceeds abundantly and far above all they ask of Him. As soon as every assembly and fellowship repairs the Fountain Gate, this powerful aspect of the church's fortress will become impenetrable. The forces of hell's host constantly tempt believers to depart from the living God. The fiery darts of the enemy repeatedly seek to contaminate the hearts and minds of God's people so that they seek elsewhere to fill their bellies with the husks that swine eat instead of waiting on the awesome faithfulness and provision of the Lord Jesus Christ.

The proclamation at the Fountain Gate is derived from understanding and admitting that every need God's people have is found in God, and that in Jesus the church has the fullness of God's provision unto all things. This chapter teaches every believer that the true fountain flows from the house of the Lord so that all the world can witness the incredible abundance and faithfulness of God:

> And it shall come to pass in that day, that the mountains shall drop down new wine, and the hills shall flow with milk, and all the rivers of Judah shall flow with waters, and a fountain shall come forth of the house of the LORD, and shall water the valley of Shittim. Egypt shall be a desolation, and Edom

shall be a desolate wilderness, for the violence against the children of Judah, because they have shed innocent blood in their land.

—JOEL 3:18–19

At the Fountain Gate, the church will finally realize that the whole world can offer nothing, and that the world's best advice leads only to shame and guilt. All worldly wisdom and reasoning leads only to empty promises. Christians must cease running after worldly answers and carnal provisions for their sustenance. The confession and proclamation discovered at the Fountain Gate is:

The LORD is my portion, saith my soul; therefore will I hope in him. The LORD is good unto them that wait for him, to the soul that seeketh him. It is good that a man should both hope and quietly wait for the salvation of the LORD.

—LAMENTATIONS 3:24–26

God's continual promise throughout Scripture is that He is sufficient to provide and help all those who wait patiently upon Him.

For evildoers shall be cut off: but those that wait upon the LORD, they shall inherit the earth.

—PSALM 37:9

I will lift up mine eyes unto the hills, from whence cometh my help. My help cometh from the LORD, which made heaven and earth.

—PSALM 121:1–2

But they that wait upon the LORD shall renew their strength; they shall mount up with wings as eagles; they shall run, and not be weary; and they shall walk, and not faint.

—ISAIAH 40:31

Therefore I will look unto the LORD; I will wait for the God of my salvation: my God will hear me.

—MICAH 7:7

Everyone who waits upon the Lord shall be refreshed with strength. They can expect to run life's journey without growing weary or fainting. The house of the Lord should serve as a model to all nations that God is sufficient to provide the resources of every good and perfect provision. Unfortunately, when Christians fail to wait upon the Lord they experience the same wretched outcome as nonbelievers. The negative consequences seen in the lives of Christians who fail to seek the Lord are later reflected in broken marriages, financial distress, and unwanted pregnancies.

Recent research shows that the likelihood of divorce is identical among born-again Christians and those who are not born again. This research reflects that many Christians tend to act like unbelievers when they choose their marriage partners. Instead of waiting for godly counsel and confirmation, they choose to follow after worldly tactics in order to quicken the process and lessen the wait.

When believers stop seeking after other cisterns to quench their thirst, they can experience true healing and abundant provision. Many churches have decided to offer the believer worldly wisdom and instruction to address present-day dilemmas. Youth group leaders are encouraged to promote new ways of entertainment, but this ends up producing superficial emotional stimuli that never cultivates effective and strong convictions in the lives of their youth. Christian youth are often swayed to compromise their convictions, taking the appearance of worldly youth without realizing that worldly youth usually revert to quenching their thirst from potholes and cesspools of life. Once the Fountain Gate is restored youth group leaders can encourage their youth to drink in God's presence. Where two or more gather in His name, the youth will find answers to their needs in prayer.

The world has nothing more to offer the church than broken dreams, broken hearts, broken lives, broken marriages, broken families, and bankrupt businesses. The church has been brainwashed into ushering worldly ways and methods into the church and enticing church members to seek for joy, peace, and prosperity just as the world does outside of God's presence and wisdom.

There is futility in trying to satisfy one's soul with any source outside of God's fountain. The Book of Ecclesiastes is a memorial to those who attempted to find fulfillment outside of God's wellspring. The words of Solomon are a true testament of the emptiness, frustration, and despair experienced by those who journey outside of God's timing to provide for their longings:

> Whatever my eyes desired I did not keep from them. I did not withhold my heart from any pleasure, For my heart rejoiced in all my labor; And this was my reward from all my labor.
> —ECCLESIASTES 2:10, NKJV

This man's diligent pursuit of seeking elsewhere for things that would bring satisfaction and fulfillment to his own personal life ended in unhappiness. Solomon's account of searching for his desires apart from God's provision and timing was so vexing that it drove him to hate the very life he lived:

> Therefore I hated life.
> —ECCLESIASTES 2:17, NKJV

> I hated all my labor.
> —ECCLESIASTES 2:18, NKJV

> Therefore I turned my heart and despaired.
> —ECCLESIASTES 2:20, NKJV

Instead of seeking for purpose, pleasure, and fulfillment away from God, there is the promise to experience a life of inexpressible joy, peace, and love that is endless. Those who drink at God's fountain will never thirst again. The promise of God to bless those who wait upon His provision is too good to pass up. The supply of God's provision is not for the elite or the prominent but for all those who call upon the name of the Lord. The Word of God affirms that God makes His sun to rise on the evil and on the good, and sends rain on the just and on the unjust.

Some people may have the privilege of drinking from exclusive sparkling water systems due to their wealth or social class, but Jesus stands with the greatest water offer of all. The Fountain Gate reminds believers that whoever drinks of the water that God gives shall never thirst again. Reading the account of the Samaritan woman, who met with Jesus at Jacob's well, gives believers insight into God's open invitation for all who thirst. Every Christian should take time to read and pray over this passage, asking God to quench their thirst so that they experience the reality of never thirsting again. This invitation may seem implausible, but God promises that He alone is the source that satiates all thirst. Those who thirst and long for their needs to be met can freely drink from God's vast supply of living water from springs that flow up into everlasting life:

> But whoever drinks of the water that I shall give him will never thirst. But the water that I shall give him will become in him a fountain of water springing up into everlasting life.
> —JOHN 4:14, NKJV

The Fountain Gate addresses an issue far beyond religious practice and ceremony. The Fountain Gate is the annunciation of supernatural provision that is able to satisfy the thirst of all who come to drink. God makes no exceptions for persons, regardless of their age, race, ethnicity, education, marital status, social status, wealth, religious background, or disability; He promises abundant provision for all. The Samaritan woman's encounter with Jesus shows that God's quenching power and provision are available to all who come and drink. God's invites all of His creation to seek Him for their provision and sustenance. Instead of trusting the Creator and Sustainer of all things, many believers turn to temporary and short-lived solutions. The greatest reward God bestows upon those who come to Him is to exchange their fruitless dependence on temporary sources of provision for a fountain that never runs dry.

Believers have been deceived into believing that God's fountain belongs to an exclusive membership of pious and worthy participants. The words of Christ stand clear that all who thirst are worthy and invited to drink. Jesus did not limit His invitation to the Samaritan woman, but offered His thirst-quenching fountain to all who would come. The Fountain Gate is not an exclusive offer for a particular few. God's invitation is freely extended to all those who are willing to come and drink.

Several days after meeting with the Samaritan woman, the Bible says that Jesus stood up in the middle of Jerusalem on the last and great day of the feast of Tabernacles to invite others to come and quench their thirst. With a loud cry, Jesus lifted up His voice and invited a great multitude to come to Him and drink for the quenching of their thirst:

> In the last day, that great day of the feast, Jesus stood and cried, saying, If any man thirst, let him come unto me, and drink.
> —JOHN 7:37

The invitation is clear: the Son of God invites all people to quench their thirst by coming only to Him. Christ's invitation gives all people the assurance that there is no thirst that cannot be quenched through God's provision.

All thirst and longing are to be satisfied and quenched in God alone. The Fountain Gate summons believers to the reality of God's invitation, which is not limited to the quenching of physical thirst. At the Fountain Gate, God satiates all different kinds of thirst, such as emotional, psychological, financial, relational, sentimental, and spiritual thirst. Anyone lingering in a perpetual state of longing or thirst can satisfy their needs at the true fountain of living waters. Christ is eager to quench all who thirst, and is able to satisfy the deepest longing of the human heart with His immense and limitless provision.

Restoring the Fountain Gate means that church leaders will teach Christians to never set their countenance toward anything but God for the meeting of all their needs. In God, the church can wait and experience His goodness for the fulfillment of all things. Once Christians begin to experience the faithful supply of God's provision and learn how their needs are faithfully met in Christ, they can turn to those outside the church and address the needs of those suffering great famines.

The church cannot meet the needs of the world if the church is turning to the world for their own provision. The church should not utilize worldly methods and techniques to satisfy the yearnings of the human soul. The only thing that can satisfy the hearts and souls of God's people is His perfect and faithful blessing. The whole world will be able to witness the faithfulness of God's promises as Christians begin to wait upon God for their provision.

During the Christian pilgrimage on Earth, God promises to be the faithful source of all their provision. In all things, God is able to satisfy in abundant measure the supply that far exceeds their imagination. In God's final greeting in the last book of the Bible, He identifies Himself as the first and the last, the beginning and the end, reminding everyone that He will give unto him that thirst of the water of life freely:

> And he said unto me, It is done. I am Alpha and Omega, the beginning and the end. I will give unto him that is athirst of the fountain of the water of life freely.
> —REVELATION 21:6

For many generations the church has been plagued by a broken Fountain Gate where Christians have recklessly and impulsively run ahead of God to seek provision elsewhere. Those who have witnessed this awful travesty have been led to believe that God is unable to keep His faithful promises to provide. Therefore many sons and daughters have been taken captive by the belief that God is not a faithful provider and that waiting upon His provision is pointless. The vulnerability caused by a broken Fountain Gate is noticed when Christians fail to believe God for their provision. I pray that the church will completely restore and forever fasten the Fountain Gate in its rightful place so that all Christians will cease to suffer loss of God's provision. As men and women begin to restore the Fountain Gate, the church will become a gloriously fortified city, adorned with the faithfulness of God's abundant supply.

PRAYER APPLICATION

Father God! Help every Christian church to restore the Fountain Gate so that every believer learns to completely trust only You for their true and faithful provision. I pray that as the Fountain Gate is restored in our church, the whole world will witness that You are a sufficient and ample source of every good and perfect gift. As we restore the Fountain Gate, all believers will begin to confidently proclaim, "My God shall supply all...need according to his riches in glory by Christ Jesus" (Phil. 4:19). Lord Jesus, from this time forward I will seek You and wait upon You alone to provide and faithfully meet all my needs from Your sovereign fountain that never runs dry.

7

THE WATER GATE

> *And the LORD shall guide thee continually, and satisfy thy soul in drought, and make fat thy bones: and thou shalt be like a watered garden, and like a spring of water, whose waters fail not. And they that shall be of thee shall build the old waste places: thou shalt raise up the foundations of many generations; and thou shalt be called, The repairer of the breach, The restorer of paths to dwell in.*
>
> —ISAIAH 58:11–12

This chapter focuses on restoring the Water Gate. In the exploration of the ancient gates of Jerusalem, the restoration of the Water Gate possesses greater vitality for the church than any other gate. The focus on the Water Gate in this chapter addresses the church's need for God's Word. As the church attempts to discern the application of the Water Gate, they must realize that the life of God is found within the confines of His Word. The Water Gate invites leaders to the great challenge of discovering how to make God's Word applicable in leading God's people.

Many church leaders fail to use the Word of God effectively in preparing the church to live for God. Rather than equipping believers with solid biblical instruction and insight into God's kingdom, many Christian ministers use Scripture to further some superficial personal agenda that promotes self-advancement. On closer inspection of the restoration efforts of old Jerusalem, one would find no evidence that the Water Gate required repair or restoration:

> Moreover the Nethinim who dwelt in Ophel made repairs as far as the place in front of the Water Gate toward the east, and on the projecting tower.
> —NEHEMIAH 3:26, NKJV

A possible explanation for this unusual phenomenon is that the Water Gate points to the perfection and accuracy only found in God's Word. The Water Gate may signify the flawless precision and faithfulness that can only be attributed to the Word of God.

The Water Gate adds incredible significance to the church, as God's people understand how the Bible plays an integral part in keeping the people of God protected and guarded against all evil. In this chapter, the church can reflect on their need to gain access to God's Word without limitation or restriction. Having access to the Water Gate means that preachers and teachers make no compromise or concession when sharing the Word of truth. In the Book of Nehemiah, the historical record reveals that the Water Gate needed no repair, but played a vital role in strengthening God's people. After the restoration efforts were completed, Nehemiah wrote that everyone assembled in front of the Water Gate:

> Now all the people gathered together as one man in the open square that was in front of the Water Gate; and they told Ezra the scribe to bring the Book of the Law of Moses, which the LORD had commanded Israel. So Ezra the priest brought the Law before the assembly of men and women and all who could hear with understanding on the first day of the seventh month. Then he read from it in the open square that was in front of the Water Gate from morning until midday, before the men

and women and those who could understand; and the ears of all the people were attentive to the Book of the Law. So Ezra the scribe stood on a platform of wood which they had made for the purpose; and beside him, at his right hand, stood Mattithiah, Shema, Anaiah, Urijah, Hilkiah, and Maaseiah; and at his left hand Pedaiah, Mishael, Malchijah, Hashum, Hashbadana, Zechariah, and Meshullam. And Ezra opened the book in the sight of all the people, for he was standing above all the people; and when he opened it, all the people stood up. And Ezra blessed the LORD, the great God.

—NEHEMIAH 8:1–6, NKJV

The Word of God is the only substance that gives the church true vitality and strength so that God's people are spiritually nourished with the heavenly manna of God's life. When the Word of God fails to issue forth, God's people are visibly wearied, wasted, and without energy or power to live the Christian life. In restoring the activity before the Water Gate, every believer should realize the significance of Christ's words when He uttered that man was not to live by bread alone but by every word that proceeds out of the mouth of God:

But he answered and said, It is written, Man shall not live by bread alone, but by every word that proceedeth out of the mouth of God.

—MATTHEW 4:4

In the Book of Nehemiah, seventy years had passed since the people of God heard the Word of the Lord in the open square. After returning from a long exile, God's people were finally able to open God's law and begin publicly reading aloud. Restoring the Water Gate symbolizes repairing the access that God's people have to faithful ministers who are willing to proclaim the purity and truth of God's Word with unfettered, unhindered, and unlimited human manipulation or philosophical religious rhetoric.

The Word of God was never meant to have been entrusted to

religious spin doctors or religious hypocrites who desire to obtain personal gain or advantages. When unstable and untaught people twist the Word of God, the church can only expect to suffer destruction. The apostle Peter understood all too well how God's Word can be used by unscrupulous men who refuse to rightly divide the truth of God's Word:

> ...which untaught and unstable people twist to their own destruction, as they do also the rest of the Scriptures.
> —2 PETER 3:16, NKJV

In this passage, Peter warns the church to be careful because certain wicked men were leading others away, causing them to fall from their steadfastness before God by twisting Scripture. Visiting the Water Gate requires the church to repent for having allowed the Word of God to be watered down, and for exchanging biblical truths for easygoing religious oratory and fables. The Water Gate is a call for the church to turn away from those things that hinder dialogue with God and prevent God's people from knowing His Word.

The vain exercise of intellectualizing God's Word for theological discourse and scholarly expository may serve academic interest, but it has rendered the church unfruitful. Likewise, expounding on superfluous topics of sociocultural philosophy or secular humanistic ideas pollutes the proclamation of God's Word rather than purifying the heart's of God's people. Bold proclamation of God's truth in love can lead God's people to the vast fortunes of His grace. There is very little interest in the body of Christ for profound and in-depth understanding of the truths in God's Word. Christian churches and other parachurch organizations prefer a superficial diet of learning Christian clichés rather than the truly nutritious substance of God's Word, which is able to minister true deliverance. Very few Christians rely upon solid foundations of biblical truth and therefore cannot withstand the storms of life.

The world is seeing an ever-abundant growth of Christian ministries that are more focused on events, activities, and talent—all of which are able to establish temporary Christian styles, fads, and fashions, but have little or no concern for obedience to God's Word. Many of these ministries have become all hype and no substance. Any ministry, spiritual vocation, or Christian work that is unable to integrate its membership into the body of Christ has missed the mark. The famine of God's truth in the body of Christ has been brought about by people manipulating the multitudes away from the church to pursue personal gain that is contrary to God's Word. Christians are closer than ever to witnessing the fulfillment of the most horrific prophecy concerning the incredible absence of God's Word upon the earth:

> Behold, the days come, saith the Lord GOD, that I will send a famine in the land, not a famine of bread, nor a thirst for water, but of hearing the words of the LORD: And they shall wander from sea to sea, and from the north even to the east, they shall run to and fro to seek the word of the LORD, and shall not find it.
>
> —AMOS 8:11–12

Sadly enough these prophetic words ring very true in many Christian denominations and ministries around the world where the relics, remains, and artifacts of yesteryear revivals are present even though they presently remain in lifeless form. When God's Word is absent, Christians go through religious motions and exercise without fire, passion, or zeal. Circles where the Word of God is no longer heard or proclaimed become a haven for jackals and vultures to prey upon the dead. The Water Gate can be restored in the church when Christian ministers become zealous stewards of God's Word and begin passionately proclaiming the Word of God without alteration. The Water Gate shows believers that there is authentic power in God's Word every time the Bible is quoted, thus allowing the church to establish inerrant, infallible, and immovable lives that are steadfastly grounded in God's truth.

The church has suffered greatly by the many times God's people have decided to replace the Bible with cheap substitutes such as humanism and therapeutic psychobabble or intellectual religious philosophy. The body of Christ has suffered irreparable harm by the many generations of previous church leaders who saw fit to withhold the Word of God and appease the appetite of believers who would not endure sound doctrine because of their itching ears.

The Water Gate can be rendered truly ineffective when a ministry decides to adopt man's wit over God's wisdom. Many ministries have chosen to implement psychological evaluations and analysis as a means of providing therapeutic counseling sessions instead of utilizing the wisdom of biblical instruction and prayer. The practical instruction of biblical counseling and prayer has been replaced by the hiring of Christian psychologists. To help believers, these psychologists implement worldly methods of modern psychology that focus on nonbiblical principles and values.

Without the Water Gate the church cannot provide the protection that God promises His people. As long as the church continues to permit ministers to replace God's counsel for human wit and humor, Christians have no chance of prevailing against hell's gates. Every church minister that eliminates the sincere preaching, teaching, and ministry of God's Word for social or academic discourse or theological dissertation will eventually render the Word of God totally ineffective. The consequences of withdrawing God's Word from the church body are fatal. When the Word of God is shallow and superficial, no longer adequately challenging believers to faithfully obey, worship, and serve God, then believers fall into untold dangers and suffer incredible loss that ultimately effects the entire body of Christ.

The effective teaching of God's Word is the only method designed to safeguard God's people from the dangers that seek to destroy and plunder their persons and possessions. Every attempt to protect God's people is rendered ineffective if they are kept far from the protections of biblical instruction and teaching. The church's attempt to editorialize the proclamation of God's Word to accommodate others has caused the character in the body of Christ to plummet to the lowest levels of degradation. On the other hand, when Christian leaders are faithful to allow the Word of God to flow freely and issue forth unhindered or distorted by human restraint, the hearts of those in the body of Christ will transform into Christ's image and character.

Sadly enough, many church leaders have chosen to reduce the intensity and significance of God's Word to accommodate believers who prefer a milder and more lenient approach. When "seeker-friendly" services and other marketing schemes take preference over the faithful preaching of God's Word, Christians will be precluded from ascending to the heights of God's standards for spiritual success and godly character. The only hope for the regeneration of ungodly character found in the body of Christ is by the intense fire and hammer of God's Word. The bland spiritual food sought by half-committed Christians is being gladly served by mild-mannered ministers who fear challenging believers lest they carry out their threat of abandoning the flock for a more easygoing place of worship.

The church must avoid appointing ministers that are mere hirelings who claim job security as the justification for keeping their flocks biblically ignorant and malnourished on dismal diets of preschool-like services and meetings. The minister who perverts the ministry of God's Word to their church assemblies in order to validate and accommodate the waywardness of a few immature, uncommitted, and obstinate members may ruin the opportunity for those who hunger and thirst for legitimate dialogue with God. Some Christian ministers err by purposefully teaching their congregations that honoring God is possible by offering second-rate spiritual worship that is most often torn, lame, and sick. Sermons of self-denial are no longer acceptable to those who attend contemporary worship services, neither is the concept of forsaking all things to follow Jesus.

The basic premise of fellowship with God in the Bible is a call for total surrender. Every minister that has turned the Word of God into a Bible buffet of all-you-can-eat, pick-and-choose spiritual food renders a total disservice to the body of Christ. Teaching the truth in love is the only way that God designed for the body of Christ to grow in godly maturity and character. (See Ephesians 4:15.) The vast lack of spiritual growth and maturity in many sectors of the body of Christ throughout the world is the result of Christians not desiring to speak the truth in love as the Bible instructs.

The absence of restoring the Water Gate in many churches has created a generation of Christians that fails to understand the ministry of God's Word. When the Word of God is present in the church, God's people will feel the quick, powerful, and sharp edge cutting away and circumcising various areas of their lives. God's Word brings clarity and is able to divide the depth of the soul and spirit of man. When the thoughts of men are being discerned, and even the intents of his heart are made manifest, many people would rather run than have their wickedness exposed. In the Book of Hebrews, the Word of God is compared to a quick, powerful, and sharp double-edge sword:

> For the word of God is quick, and powerful, and sharper than any twoedged sword, piercing even to the dividing asunder of soul and spirit, and of the joints and marrow, and is a discerner of the thoughts and intents of the heart.
>
> —HEBREWS 4:12

In this passage of Hebrews, the author purposefully selects the Greek word *machiara*, which is translated into the English language as "sword." The origins of this word define a dagger-like instrument utilized by Jewish priests to prepare the animal sacrifices that were offered to God in His temple. The machiara was a small, razor-sharp dagger with two edges that Jewish priests repeatedly used. It was similar to a surgical scalpel, and was effectively used to cut away the ligaments, sinews, tendons, and muscle tissue of every sacrificial animal that was presented to the Lord by His people.

The fame of this small, powerful "sword" spread among the ancient peoples. Warriors began to use the machiara in battle because it was an effective and devastating weapon. The dagger was quite capable of shearing a bronze helmet worn by an opposing soldier, and was often used in hand-to-hand combat. Despite its small size, the machiara struck terror into the toughest foe.

In the light of this understanding, a ministry remains unfruitful when God's Word is purposefully dulled, diminished, or blunted by lethargic and sluggish ministers. When the Water Gate is not restored, the Word of God becomes slow, impotent, and like a blunt instrument. It becomes like an ordinary butter knife, unable to pierce or draw a line between soulish and spiritual, and never being able to discern or cut away those things that entice the hearts and thoughts of God's people to follow after the ungodly, unspiritual, and unclean.

No other attitude destroys the strength and vitality of the body of Christ like rendering God's Word of no effect. Denominational groups all over the world have chosen to prefer the traditions of their fore-fathers' faith, which have been adopted into the ministry, and not God's Word that abides forever. When religious traditions and church customs are embraced instead of the Word of God, every member becomes ineffective and God's movement is totally immobilized to a large crowd of people going nowhere. The Christian church has some-times been called the "sleeping giant."

Church leaders must be reminded to restore the Water Gate by com-municating God's Word with accuracy. They must show themselves approved unto God as workmen that need not be ashamed of rightly dividing the Word of truth. The Christian church can no longer afford to shut out the immense force and power contained in biblical instruc-tion. It cannot continue to keep those who form the "sleeping giant" nodding off in their pews. When clergy refuse to activate the power of God's Word to convince, correct, rebuke, exhort, instruct, admon-ish, and purify by the fire upon God's alter, the church has no hope of becoming wiser, stronger, and better able to fulfill God's call.

Believers should be careful not to dismiss the Word of God as the secondary, whimsical rhetoric of those who like to listen to themselves preach. By allowing other pressing matters to drown out the day's ser-mon, the church makes the Word of God irrelevant and of no effect.

Jesus personally warned the leaders of His day that traditions and ceremony can render the commandments of God null and void, neutralizing the effect of God's Word:

> Making the word of God of none effect through your tradition, which ye have delivered: and many such like things do ye.
> —MARK 7:13

In today's society, many people hide or sugarcoat the effect of God's Word so that sermons become hollow, losing any relevance and application to the present culture. Instead of reducing the Word of God to ineffectual religious cliché and vain repetition with no obedience, the Christian church should honor God's Word in practice to inherit the full benefit and impact of God's desired expression. In the above passage, Jesus warns that believers can corrupt the Word of God and make biblical instruction of no effect by failing to properly implement and obey.

To corrupt the Word of God is to reject God's counsel. Sunday worship services have become a favorite pastime or hobby. Christians come to hear God's Word but later reject His instruction. They are unable to endure the sound teaching of God's instruction. However, when the Word of God issues forth in transparent application and force, the church can hope to produce a harvest of righteousness that will glorify God in heaven.

The Word of God demands a passionate, relevant, and zealous delivery. It demands a bold proclamation in season and out of season, so that Christians can apply God's truth to every aspect of spiritual growth and development. Some ministers think that God's Word is a means by which to obtain monetary gain for capitalist business ventures. They desire increase in matters totally unrelated to the kingdom of God or the church. Many times biblical principles and teachings are vehemently directed toward unscrupulous, ungodly, impenitent businessmen for the purpose of seeking financial increase and greed-related prosperity without repentance. This becomes a severe problem when those engaged in immoral and ungodly activities think that by tithing and giving offerings to the kingdom of God their ungodly and wicked enterprises and lives will prosper.

Many times the biblical instruction ministered in some churches is so dull and boring that it does not even begin to cut the believer's umbilical cord to sin, much less circumcise their heart from ungodly ways. Through God's Word, the Spirit is able to deeply cut away and perform precise removal and circumcision of the heart related to issues that require God's hand. Through the ministry of those who faithfully preach God's Word, the Holy Spirit, as God's finger, can point to the areas of a believer's life that are unpleasing or unprofitable and remove them with surgical precision. God's Word, like the machiara, continues to prepare God's people to be a fragrant, well-pleasing aroma in His presence as they live out their lives upon the earth.

Those fearing the ministry of God's Word cannot endure sound doctrine working as a machiara in their lives. They will run after their own lusts heaping up teachers for themselves. The Word of God was never intended to stunt the growth and development of God's people. On the contrary, instead of passively persuading the populace with words of flattery and eloquent tickling, preachers need to proclaim God's Word by challenging and correcting Christians so they quickly move into God's sovereign plan and direction before it is too late. Many times preaching the Word of God has become difficult because believers have already decided to move in another direction. They justify their contrary actions by carrying a Bible in hand and quoting self-serving Bible verses that are totally out of context.

To restore the Water Gate, Christians must cease refusing to welcome the serious study and delivery of God's Word through sober messages delivered from God's throne. Those churches whose membership cannot endure the legitimate ministry of God's Word and sound doctrine will obligate the pastors to establish a church more akin to kindergarten. In these churches, Bible stories are shared like nursery rhymes. Sermons have no effect on transforming the character and heart of the congregation. If the church membership does not learn to endure the sound doctrine and true ministry of God's Word (allowing Scripture to reprove, rebuke, exhort, correct, instruct, convince, and establish God's truth in love), then the church will not be able to restore the Water Gate.

Rather than allowing God's Word to penetrate with intense and purposeful depth, many ministers are entertaining their congregations by providing diversionary amusement that does not involve godly instruction. The lack of godly stewardship and administration of God's Word in many ministries has diminished the church's stature to a second-rate local rehabilitation center for Christians who are addicted to self-pity and need a quick fix of conscience soothing.

As each church willingly steps toward restoring the Water Gate, they must courageously stand before ministers who proclaim God's Word without compromise or whitewashing. Pastors must see the obligation of their ministry as feeding God's sheep so that they desire green pastures and still waters of God's truth. In restoring the Water Gate, the church will see the constant replenishing of God's people with a fresh supply of God's uncompromising truth.

When the Christian church is exposed to the authentic ministry of God's Word, Christians will begin to gravitate toward God's eternal design, showing forth glorious fruit that is consistent with God's wisdom, maturity, and perfection. The Bible begins with a clear look, in the Book of Genesis, at how God's spoken word is able to delineate a course for His creation that is more akin to paradise. In the first chapter of Genesis, the church can catch a glimpse of the reality that occurs when God's words are spoken and welcomed by His creation. The formless, empty existence of all things is transformed according to His commands—everything returns to the form and order that radiates His majestic glory, power, and might:

> In the beginning God created the heaven and the earth. And the earth was without form, and void; and darkness was upon the face of the deep. And the Spirit of God moved upon the face of the waters. And God said, Let there be light: and there

was light. And God saw the light, that it was good: and God divided the light from the darkness.

—GENESIS 1:1–4

The omnipotent God of the universe begins restoring all things upon the earth by speaking His words. In the very beginning when disorder, emptiness, and utter darkness prevailed, God decided to deliver His word to change the entire cosmos. Church leaders need to realize that they cannot expect to transform the lives of God's people without access to God's Word. When God's Word is absent, the church is filled with philosophical, religious rhetoric that often produces confusion, darkness, and chaos.

The Bible records that during a time in the earth's prehistoric existence, the earth was without form; it was void and darkness. In this chaotic condition, God was able to unleash His word and start a massive revolution, transforming all things to a pristine paradise—a perfect dwelling place that was the precise setting for man's existence to fellowship with God. All things were divinely appointed to bring about a harmonious environment fit for man's development and growth. The Word of God brings all things into God's glorious and divine order to be enjoyed by those who take the form of His commanding truth.

The Word of God has the power to regenerate all things toward divine order. Without the Word of God, the church produces only confusion and disorder. The failure of God's people to meet before the Water Gate deprives the church body of the only hope Christians have to be restored. Since the beginning of time, God has instructed man with His word so that man might walk in a peaceful paradise obtaining victory in ever area of his earthly existence.

The first chapter of the Book of Genesis shows the world the power of God's Word to transform complete disorder and utter chaos into perfect order and serenity. When God's Word is stifled or fails to issue forth unpolluted, the body of Christ has no strength to establish the kingdom of God in the hearts of God's people. The only hope the church has of becoming a people transformed into the image and reflection of God's glory is by welcoming Scripture into their lives. Behind the Water Gate lies God's secret to overcoming sin for those in the body of Christ.

Years ago, as a young and upcoming Christian, I noticed that everything I enjoyed in life at that time involved sin. I thought to myself, I could never stop sinning—ever! Years later, I discovered the secret of being delivered from sin. I kept on planting God's Word in my heart, to cultivate a harvest of righteousness. The only answer for the travesty of fallen man's selfishness and sinful state is to welcome God's Word and allow His instruction to come within the human heart. The secret to being delivered from sin is found in Psalms. In Psalm 119, King David pays tribute to the importance of God's Word in the hearts of God's people. The only preventive measure found by David to help him stop sinning against God was to hide God's Word in his heart:

> Thy word have I hid in mine heart, that I might not sin against thee.
>
> —PSALM 119:11

This is a powerful truth. The more of God's Word that leaders can deposit into the hearts of God's people, the less they are going to miss the mark. That is what the word *sin* means, "to miss the mark." As long as ministers plant and cultivate God's Word into the hearts of their church members, this impartation will prevent them from sinning against the Lord. After years of having the Word of God sown into my heart, today I find myself much more able to resist the temptations to sin against God. To the degree that the Word of God has been planted into my heart, I can deter sin's ability to have its way in my life.

The Water Gate's restoration allows Christians the power to honor God and avoid sin by embracing the genuine impartation from the Word of God so that church might be delivered from their enemies. At the Water Gate, the church learns that whenever there is disorder, only the Word of God can restore order and heal. Churches that suffer continual problems with dysfunctional families and broken marriages must seek relief in God's Word.

Neglecting the Word of God causes havoc and irreconcilable differences for families and marriages. If believers are experiencing problems with their children, they must trace the problem to the area of their lives that lacks obedience to the Word of God. If believers suffer financial difficulties, they most likely violated a principle in God's Word that was intended to keep them stress free and financially sound. When God's people seek His Word to address their finances, they will find sound instruction on proper administration of their economy and enjoy the blessing of His abundant provision and peace. God's desire is that the church might fully understand the principles of His Word so that they can be set free from any financial snare or ongoing deficiency.

As God's truth is continually escorted toward God's people, the church can experience freedom from all sorts of bondages and snares. Jesus expected His followers to find and experience true freedom as each believer came into intimate contact and fellowship with God's Word:

> And ye shall know the truth, and the truth shall make you free.
> —JOHN 8:32

As daily problems arise trying to take believers by surprise and into captivity, the Spirit of God can minister God's Word so that they can be set free by the light of His counsel.

There are many references in the Bible that teach the church that the purpose for water is not only to quench thirst but to purify and cleanse that which is polluted. The restoration of the Water Gate also speaks of a place where the church can be cleansed and purified by washing with the water of God's Word:

> That He might sanctify and cleanse her with the washing of water by the word.
> —EPHESIANS 5:26, NKJV

When the Water Gate is absent, there is an inability to purify the hearts of God's people. In this passage, the Bible says that God is able to use His Word to wash with water to sanctify and cleanse His church. When the church has access to God's Word, cleansing and sanctifying are made possible. The church that places little emphasis on God's Word becomes defiled and polluted with all kinds of contaminants. When the Water Gate is restored, the church has an assurance of sanctification and cleansing by the power of God's truth. Right before departing, the Lord made a specific request to God the Father in His prayers. He prayed that God would sanctify His followers and that the method of true sanctification would be His Word:

> Sanctify them through thy truth: thy word is truth.
> —JOHN 17:17

This passage in the Bible helps Christians appreciate God's Word as the instrument needed to perform an integral part in sanctifying each believer. In other words, every believer who opens his or her heart and honestly welcomes and receives the truth of God's Word will experience a sanctifying separation from sin, with the hope of becoming part of Christ's glorious church. When Christians begin to search out the wisdom of God's truth, they will begin reflecting the joy, love, and peace God always intended for the church. If the church begins to take on the form of God's design and the purity of His character, Christians can expect to become a glorious and overcoming church.

The Word of God will direct all Christian men to line up as godly husbands and fathers to fulfill what God intended with the creation of these institutions. When the church fails to provide the light of God's Word to the darkness and chaos facing man's dilemma of having no idea of how to become a good husband or father, then broken homes ensue. When the light of God's Word shines bright, darkness does not prevail any longer, evil burdens are lifted, and sadness is gone. This is only possible if the church is able to take the form of God's Word and instruction. As women decide to honor their calling as mothers and wives who line up with God's truth, they can eliminate all darkness and void in their households. God always intended for His Word to define the human existence so that men and women could walk in His perfect design. When Christians take on worldly forms, the restoration of the Water Gate fails and other believers are deprived of the forms and orders God intended for them to embrace.

As long as the church is unsettled with accepting God's Word at face value, Christians will continue replacing biblical instruction with sociocultural norms, mores, or evolution. This repudiation of God's way of life always leads men and women to continue living outside the parameter of God's desired blessing and plan:

> That He might present her to Himself a glorious church, not having spot or wrinkle or any such thing, but that she should be holy and without blemish.
> —EPHESIANS 5:27, NKJV

The Water Gate helps Christians focus upon the preparations needed for the church to be presented to Christ without blemish, spot, or wrinkle. The water prepares the church to meet God. The Word of God prepares Christians to meet their Maker. Only through God's Word can the church prepare to line up with God's truth so that when they stand in the presence of almighty God they are thoroughly prepared in every aspect. Without God's Word issuing forth in the churches, many Christians are going to be unprepared because they have not attained the form of God's pleasure. At the Water Gate, the church asks the Lord to help them become what He desires, instead of the likes of an earthly business entity.

When the church continues to function without paying serious regard to the Word of God, the Water Gate cannot be restored. This causes Christians to be ineffective at prevailing against the gates of hell and darkness. The lack of God's Word in many congregations causes the church to drift away from God's model toward a more secular business-like model. Many churches operate as secular businesses where pastors are not pastors but CEOs, deacons are executive assistants, and bishops are regional managers. Every instruction from God's Word that is replaced by secular concepts will bring a cloud of darkness that casts shadows on this glorious city God intends to build.

Without repairing the Water Gate, the Christian church is destined to become something other than what God intended. God did not establish the church to become a business franchise or subsidiary of some ecclesiastical multinational corporation. He intended His church to be the living proof of His existence; for each member, cell, and instrument to breathe His breath.

The purpose of restoring the Water Gate is to fill the church with God's knowledge so that believers can embrace their true identity. The church will walk in divine integrity with both the leadership and membership transformed into one body—the body of Christ. God intended the church to become the model for the nations, not follow-ers of corporate America. The purpose of the church was to create a model to teach all nations the manifold wisdom of God, not the fool-ishness of cunning men.

Standing before the Water Gate allows the church to reflect heav-enly wisdom and glory as they walk in keeping with God's Word. Failure to stand before the Water Gate forces the church to con-tinue catering to worldly demands of contemporary fads. When the Word of God is diluted to accommodate worldly reasoning, the church loses its authority and power. As the church takes its proper stand before the Water Gate, the tolerance for worldly ways is eliminated. Christians are then catapulted to the forefront of God's work upon the earth.

Churches founded on men's wisdom cannot withstand the devil's opposition. Churches founded on God's Word shall prevail against every scheme of the evil one. God promises His people large rec-ompense and blessings when they are willing to hear and obey the instructions in His Word. The incredible favor and blessing that will follow and overtake God's people as they keep God's Word is summed up in Deuteronomy 28:1–14.

God's continued promise was that if His people would keep His Word and carefully observe all His instruction, then God would set them on high, above all other nations of the earth:

> Now it shall come to pass, if you diligently obey the voice of the LORD your God, to observe carefully all His commandments which I command you today, that the LORD your God will set you high above all nations of the earth.
> —DEUTERONOMY 28:1, NKJV

God has always promised His people that if they are willing to obey His Word, He will prosper them in all the works of their hands until they become the head and not the tail:

> And the LORD shall make thee the head, and not the tail; and thou shalt be above only, and thou shalt not be beneath; if that thou hearken unto the commandments of the LORD thy God, which I command thee this day, to observe and to do them.
> —DEUTERONOMY 28:13

Time and again, God reminds His people that the ultimate source of keeping His favor and blessing is in their adherence to diligently observing and obeying all His words. In these passages, Christians can see the promise of rich blessing, abundance, and prosperity for all those who keep God's Word. On the other hand, God warns His people that upon ignoring or neglecting God's truth they would fall from favor to disgrace. Every believer should pay close attention and make a heartfelt reflection at the importance God places on the keeping of His Word as it relates to Deuteronomy 28.

The effects of a fallen Water Gate are readily evident in the problems that are listed in Deuteronomy 28:15–68:

> But it shall come to pass, if you do not obey the voice of the LORD your God, to observe carefully all His commandments and His statutes which I command you today, that all these

curses will come upon you and overtake you.

—DEUTERONOMY 28:15, NKJV

The consequences of despising the Word of God are delineated in Deuteronomy 28:30–32, wherein God warns that disobeying His Word causes devastation in every area of human life, especially the family nucleus. Some of the curses upon those who forsake God's Word are disease, mental problems, marital infidelity, loss of income, loss of property, loss of prosperity, loss of children, and the total disintegration of all things.

As churches move toward restoring the Water Gate, they will run into defiance from those who prefer the path of least resistance and to carelessly cater to the appetites of the flesh. The church has been called to be the head, and not the tail. A church that allows the Water Gate to remain in ruins is not a leader but a follower. The apostle Paul taught that if the Word of God proves to be false, then believers are to be the most pitied among men. In other words, if the Word of God cannot become reality, those who live for Christ are the biggest fools of all. If the church cannot show the practical relevance of God's Word, they are the ones to be most mocked among men:

> Therefore whosoever heareth these sayings of mine, and doeth them, I will liken him unto a wise man, which built his house upon a rock: And the rain descended, and the floods came, and the winds blew, and beat upon that house; and it fell not: for it was founded upon a rock. And every one that heareth these sayings of mine, and doeth them not, shall be likened unto a foolish man, which built his house upon the sand: And the rain descended, and the floods came, and the winds blew, and beat upon that house; and it fell: and great was the fall of it.
>
> —MATTHEW 7:24–27

As the church illustrates a true stand of living in obedience to God's Word, the Water Gate in God's dwelling can show the world that those

174

who live by God's Word shall prosper in all things. When Christian youth begin to hear and apply God's Word taken from powerful pulpits across the globe, they will learn to walk in obedience in God's righteousness as a mighty army arising to become an unstoppable force. The Water Gate calls preachers and teachers in the church to proclaim God's eternal truths; not momentary, fleeting, transient tales that are short lived and impermanent.

The church has paid an awful price by becoming a people who will not endure God's Word and would rather pursue after crafty men who are willing to preach humanistic philosophy and postmodern values that cater to men's lusts. Once the world sees preachers honestly teaching and proclaiming God's truth, instead of peddling deceitful cunningness for self-gains, then the church will experience a different harvest. The Water Gate is an opportunity for those willing to preach and teach God's Word to do so with all sincerity. It is not for those who twist and pervert Scripture to their own advantage and benefit. The apostle Paul was able to assure that he was among the few that spoke God's Word with all sincerity, as if God Himself were present during his sermons:

> For we are not, as so many, peddling the word of God; but as of sincerity, but as from God, we speak in the sight of God in Christ.
> —2 CORINTHIANS 2:17, NKJV

A fortified Water Gate leads the church to firm footing upon God's infallible counsel forever, instead of wading through the quagmire of flattering words and fair speech. Only God's Word and counsel stand the test of time and the storms of life.

The Water Gate shows that God desires to bring His Word before His people so that they might live in His purpose and within His design. The Water Gate's restoration points to the church removing the fleeting fantasies of perilous preachers. It encourages the church to seek godly men that are willing to live and teach His Word in order to establish spiritual foundations that will render His people stead-fast, immovable, and unshakeable. A church without the Water Gate is severely lacking God's truth as He intended.

The Water Gate is where we stand to hear the voice of God instead of trying to squelch or stifle it. At the beginning of my pastorate, I was invited to attended a large pastor's conference with well over several thousand pastors in attendance. As I began to converse with some of these seasoned pastors, I realized they no longer governed church affairs or matters by the Bible. Instead, they had chosen to govern and lead church affairs using standard church bylaws and corporate regulations. When I asked why this was their preference they told me that any deviation from the bylaws would cause them to lose their jobs as professional clergy within their church denomination.

Sadly, the Christian church has come to a place where men of God prefer to exchange the biblical truth of God's Word for the convenience of ecclesiastical employment. The Word of God has been hidden from too many pulpits and sanctuaries in order to establish the proper elements of religion. For many churches, the Bible becomes a sacred relic that serves only to decorate and commemorate former years when God's Word was relevant and applicable. Famous Bible quotes used by well-known preachers during the Reformation and famous missionaries are now showcased in museum-like furniture as if God's Word is no longer applicable.

Instead of the ever-flowing source of God's omnipotence, the Bible has become a religious artifact better served in city museums. Many churches are unwilling to bring their people to stand before the Water Gate. Rather than proclaiming God's Word vibrantly and passionately to rend hearts with transforming truth, many churches have opted to minimize the effect of God's Word through boring, monotone exposition of theological rhetoric and vain repetition. Many churches are satisfied to leave the Word of God solely in physical exposition in the foyer or on a fancy pulpit so that the controversial truths of God's Word might not frighten parishioners off. The Water Gate speaks of having access to God's Word so that His people are not inundated by irrelevant, religious rhetoric, theological exposition, or ecclesiastical liturgy. The importance of delivering God's Word is crucial to freeing God's people from destruction and delivering the church out of darkness.

The Bible was not given by trickery of men, but it is the inspired, breathed Word of God:

> For prophecy never came by the will of man, but holy men of God spoke as they were moved by the Holy Spirit.
> —2 PETER 1:21, NKJV

Every part of the Word of God comes not by the design or will of men, but is given by God through His Spirit. The Word of God has always been the believer's source of blessing and victory. Every word of God has been given to protect, prosper, and bless those who obey Scripture without excuses. The apostle Paul understood the importance of Scripture as the hope of God's people getting prepared and thoroughly equipped and complete to participate in every one of God's good works:

> All Scripture is given by inspiration of God, and is profitable for doctrine, for reproof, for correction, for instruction in righteousness, that the man of God may be complete, thoroughly equipped for every good work.
> —2 TIMOTHY 3:16–17, NKJV

When the Word of God is absent or censored, the church loses the ability to teach, rebuke, correct, and train for instruction in righteousness. The inability to call God's people before the Water Gate renders the armies of God ill equipped for every good work. This present generation suffers from the unskilled multitudes of Christian ministers that were never thoroughly trained for the exercise of rightly discerning or dividing the Word of truth so that their members are deprived from the benefit of distinguishing between good and bad for their life choices and decisions.

The apostle Paul understood the importance of having God's Word preached at all times and in this way. Scripture was able to produce an excellent fruit in the hearts, minds, and souls of God's people:

> Preach the word; be instant in season, out of season; reprove, rebuke, exhort with all longsuffering and doctrine. For the time will come when they will not endure sound doctrine; but after their own lusts shall they heap to themselves teachers, having itching ears; And they shall turn away their ears from the truth, and shall be turned unto fables.
>
> —2 TIMOTHY 4:2–4

Pastors should know that no other expression given by man can perform the transforming work of God's powerful pleasure and mighty work. Because of this, they should become experts at proclaiming God's Word without intimidation, restraint, or consternation. The world chases after storytelling comedians who mock all truth with colored and distasteful expression to appease the multitudes with entertainment. God's preachers, on the other hand, must learn to proclaim the sober, somber, solemn, thunderous truth of God's Word. When God's Word issues forth in the sanctuary with the anointed essence of God's truth the foundations of futility will shake, and lust for earthly things will vanish.

Too many preachers fill their sermons with feel-good comments and opinions on earthly gain and prosperity, which have little or nothing to do with the true eternal purpose of God's success. As the church mimics the world, using an arsenal of patterns, models, methods, steps, formulae, principles, stages, and levels to obtain earthly goals and worldview, they lose the reference to the standards of God's Word. There is ample evidence that the Water Gate is unattended when God's people fail to receive the essence and substance of God's Word and revelation. Restoring the Water Gate is important to the church's beginning to overcome and manifesting the ability to prevail.

Many believers that attend church today dislike any appeal for obedience to Old Testament biblical instruction or teaching. The inability of these believers to glean wisdom from Old Testament instructions is founded upon their unwillingness to take personal responsibility for their inappropriate and irreverent lives. The time must come for the church to wake up and realize that the God of the Old Testament ratifies His truth in the New Testament.

Unscrupulous gainsayers have erroneously taught many Christians that their actions are of no consequence because of God's grace. They assume that grace overrides their need to live godly lives that please the Lord. The New Testament epistle that most corresponds to the concept of grace is the Book of Galatians. Therein the apostle Paul declares that God's grace is indispensable. Without grace, one can barely aspire to live the Christian life. However, Paul concludes his epistle by warning man to be careful because they only stand to reap what they have sown:

> Do not be deceived, God is not mocked; for whatever a man sows, that he will also reap. For he who sows to his flesh will of the flesh reap corruption, but he who sows to the Spirit will of the Spirit reap everlasting life.
> —GALATIANS 6:7–8, NKJV

Every Christian must understand the importance of restoring the Water Gate to remain in God's truth.

God gave His people His Word to set them high above all the nations of the earth. The Word of God has been called the Good Book, the Words of Christ, the Words of Truth, the Holy Scriptures, the Scripture of Truth, the Book of the Law, and the Sword of the Spirit. Regardless of the name given, the Bible is the single most important component needed to edify the church. It is in each Christian's best interest to own a Bible and occupy their time with searching Scripture. The following Psalm is another all-time favorite reference to the advantages of having access to God's Word:

Blessed is the man Who walks not in the counsel of the ungodly, Nor stands in the path of sinners, Nor sits in the seat of the scornful; But his delight is in the law of the LORD, And in His law he meditates day and night. He shall be like a tree Planted by the rivers of water, That brings forth its fruit in its season, Whose leaf also shall not wither; And whatever he does shall prosper.

—PSALM 1:1–3, NKJV

Many church members cater specifically to receiving the counsel of the ungodly standing in the path of sinners. At times church programs and sermons surround the feel-good theme of pleasing carnal Christians who would rather take the low road and follow near to the path of sinners. For this reason, many churches lack the blessings of prosperity spoken of in the first psalm. While some churches have a fortified Water Gate that refreshes and blesses the flock, others have a weak Water Gate that is the result of leadership that has departed from in-depth biblical study and counsel.

In the past, church leaders preferred to counsel others using all kinds of self-help instructional booklets and manuals that integrated concepts like the power of positive thinking instead of searching Scripture for God's insight and instruction. The study of God's Word among clergy has been neglected. This has led them to deliver ungodly, worldly advice, secular methods, and humanistic approaches when counseling the hearts and minds of God's people.

The Water Gate becomes all the more vulnerable as church elders and ministers spend more time reading books on the secrets of self-help, and implementing programs that are founded on secular principles of prosperity instead of delighting in the law of the Lord day and night. Many church leaders spend more time reading *Fortune* magazine and *The Wall Street Journal* or other periodicals rather than submerging themselves in God's wisdom in Scripture. Many leaders think that by looking at these carnally-generated treatises, filled with earthly insight, their God-inspired church enterprises are going to prosper. These insights may give them some kind of prosperity, but not according to God. Corporate business methods will take God's people in some direction, but they will end up nowhere near the place God would like to lead them.

The Word of God promises blessing for those who decide not to walk in the counsel of the ungodly nor stand in the path of sinners. Continual meditation in the law of the Lord will help God's people be like trees planted next to the rivers of waters, bringing forth fruits in season, causing their lives not to wither but prosper in whatever endeavor they pursue. What a tremendous promise that God desires for the Water Gate to transfer worldly counsel to the counsel of the Most High God! The Water Gate reminds the church to replace every ungodly book of foolish worldly counsel with the good book of God's wisdom, remembering that even the foolishness of God surpasses the wisdom of men.

When I was a child, my mother tried to fix her twenty-four-year-old marriage relationship by reading various books on making your marriage work and other reconciliation manuals. She went to the town's public library and checked out books on family journals, sociology, family counseling and therapy, and psychology for the family, but her marriage only became worse and deteriorated further. Finally, in 1983, God allowed her to stumble upon a Bible. She traded her entire library of family self-help books for the Word of God, and God began to speak into her life. Upon reading and seeking the counsel of God's Word for her dysfunctional marriage, she found the answer to every dispute faced in marriage. From that time forward her marriage was reconciled and restored without further threat of separation or divorce.

When church leaders proclaim, teach, and encourage the obedience of God's Word, the church will arise to take her stand as the people of God; people of character, people who walk in integrity, people who love truth, and men who exemplify truth and pursue every good thing for their families, their church, and their communities. The Water Gate is restored as the church decides that the

Bible is the indispensable counsel for all instruction, and that secular books only contain human rationale and methods that must take a backseat to God's Word.

The church that decides to replace the Bible with books that foretell patterns of prosperity and success without the fear of the Lord is setting itself up for major catastrophe. The church as a whole must realize that hearing, learning, and keeping God's Word is the true mark of prosperity and success. The only hope of genuine prosperity and growth for the church as God intended is in keeping His Word.

The church can recognize bestselling authors, but it should never forget *the* bestseller of all time—the Bible. When the Bible becomes a foreign text and an unfamiliar document, the church should only expect great foolishness and confusion to befall the body of Christ.

One of the best-known motivational speakers of our time is Anthony Robbins. For years, he taught courses on obtaining success by following the power of personal growth. Several years later, Mr. Robbins' marriage fell apart and he was divorced from his wife. In the Gospel of Matthew, Jesus teaches His followers the importance of building their lives in obedience to God's Word. The Word of God promises that those who hear and obey the Word of God shall establish their lives on the rock, and those who fail to do so build upon sand:

> Therefore whoever hears these sayings of Mine, and does them, I will liken him to a wise man who built his house on the rock: and the rain descended, the floods came, and the winds blew and beat on that house; and it did not fall, for it was founded on the rock. Now everyone who hears these sayings of Mine, and does not do them, will be like a foolish man who built his house on the sand: and the rain descended, the floods came, and the winds blew and beat on that house; and it fell. And great was its fall.
>
> —MATTHEW 7:24–27, NKJV

Neglecting the Word of God as the true foundation of church causes the house to fall. When the Word of God is merely incidental to church planting instead of foundational, church leaders should expect incredible suffering, ruin, and great loss as the rains descend, floodwaters rise, and storm winds blow. The only way to be truly successful and prosperous is to walk in line with the teachings of God's Word.

Many multimillionaires have spent their lives growing and developing their wealth only to lose their families by failing to build their treasures according to God's wisdom. Believers who follow godly instruction and walk in stride with the Word of God are truly prosperous and successful. As they keep God's Word, they are continually blessed with the favor of God's instruction for every season of life. The Word of God is instruction for all peoples everywhere without exception. The challenge therefore is this—once the Water Gate is restored and functioning properly, the church will be able to show forth that Christ's words are faithful to sustain and render all things prosperous.

Regardless of anything else, no other instrument preserves a Christian's life, family, marriage, church, and finances like obedience and adherence to God's Word. Those things kept by the power of His Word will remain under God's care and protection. When Christian people begin to live their lives according to obedience to God's Word, they can assure their union will be inseparable and enjoy a true marriage made in heaven. Thanks to God's ultimate design, His Word allows the church to overcome and prevail against any obstacle or oppositional force.

God gives clear instruction to His people so that the church need not add or take away from His Word, lest they suffer the consequences. Some preachers think they have to sensationalize God's Word by adding mystical phenomena to make it zestier. The Lord's commandment is clear that they should not alter, add, or take away from His commands:

> Now, O Israel, listen to the statutes and the judgments which I teach you to observe, that you may live, and go in and possess the land which the LORD God of your fathers is giving you. You shall not add to the word which I command you, nor take from it, that you may keep the commandments of the LORD your God which I command you.
>
> —DEUTERONOMY 4:1–2, NKJV

This Old Testament commandment is repeated at the end of the New Testament, in the Book of Revelation, with fatal consequences for those who decide to add anything or take away from God's Word:

> For I testify to everyone who hears the words of the prophecy of this book: If anyone adds to these things, God will add to him the plagues that are written in this book; and if anyone takes away from the words of the book of this prophecy, God shall take away his part from the Book of Life, from the holy city, and from the things which are written in this book.
>
> —REVELATION 22:18–19, NKJV

The instruction is clear that to remove God's people from the light of God's Word is detrimental to the church's health as it is exposed to plagues unknown. The lesson at the Water Gate is to make sure that the church never changes, compromises, or simplifies the substance of God's Word. God's truth was intended to deliver His people from their enemies and correct the error of their thoughts and ways. The biblical record teaches the church a pattern that assures strength and victory when they possess the Word of God for their deliverance.

When Adam and Eve departed from God's instruction, they fell into sin. In the Gospel of Matthew chapter four, when Jesus Christ was tempted by Satan in the wilderness, Christ used the Word of God to deliver His soul. This shows the church that they too can obtain victory over the tempter when they effectively quote and rely upon God's Word. If the church is going to be able to stand up against and defeat their enemies, they need to preserve the Word of

God and learn what is written in God's Word.

Through the Water Gate, the church learns that God intends His people to defend themselves, their families, their marriages, and everything they possess with the written Word of God. We live in an age where we are constantly invited to exchange God's Word for modern philosophies or New Age instructions. In light of this, the Christian church must refuse to exchange God's Scripture, which He has preserved from generation to generation. Every challenge to forsake God's Word should be rejected as the devil's attempt to strip the church of its wealth and heritage. No other book in the world contains the wisdom, truth, patterns, and life found in the pages of the Bible. The Water Gate shows all people that only fools hate correction and despise God's counsel. To forsake God's Word is to walk as a fool in darkness, embracing destruction and lies.

When the church begins to restore the Water Gate, the church will know the importance of memorizing and keeping the written Word of God. They will then have the power needed to be delivered from their enemies and all other things that come to plunder and pillage their godly gain. The world teaches its students, saying, "If you want to make money, lend your money at high interest." The Bible says that he who lends at a high interest rate will be found and rebuked by the Lord. The Lord will confront this evil. (See Psalm 35:10.)

When the Water Gate is fully functioning, the church will begin to enjoy the strength of having open access to the ministry of God's Word. Through the Word of God, believers are exposed to and receive the power of transformation unlike any other power in the world. The benefits derived by a congregation that receives godly instruction in the fear of Lord in insurmountable. The Bible is the true hope of converting souls and making the simple wise:

> The law of the Lord is perfect, converting the soul; The testimony of the Lord is sure, making wise the simple; The statutes of the Lord are right, rejoicing the heart; The commandment of the Lord is pure, enlightening the eyes.
>
> —Psalm 19:7–8, nkjv

Restoring the Water Gate is inevitable for those churches that desire to prevail, for therein lies the hope of perfect promises that will restore the church. The people of God will rejoice over a functioning Water Gate because instead of plunder and need, they can enjoy His Word, rejoice in their hearts, and be enlightened in their eyes. An entire generation of churched people has fallen into the grips of depression, oppression, and the curse of spiritual blindness by failing to experience a rejoicing heart that comes from knowing and keeping the commandments of the Lord. The psalmist says the words of God give clarity of vision and keep God's people from going astray or stumbling. Through the Word of God, God's people are warned, reminded, illuminated, and edified. Without the Water Gate, God's people are only fit to be destroyed without warning. When the Bible is the main course of every church gathering, the Water Gate is a memorial to God's promise of rewards and the existence of great treasures that are finer than gold.

Today's church lacks integrity and influence due to its inability to show true strength in keeping God's Word. To reestablish strength and true godliness, the church must commit to revisit the ministry of God's Word with renewed passion and zeal. When restored, the Water Gate can signify that the Christian church will be able to make their future paths shine bright in the midst of deep darkness. To restore the Water Gate is to remind the body of Christ that the Word of God is not only to be heard, but is also to be obeyed. Many believers say, "I know, I've heard," or "I've read the Bible," but very few of them say, "I obey the Word of God." Many of these professing Bible scholars fail to become real doers of God's Word, and therefore concoct excuses for their ungodly acts and behavior. Similar to Satan, these ungodly Christians know the whole Bible but obey none of it. Many in the church think that simply memorizing Scripture and knowing biblical concepts makes them members of God's kingdom. Those who form part of the Christian church must be taught that when they fail to put God's Word into practice, they are no different from the devil and his host.

The Word of God is a powerful weapon for God's people. The Bible is said to contain *power*, which in the Greek translation is the word *dunamis*. This word comes from the same root word that comprises the word *dynamite*. As Christians speak and keep the Word of God, they can enjoy the real work of God's powerful impartation of knowledge to them, which is as intense and awesome as the force of dynamite.

The church should teach Christians that they can quote Scripture whenever they are confronted by adverse situations or problems. Doing this releases an incredible force of power to help them overcome. As the church learns to embrace the Word of God, they will notice the self-contained power and strength to project an effective force and energy toward the surrounding elements that oppose them. As the Word of God is proclaimed, there will be a definite and lasting effectual work in the hearts of His people. While many Christian leaders may desire to implement the use of other good words to counsel or instruct believers, I pray they realize that no words have more lasting significance and effect than those found in the Bible.

The Bible contains the most reliable and infallible words known to man. They are useful for every situation. By learning the teachings of the Bible, believers are able to walk in credibility and reliability wherever they go and in whatever they do. When church leaders begin to speak the Word of God into the lives of their followers, there remains hope that all problems will get resolved and every situation that arises will be an opportunity to walk in the Lord's counsel.

The Word of God is the truth that can set teenagers free from peer pressure by establishing standards that will not fade or change with the fashions. The Word of God lays a foundation that is immoveable, permitting Christians to build strong lives. The Water Gate establishes strong families, strong marriages, strong friendships, and strong relationships that are healthy and safe.

The Bible teaches believers not only to be hearers of the Word of God but doers as well. Hearers of the Word that do not obey only deceive themselves. The Bible calls the church to love the Word, to delight in the Word, and to regard it as sweet and not bitter. The Word of God is to be esteemed above all else. The church should seek after God's Word and yearn for sound biblical teaching because God's Word causes all things to flourish and grow in the purpose and light of His counsel. Besides committing God's Word to memory, believers should grieve when other believers despise and disobey the Word of God.

The church is supposed to rejoice in God's Word and trust in God's instruction. Christians should consider God's Word as a light unto their feet and a lamp unto their path. The Word of God can renew, restore, repair, and preserve the Christian church from ruin if they are able to make a commitment to restore the Water Gate, thereby allowing God's Word to flow richly into their lives. The apostle Paul teaches, in his epistle to the Colossians, that God will not force His Word into the Christian heart. Rather, this is a voluntary act of the will:

> Let the word of Christ dwell in you richly in all wisdom, teaching and admonishing one another in psalms and hymns and spiritual songs, singing with grace in your hearts to the Lord.
>
> —COLOSSIANS 3:16, NKJV

The first word in verse 16 is *let*. This word refers to the attitude of the heart that must be present to allow or permit. There are a lot of churches that do not let the Word of God dwell richly inside the assembly. Delivering God's Word to the church requires every member to extend an invitation from the heart so that each church member gives the Word of Christ permission to dwell therein. The church must renew their attitudes and begin to pray, *Lord, I want to let Your Word have its way.* Apart from all other instruction the church continually gives, the Word of God is the most important to have dwelling richly in the Christian heart. The church may have learned a lot of Christian clichés, slogans, and even honorable advice from grandpa, but they must forego all and let God's Word dwell richly within their hearts in all wisdom, teaching, and admonition. This means more than a once-a-week, superficial, twenty-minute sermonette experience or exposure to God's Word. The church must begin to grow an appetite for God's Word so that Scripture dwells, abides, and sinks down into the depths of the Christian heart. Church members must allow the Word of God to saturate the existence of their entire being.

The wicked constantly trample upon God's Word because Scripture always establishes the rightful record of their wickedness. The Word of God serves as either a stepping-stone or stumbling block, because by it Christians will either step up and over or stumble and fall. As ministers understand the need to provide adequate provision of God's truth to His people, believers can then strive to gain God's favor and take their rightful place to obtain their spiritual inheritance.

The apostle Paul instructs believers to devote themselves to the public reading of Scripture. Reading God's Word protects the Christian believer from being deceived or enticed to follow after other things:

> Till I come, give attention to reading, to exhortation, to doctrine.
> —1 TIMOTHY 4:13, NKJV

Paul's instruction to Timothy should be interpreted as God's encouragement for Christians to always come before the Water Gate and give attention to the continual reading of Scripture. When every Christian believer realizes the importance of restoring the Water Gate, and Christian ministers are able to faithfully deliver, without self-serving manipulation, the Holy Scriptures to hearts that are willing to hear God's truth, then the body of Christ can hope to receive the wealth of God's truth that prepares God's people to prevail against every enemy.

PRAYER APPLICATION

Father God! Help every Christian church to call their assembly back before the Water Gate to hear God's Word. Lord, I pray that the church stands together as one before the Water Gate and opens their hearts to hear the holy commandments and instruction found in Scripture. Jesus, please expose and remove every Christian minister from the body of Christ who manipulates, hinders, or holds back biblical truth. Allow God's Word to continually prosper and flow unfettered by flattery or trickery to the hearts and lives of church members. Holy Spirit, yearn within the hearts of God's people, giving them hunger and thirst for God's Word so that their lives are thoroughly nourished with the true manna that comes from heaven. Lord, may the church always remember that men cannot live by bread alone but by every word that proceeds out of the mouth of God.

8

THE HORSE GATE

The appearance of them is as the appearance of horses; and as horsemen, so shall they run. Like the noise of chariots on the tops of mountains shall they leap, like the noise of a flame of fire that devoureth the stubble, as a strong people set in battle array. Before their face the people shall be much pained: all faces shall gather blackness. They shall run like mighty men; they shall climb the wall like men of war; and they shall march every one on his ways, and they shall not break their ranks.

—JOEL 2:4–7

This chapter on the Horse Gate focuses on an aspect of the local church that involves preparing each member of the body of Christ to become a spiritual warrior capable of taking on spiritual battles and withstanding attacks against the host of hell. Restoring the Horse Gate will determine whether or not a church is ready, willing, and able to wage spiritual battle and withstand the many wiles of the evil one. The necessity of repairing the Horse Gate is evident by the great number of Christians who have little to no ability to fight the good fight of the Christian faith as soldiers of Jesus Christ.

The ever-growing challenge in restoring the Horse Gate requires Christians to know and understand that the church does not wrestle against flesh and blood, but against wicked principalities, against powers, against the rulers of the darkness of this world, against spiritual wickedness in high places, and the remaining host of hell in the heavenly realms. (See Ephesians 6:12.)

During the restoration process in the days of Nehemiah, the Bible mentions the existence of another gate in Old Jerusalem called the Horse Gate:

> Beyond the Horse Gate the priests made repairs, each in front
> of his own house.
>
> —NEHEMIAH 3:28, NKJV

To a large degree, the Bible contains symbolism to help God's people understand key concepts that would otherwise be too difficult to even imagine. Most of the time the Bible adequately provides sufficient and meaningful representation in regard to assisting readers in discerning the significance behind every scriptural symbol. For purposes of restoring the Horse Gate, the church need not look too far to extract meaningful imagery from Scripture.

The horse is very well described throughout the Bible as the preferred animal for battle. The horse was distinctly characterized as the ideal animal for those engaged in war. Therefore, as the church restores the Horse Gate, Christians must learn and expand their awareness to every aspect of waging spiritual battle to become proficiently combat worthy. God's people are obligated to progress courageously into battle, fighting with all readiness and skill to obtain victories for the Lord. The Horse Gate is a memorial to the fact that God expects the church to fight spiritual battles to protect and defend His people from all their enemies. Every member of the Christian church has been recruited and enlisted into the Lord's army, and not a single soldier of the Lord is exempt from spiritual battles and conflict. By restoring the Horse Gate, the people of God begin to show a willingness to fight the spiritual battles of the Lord and overcome every conflict.

A broken Horse Gate signifies frailty in spiritual battles and the unwillingness to overcome defeat and opposition. When the Horse Gate is fully restored, God's people will willingly advance from victory to victory, triumph to triumph, and from glory to glory. The greatest description and imagery found in Scripture of a horse is in the Book of Job:

> Have you given the horse strength? Have you clothed his neck with thunder? Can you frighten him like a locust? His majestic snorting strikes terror. He paws in the valley, and rejoices in his strength; He gallops into the clash of arms. He mocks at fear, and is not frightened; Nor does he turn back from the sword. The quiver rattles against him, The glittering spear and javelin. He devours the distance with fierceness and rage; Nor does he come to a halt because the trumpet has sounded. At the blast of the trumpet he says, "Aha!" He smells the battle from afar, The thunder of captains and shouting.
>
> —JOB 39:19–25, NKJV

Throughout the Bible, horses are mentioned in relation to warfare. No other biblical passage could more accurately describe a horse's function like the one above. The extraordinary attributes of a horse's makeup are clearly visible in the face of battle. From the earliest of times, horses have been used in combat more than any other animal known to man. This is because of their astonishingly ideal performance in the midst of battle. The horse is generally useful in battle because of its enduring strength and amazing agility, which make it incredibly beneficial to those headed for conflict.

The Book of Job describes a horse as a fast and furious animal designed as such by God and perfected for battle. In battle, the horse charges fiercely in the face of danger without being frightened or easily intimidated. This description of a horse in Job permits God's people to perceive that God desires His church to advance with similar character and temperament. In fact, God reveals to the apostle John in Revelation 21:8 that no cowards or fearful people will be permitted to enter the heavenly Jerusalem. Thus, the Horse Gate in the old Jerusalem reminds God's people that cowards will have no place in the city of God.

Why would God choose to name one of the gates of old Jerusalem the Horse Gate? Is it plausible that God desired for the church to have the essence and innate character of this animal? Apparently, the Horse Gate in old Jerusalem was utilized to deploy the military forces that defended God's dwelling place and people. The God of Israel continually instructed His people to be courageous and fight fearlessly, as a mighty people of war. The old Jerusalem contained treasures and wealth that required protection against enemy combatants who frequently laid siege upon the people of God to plunder their belongings. In the same manner, God expects the church to prepare and engage battle to fiercely defend and safeguard the things entrusted to them.

The general characteristic of a good warhorse is exemplified by their gentle submission to their rider, while remaining ready to show forth great strength and endurance in battle. While under full submission to its rider, a horse is willing to be led into dangerous combat. When training a horse for battle, a rider would generally address its responsiveness to being controlled without reins, tolerance for the noises of battle, and its adaptability. Some warhorses were also trained to kick, strike, and even bite on command, thus becoming weapons in the extended aspects of conflict. A horse is never intimidated and it conducts itself with the same courage of its rider.

The Horse Gate speaks to the church that God desires a strong and courageous people willing to wage warfare and engage in battle against the enemies of God. The Christian church is not a place for cowards or cowardly fearful men and women. Every member called to join the ranks of God's army in the body of Christ must develop a fierce and fearless character in order to withstand the challenge to confront wickedness and encounter opposition fighting the good fight of faith on every battlefront.

In the Book of Revelation, we are given a glimpse of God's final judgment from which we can clearly understand that God does not intend to welcome cowards into His kingdom. Any believer who continues displaying cowardice in His character will not be permitted to enter the city of God. Christians who truly desire to one day enter the realm of the heavenly Jerusalem must reconsider whether or not they have conducted themselves worthy of God's acceptance by developing a character of courage rather than cowardice. Believers who justify their tendency to act cowardly and consider fearfulness not equally as bad as killing a person or committing a heinous act of gross wickedness must realize that being a coward is just as sinful. The apostle John was given a specific list of the people types that would perish in the lake that burns with fire and brimstone:

> But the cowardly, unbelieving, abominable, murderers, sexually immoral, sorcerers, idolaters, and all liars shall have their part in the lake which burns with fire and brimstone, which is the second death.
> —REVELATION 21:8, NKJV

The Bible clearly categorizes the "cowardly" in the same column with every other type of evil deviation. Cowardice, otherwise known as "fearfulness," is listed in God's Word at the forefront of all ungodly conduct. God did not intend for Christians to possess the character attributes of an ostrich. So often, church people talk about "Christians" who prefer to hide out, undercover, in fear of reprisal. They say, "Oh, be careful, they might think that I am a Christian." Other believers withdraw from Christian identity hoping that no one labels them as a person who lives for God's honor.

Every Christian leader is entrusted as a steward of God's divine administration upon Earth, accurately representing and furthering the interest of God's kingdom. Therefore, church leaders who desire to restore the Horse Gate have an obligation to teach God's people that cowards will not be welcomed into God's eternal dwellings. Furthermore, welcoming cowards to participate in church affairs and membership without heartfelt repentance and restoration is a serious infringement of God's trust. In fact, the Bible record reveals that cowards are ultimately deserving of hell and will be tossed directly into the lake of fire. Christians everywhere need to be informed that unrepentant cowards will find their names at the forefront of God's list, among the worst group of wicked people, heading to the lake of fire.

Many churches encourage cowardly Christians to remain uninvolved and reservedly sitting back in church pews doing nothing because they are fearful. Every Christian has been called by God to actively participate in the realties of spiritual warfare assisting the host of heaven to overcome against the enemy. When the Christian church restores the Horse Gate, every believer will be encouraged by the opportunity to have their character transformed into the fierce and valiant character of a warhorse. The Horse Gate prepares Christians to fight the good fight of the Christian faith understanding that victory belongs to the Lord. Restoring the Horse Gate will teach Christians that God's people have nothing to fear because Scripture promises them that God goes with them to fight for them against their enemies to give them victory. Consequently, restoring the Horse Gate helps the church instruct believers that every fight they wage must be fought with the tenacity and courage of a warhorse.

Another biblical passage that illustrates God's desire for a courageous people is found in the Old Testament Book of Deuteronomy. Before going to war, God's people were thoroughly instructed to understand the rules of engagement. In this passage, God instructs His leaders to disqualify certain men from battle and render them ineligible to participate because of certain character flaws. The Lord instructed His military leaders to dismiss from battle those warriors who exhibited inappropriate behavior because they threatened the success and safety of all others:

> When you go out to battle against your enemies, and see horses and chariots and people more numerous than you, do not be afraid of them; for the LORD your God is with you, who brought you up from the land of Egypt. So it shall be, when

you are on the verge of battle, that the priest shall approach and speak to the people. And he shall say to them, "Hear, O Israel: Today you are on the verge of battle with your enemies. Do not let your heart faint, do not be afraid, and do not tremble or be terrified because of them; for the LORD your God is He who goes with you, to fight for you against your enemies, to save you."

—DEUTERONOMY 20:1–4, NKJV

The instructions given to God's people in this passage of Scripture remind Christians to take courage when going to battle. They must understand that God is on their side, fighting for them against the enemy. This divine preamble was proclaimed aloud every time God's people were faced with the stark reality of going to war. The uneasiness felt by warriors on the verge of battle would vanish upon hearing the declaration of God's incredible encouragement that He would save and deliver them from their enemies. Likewise, God has given the church similar pronouncements that assure the body of Christ victory every time they face difficult situations. Every time the church faces a major decision regarding ministry, purpose, direction, or position, church leaders must make sure that there are no fearful and cowardly warriors on the battlefield lest they discourage the other brethren.

On the verge of every spiritual battle, the body of Christ must learn to eliminate every matter that promotes fear and dismay. The Lord knows that His people have a natural tendency to be scared and dismayed on the verge of every battle. For this reason, God desires the church to restore the Horse Gate so that Christians begin embracing the character of a horse prepared to go to battle. God requires the church to be thoroughly instructed in the ways of spiritual warfare. God's heart is that His people be strong, formidable, and able to wage spiritual warfare against the host of hell. The historical rules of engagement remind God's people that He is with them to fight their battles and that they are not to be afraid. The Bible record further shows that the priest would speak to the ranks of God's army with specific instructions to prevent any distraction or hindrance to victory:

> And he shall say to them, "Hear, O Israel: Today you are on the verge of battle with your enemies. Do not let your heart faint, do not be afraid, and do not tremble or be terrified because of them; for the LORD your God is He who goes with you, to fight for you against your enemies, to save you." Then the officers shall speak to the people, saying: "What man is there who has built a new house and has not dedicated it? Let him go and return to his house, lest he die in battle and another man dedicate it. And what man is there who has planted a vineyard and has not yet eaten of it? Let him go and return to his house, lest he die in the battle and another man eat of it. And what man is there who is betrothed to a woman and has not married her? Let him go and return to his house, lest he die in the battle and another man marry her." The officers shall speak further to the people, and say, "What man is there who is fearful and fainthearted? Let him go and return to his house, lest the heart of his brethren faint like his heart."
>
> —DEUTERONOMY 20:3–8, NKJV

Apparently, fearfulness and faintheartedness are very contagious conditions. Therefore, God emphatically states that He does not want fainthearted people to participate in the battles of the Lord. God understands that the warriors who are busily occupied with thoughts of new houses, relationships, or chores usually distract others from fighting the good fight. Christians that are busy seem to have problems committing and are not able to concentrate their efforts while in the line of fire. When soldiers are occupied with extracurricular activities, they have a tendency to let down their guard in crucial situations instead of being alert and vigilant in the midst of conflict. God desires an army readily attentive and prepared for every aspect of spiritual battle.

Today in the body of Christ there are two particular factions that distort the church's focus on the issue of spiritual warfare. First, the

Christians who believe that spiritual battles are unnecessary because all battles have been won by God's grace. Therefore, any mention of "spiritual warfare" or "a call to arms" is the product of paranoid exaggeration coming from delusional believers. Second is the group of Christians who elevate their "call to arms" toward the physical realm and actually store up physical weapons aimed at human, political, or social adversaries. This second group willfully forgets that their battle is not against flesh and blood, but against principalities and powers in spiritual realms. Satan has duped many Christians with their failure to discern between flesh and blood. Instead of confronting the spiritual host of darkness, they are rendered totally ineffective by concentrating their attacks upon physical targets. The devil has masterfully deceived and distracted the latter group with issues concerning flesh instead of putting on the full armor of God to withstand the evil one in the spiritual realms.

Many people believe that Christ came to bring peace upon Earth and therefore any mention of fighting is totally inconsistent with their understanding of Christ's peace plan. However, any concept of peace intrinsically involves a clash with those who persist in opposing peace. When Christ came to declare peace to humanity, He had to declare war on the devil. The Bible states that Christ disarmed the principalities and powers, triumphing over them victoriously:

> Having disarmed principalities and powers, He made a public spectacle of them, triumphing over them in it.
>
> —Colossians 2:15, nkjv

The Horse Gate fosters the idea that Christians should engage in every form of spiritual combat necessary until they are able to disarm the host of hell, and this is not possible without a fight. For light to prevail over darkness they must first engage in a disputed confrontation. First and foremost, light must encounter and declare war and engage in battle. The word *prevail* indicates that a conflict has occurred and one party has been the victor over the other. The light engages in war by challenging darkness with the declaration, "This area does not belong to darkness," thus exposing the darkened area. Light must then confront the dark areas and overcome darkness. The Bible teaches that light always prevails over darkness. When truth advances against the lie, the lie will flee, but not without a battle. The Bible states that when Christians resist the devil, he will flee from them. (See James 4:7.) In other words, when Satan comes against the church, every member must stand firm and resist him. When they have steadfastly resisted the enemy, he will flee from them.

To belong to God is to declare war on everything that is not of God. Christians will not be numbered among heaven's host if they continually befriend the enemies of God. The Bible states that the world and God are in enmity with each other, therefore whoever loves the world is an enemy of God. (See James 4:4.) Anyone who loves God has to see the world as His enemy. The Bible teaches followers of Christ that there is a continual conflict with the sinful nature of their flesh. Christians should remain steadfast in their faith being prepared to war constantly against the members of their own body. The Horse Gate reminds the enemies of God that those who oppose God and His kingdom will not prevail because of the fierce character and courage of God's people. When the body of Christ restores the Horse Gate, Christians can begin to overcome triumphantly any opposition that arises against God's people.

Once again, the Horse Gate is a reminder to every believer that good warfare is essential for every believer in the body of Christ to overcome against all their opponents. Many Christians may have been led to think that "warfare" is an Old Testament concept that is no longer applicable to today's Christian walk. Still the apostle Paul writes to his young apprentice Timothy with specific words on how to engage effectively in good warfare:

> This charge I commit unto thee, son Timothy, according to the prophecies which went before on thee, that thou by them mightest war a good warfare.
>
> —1 TIMOTHY 1:18

For Christians to continue growing in faith and maintaining a good conscience requires a constant state of awareness in spiritual battles. Even though Paul reminds Timothy to wage good warfare, for many this concept of fighting is not taken well. They do not understand the reality of this continual conflict. In every area of the Christian's life, there are battles to overcome. Through these battles, the church is able to receive God's inheritance. For example, to preserve a godly home a Christian must be tenacious in battles over all the elements that want to flood the home with ungodliness.

The spiritual battles fought by the present-day young people in the body of Christ will determine the future for the church in many respects. There is a fierce battle raging for the hearts and minds of this generation's youth. For many Christian teenagers, spiritual battles are evident in the horrible things taking place in today's public schools. When Christian teenagers declare that they go to church and obey God's Word, they defy the tide of wickedness that has engulfed many sectors of today's youth. The proclamation of loving Christ and keeping His Word is a declaration of war in today's youth culture. When Paul addressed Timothy in the course of his writings he reminds the young disciple that as a good soldier of Jesus Christ he is to continue fighting the good fight.

In the letter to the Ephesians, Paul wrote that the Christian battle is not directed at other people:

> Put on the whole armour of God, that ye may be able to stand against the wiles of the devil. For we wrestle not against flesh and blood, but against principalities, against powers, against the rulers of the darkness of this world, against spiritual wickedness in high places.
>
> —Ephesians 6:11–12

Many Christians fail to realize the existence of spiritual battles and that the fighting is not merely theoretical, but a genuine aspect in the lives of all who desire to stand up for Christ against the hellish tide of wickedness. The call of a Christian is to fight against principalities and powers; therefore, God has forewarned His people to put on the full armor of God:

> Wherefore take unto you the whole armour of God, that ye may be able to withstand in the evil day, and having done all, to stand.
>
> —EPHESIANS 6:13

One of the reasons many Christians are ineffective in their warfare against wickedness is their constant resorting to carnal weapons. In 2 Corinthians 10:3, Paul wrote to the Corinthian believers that their weapons of warfare should not be carnal. Many Christians attempt to engage in spiritual battle by utilizing human wit or carnal weapons. Many times Christians scream and yell in the presence of a devil and his demons, fighting on a natural plain, thinking that evil spirits suffer from some type of hearing impairment. But the Bible instructs Christians that they should not war according to the flesh:

> For though we walk in the flesh, we do not war after the flesh: (For the weapons of our warfare are not carnal, but mighty through God to the pulling down of strong holds;) Casting down imaginations, and every high thing that exalteth itself against the knowledge of God, and bringing into captivity every thought to the obedience of Christ; And having in a readiness to revenge all disobedience, when your obedience is fulfilled.
>
> —2 CORINTHIANS 10:3–6

At the Horse Gate, the church begins to glean wisdom and understanding from the biblical principles on waging good warfare in their daily efforts of overcoming the evil one. Before becoming Christians, people have no idea the extent to which wickedness influences their lives. Having no previous knowledge of how to overcome these evil spirits, which flooded their daily existence, Christians must now learn how to protect themselves. A vast majority of Christians contend with similar spiritual battles in their lives, which causes them to do things they would never otherwise do. Rather than suffering casualties and loss, the body of Christ must learn to wage effective and strategic spiritual battles. God desires that His people stand up as victorious warriors overcoming the clash between good and evil. God desires the church to regain the full authority and garments of war and confront their enemies at every turn, telling them that the body of Christ is more than conquerors. The Spirit of the Lord calls Christians to vest themselves of the full authority of God's kingdom, and govern the whole earth not by power or might but by the Spirit of God that resides within them.

At the Horse Gate, the church understands they will never be able to exercise their God-given authority unless they are willing and able to go to battle. Christians must begin to identify their enemies and recognize the opposition. The church must understand that each member of the body of Christ has a different enemy who contends against their vulnerability to affect the whole body. For youth, the weakness might be loneliness, despair, peer pressure, drugs, hopelessness, or promiscuity. These are all terrible giants for youth to overcome. Adults may have other enemies such as pride, alcoholism, depression, anxiety, divorce, or financial conflicts.

Regardless of the enemies that stand to oppose God's people, Christians both young and old must be trained in tactics of spiritual warfare to ultimately overcome. God has the ability to train you for the battle and make you strong and fiercely competent for war. David writes, "He teacheth my hands to war, so that a bow of steel is broken by mine arms" (Ps. 18:34). Christians should always be reminded that Jesus Christ is the Lord of God's host and Captain of the Lord's armies. Jesus is always willing to go before His people, conquering and taking all the land that He has promised them. As Christian leaders effectively restore the Horse Gate, the church can expect to know that the battle belongs to the Lord. Regardless of what kind of battle rages against Christians or the kind of warfare that faces the body of Christ—victory is theirs in Christ. The church must be reminded at the Horse Gate that God is always victorious and has never lost a battle.

The church must never lose sight of the fact that they are God's people and as such, they have enemies. If Christians become too shortsighted to notice the enemies on the horizon, they run the risk of leaving themselves exposed to terrible destruction. On September 11, 2001, the United States of America was attacked by a group of terrorists called Al-Qaeda. Many experts have argued that American authorities failed to give serious attention to years of serious threats made by these terrorists, including various declarations of war made by various segments of these terrorist zealots.

In the same manner, Satan has declared war on the body of Christ. His desire is to kill, steal, and destroy those enlisted in the Lord's army. (See John 10:10.) If Christians permit the enemy to have his way, the devil will take everything God has given them. The devil's desire is to oppress believers and plunder all that is theirs. The church cannot pretend that this threat of conflict is merely philosophical and not a reality. The Bible confirms the intensity of this plight, warning every Christian to be constantly on guard because the devil roams about like a roaring lion, seeking whom he may devour. (See 1 Peter 5:8.) The Bible reveals this reality with the purpose that every Christian can prepare for a real and specific attack by the enemy and not be caught off guard. The church must be trained and equipped so that they are not surprised when the enemy engages them in conflict. Paul wrote to the Corinthian church advising them that his training and preparation was such that he never missed his target when he fought:

> I therefore so run, not as uncertainly; so fight I, not as one that beateth the air.
>
> —1 CORINTHIANS 9:26

Consider the travesty of those who fight and always miss their target when they launch their assault. Paul warns Christians that they must concentrate their efforts on effective warfare, not like warriors who miss their target. When the church launches an attack, they must hit their target with all purpose and force. When the Horse Gate is broken, the church cannot challenge the devil to any contest because after swinging twenty times and hitting nothing they retreat in all defeat. The Horse Gate calls for spiritual training in warfare so that the Christian church begins to aim their efforts to obtain successful results and achieve God's victories in every competition.

The Horse Gate was assigned to protect old Jerusalem by launching a horse battalion against enemy combatants that threatened the cities inhabitants. Every church should develop a special task force or division ready to address the spiritual battles and needs that confront the church from time to time. This group of spiritual soldiers should be ready to oppose enemy attacks and fiercely contend with those elements that desire to destroy the body of Christ.

In the American military, there are specially trained men prepared for special operations and sophisticated battle engagements and warfare tactics. Over the years, the American military has formed specialized military groups such as the Green Berets and Navy SEALs to effectively ward off enemy combatants. In the body of Christ the church needs "Cross Berets" or "Christian SEALs" that take after the character of the U.S. military, ready to engage and deploy at a moment's notice. The body of Christ must train Christian men and women to be prepared to leave whatever they are doing and launch an offensive against any spiritual attack against the host of hell. Whenever a spiritual battle or attack occurs in the surrounding community, Christians should be able immediately to call these specialized forces into action. They should be able to provide them with a quick briefing, and off they go to confront the opposition. The church cannot send any ordinary person. Without the proper preparation to participate in a spiritual battle, the believer may suffer an embarrassing defeat. Unprepared and untrained Christians would not know what to do, and their involvement would cause more problems than help.

Several years ago, a family in the south Florida area summoned the church to their residence to assist with the immediate removal of articles of witchcraft and satanic worship valued at more than one hundred thousand dollars. For several hours all types of detestable objects were removed that were formerly utilized in occult practices to perform enchantments, rituals, and demonic ceremonies. As the pastor of the church, I was weary to take members of the church that were not prepared to confront such a tremendous spiritual battle. Several members of the church were selected who had previous experience and the maturity to be able to confront these wicked principalities and powers of darkness in the name of Jesus. This family had invested large sums of money into acquiring all sorts of ungodly items to conduct sacrifices and appease the evil spirits they served.

Knowing that this kind of spiritual battle required a strong ministry team to avoid distractions, I could not select just any ordinary believer to help. This particular mission required people who were prayed up and walking in purity. In a situation like this, the church is confronting very strong evil spirits, walking into their territory declaring the end of their reign of terror. In order to confront the wicked host of hell that gripped this family with years of various types of blood covenants and animal sacrifices, we came in the residence with the authority of God, led by the Spirit and under the blood of Jesus Christ. The entire process of removing these wicked objects involved guarding our hearts and thoughts, keeping them in obedience to the Lord so that the devil could not intimidate or influence them.

Until the church becomes a strong people of battle, the cities and countries of this world will continue to be held in captivity to darkness and all types of evil. Miami is one of the largest occult cities in the world. Much witchcraft takes place through the Santeria religion and similar religions with roots in Afro-Cuban rituals. If the church intends to participate as the elect of God's host, they must be ready as an army dressed for battle. The Horse Gate reminds the church to revisit their true source of strength and vitality; to restore what otherwise may be a demoralized, disorganized, unprepared battalion. Jesus taught His followers to take inventory prior to going to battle so that they need not retreat in the face of battle:

> Or what king, going to make war against another king, sitteth not down first, and consulteth whether he be able with ten thousand to meet him that cometh against him with twenty thousand? Or else, while the other is yet a great way off, he sendeth an ambassage, and desireth conditions of peace. So likewise, whosoever he be of you that forsaketh not all that he hath, he cannot be my disciple.
>
> —Luke 14:31–33

The clarity of this parable associates the Christian walk with a king going to make war against another king. God desires His people to take formation as an army that is not distracted and has counted the costs of battle. For Christian leaders, the Horse Gate represents preparing a church full of courageous people ready to fight the good fight of the Christian faith. Even young people within the church are expected to develop the character of a soldier. The Horse Gate reminds them to walk in the character of the true church, requiring each member to fight a daily spiritual battle to further the kingdom of God. The Horse Gate is a memorial to the church reminding them that the Christian life is filled with spiritual fights at each moment of every day, and that preparation must be made to face these fights. Every Christian that becomes a part of God's army must understand this truth. The Christian church is about to fight the greatest battle of all time. Therefore, Christians are called to march faithfully to the drumbeat of God's battle cry and stand firmly against the enemies they confront each day.

There is no better description for a disciple of Jesus Christ than a soldier. Once enlisted, a soldier never does his own thing. The main attribute of a good soldier is the ability to be ready for the call of duty. They have to be tested to see if they are equipped. Their training consists of officers demanding excellence.

In 1 Timothy 6:12, Paul tells Timothy, "Fight the good fight of faith."

Later, he adds, "Thou therefore endure hardness, as a good soldier of Jesus Christ" (2 Tim. 2:3). When a country prepares their soldiers for war, they do not take them to a Caribbean resort to hang out and catch up on some rest and relaxation. No, the soldiers' training for battle is in a hostile environment where conditions simulate war, explosions are loud, and events take the character of real combat. With a multitude of distractions during training, a soldier is forced to concentrate to accomplish his mission.

The word Paul utilized to prepare Timothy was *endure*. Why endure? A good soldier must be able to endure hardship, and a soldier of Christ must have the capacity to endure hardship like a faithful follower of Jesus Christ. Paul told Timothy that soldiers involved in daily combat with spiritual affairs should avoid:

> No one engaged in warfare entangles himself with the affairs of this life, that he may please him who enlisted him as a soldier.
> —2 TIMOTHY 2:4, NKJV

Christians may think, *Lord, give me a short break because I have to go do something that is going to take me a while, and I'll be right back.* A true soldier of Christ wants to bring pleasure to God's heart. He therefore does not entangle himself in the affairs of this life. For this reason, Christians must begin to ask themselves, "Am I willing to endure hardship?" Have Christians entangled themselves in the affairs of this life so much that they are no longer useful to fight the Lord's battles? Are they enduring hardship to the point that they are bringing pleasure to the heart of God, to the One who enlisted them and gave them a role to play in His army?

As the Horse Gate is repaired and restored, the church must ask questions concerning the state of their armor and weapons. What inventory is there in the spiritual armory to prepare and engage in effective warfare against the host of hell? How sharp is the sword of the Spirit? When the devil comes at the church, will Christians respond by saying, "It is written..."? When Satan blows up like a giant shadow, will the church have sufficient ability to expose him by shining so much light on him that he disappears?

The Bible is a light unto the path of the righteous so that they do not stumble and fall. While this chapter did not address specific strategies for planning and conducting spiritual battle campaigns, such as movement and disposition of forces, hopefully it pointed to the our need to prepare ourselves to be a fierce and courageous people ready for battle.

Specific weapons that God has given the church can be used to overcome the evil one. Will the church mount up an air force of *forgiveness*? Will the mystery of forgiveness equip the body of Christ to stand against the host of bitterness and resentment that destroys thousands in the church each day? Many are totally foreign to the concept that forgiveness is a powerful weapon that could defuse and deactivate the works of Satan. When the body of Christ is in the quest for victory amidst a raging battle, the words *forgive me*, or *I forgive you* can be articulated to bring about sudden conquest. Forgiveness instantly destroys the works of the evil one.

How about when a Christian is able to walk in love? The Bible teaches that love conquers all, and love never fails. The Horse Gate reminds the church that if God is for them who can be against them? The body of Christ needs to be reminded that God is constantly fighting all their battles for them.

There are all sorts of evil spirits that come up against the people of God. The church must begin to discern evil spirits that besiege God's people:

> ➤ To be able to walk into a house and know what spirit is governing there
>
> ➤ To be able to call each spirit after their name and kind

> ➤ Interact with a person having a problem and know what is operating behind the scenes

> ➤ Be able to call those spirits by name and rebuke them and cast them out in the name of Jesus

Every Christian must prepare to wage spiritual battles because the enemy makes no exception of persons and takes no prisoners. Unless the church restores the Horse Gate, the enemy will continue to ransack the city of God because he knows that no horses reside in there to defend the people. The devil will know that no troops are present to fight God's battles. The broken Horse Gate tells Satan that the church continues unprepared, showing an absence of courageous soldiers to defend the house of the Lord against the unworthy elements that desire to besiege the body of Christ.

From time to time, the enemy threatens to stand victoriously over God's kingdom, scaring God's people into fearful submission. For this reason, the body of Christ must be reminded that the kingdom of God and their host will prevail ultimately over all the kingdoms in the heavens, on the earth, and beneath the earth. All kingdoms will submit themselves to the lordship of Jesus Christ. The church, as the body of Christ will reign with Christ:

> Now I saw heaven opened, and behold, a white horse. And He who sat on him was called Faithful and True, and in righteousness He judges and makes war. His eyes were like a flame of fire, and on His head were many crowns. He had a name written that no one knew except Himself. He was clothed with a robe dipped in blood, and His name is called The Word of God. And the armies in heaven [you and I], clothed in fine linen, white and clean, followed Him on white horses.
>
> —REVELATION 19:11–14, NKJV

They were following Him on what? On white *horses*:

> Now out of His mouth goes a sharp sword, that with it He should strike the nations. And He Himself will rule them with a rod of iron. He Himself treads the winepress of the fierceness and wrath of Almighty God. And He has on His robe and on His thigh a name written: KING OF KINGS AND LORD OF LORDS.
>
> —REVELATION 19:15–16, NKJV

The final battle is foreseen as the battle of the End Times. A battle rages in the heavens between the armies of Satan and the armies of God. The church is called to a significant role fighting with Christ to establish the kingdom of God. The church has been called to a victorious legacy, and Jesus affirms that the gates of hell will not prevail against the church:

> I will build my church; and the gates of hell shall not prevail against it.
>
> —MATTHEW 16:18

The biblical record denotes that the followers of Christ are more than overcomers in the name of Jesus. All authority over the evil one has been given to the church. Before Jesus, every knee shall bow and every tongue shall confess, acknowledging that Jesus is Lord.

The prophet Joel recorded his vision of how God's people would take the world by storm. The Horse Gate will be an essential aspect of the church's revival in the last days. This prophetic vision describes how every member in the body of Christ will take their place in God's army. Joel describes their appearance like the appearance of horses. The church should pray as follows from this day forward:

> *Lord Jesus, let us come under Your authority and command. You are the commander and chief of this army. Lord, train and equip Your church and set us in battle formation never*

breaking ranks. May Your voice arise and sound like an alarm before Your army. Jesus, let Your church blaze a trail that glorifies Your name at all times. In Jesus' name I pray, Amen.

Blow the trumpet in Zion, And sound an alarm in My holy mountain! Let all the inhabitants of the land tremble; For the day of the LORD is coming, For it is at hand: A day of darkness and gloominess, A day of clouds and thick darkness, Like the morning clouds spread over the mountains. A people come, great and strong, The like of whom has never been; Nor will there ever be any such after them, Even for many successive generations. A fire devours before them, And behind them a flame burns; The land is like the Garden of Eden before them, And behind them a desolate wilderness; Surely nothing shall escape them. Their appearance is like the appearance of horses; And like swift steeds, so they run. With a noise like chariots Over mountaintops they leap, Like the noise of a flaming fire that devours the stubble, Like a strong people set in battle array. Before them the people writhe in pain; All faces are drained of color. They run like mighty men, They climb the wall like men of war; Every one marches in formation, And they do not break ranks. They do not push one another; Every one marches in his own column. Though they lunge between the weapons, They are not cut down. They run to and fro in the city, They run on the wall; They climb into the houses, They enter at the windows like a thief. The earth quakes before them, The heavens tremble; The sun and moon grow dark, And the stars diminish their brightness. The LORD gives voice before His army, For His camp is very great; For strong is the One who executes His word. For the day of the LORD is great and very terrible; Who can endure it?

—JOEL 2:1–11, NKJV

The Horse Gate allows the church to boldly mount up with the courage of King David and dismiss the cowardly as unfit for battle. The church cannot restore the Horse Gate without joining the ranks of God's army in the End Times. Christians should be encouraged to stand and ask God to give them the courage of a lion. The Bible states, "The righteous are bold as a lion" (Prov. 28:1). First, every Christian must learn to fight their personal spiritual battles, then those of their immediate family, and finally those of the local church. Lastly, the Christian church can direct effective efforts at fighting the spiritual battles within their local communities, states, nation, and to the ends of the earth. For this reason, the church must take serious steps toward restoring the Horse Gate in the local church.

PRAYER APPLICATION

Father God! Help the Christian church to restore the Horse Gate. Lord Jesus, prepare Your church as a mighty and strong army filled with courageous men and women that have the character attributes of warhorses, prepared and willing to fight the good fight of the Christian faith. I pray that the body of Christ begins to obtain victory after victory in every spiritual battle they face. May all the enemies of Your people be confounded and unable to withstand those that serve You faithfully as good soldiers of Jesus Christ. Lord, allow Your church to finally put on the whole armor of God so they can thereby withstand and wrestle against every spiritual host of darkness confronting the body of Christ, and ultimately prevail over the enemy as more than conquerors.

9

THE EAST GATE

> *Afterward he brought me to the gate, even the gate that looketh toward the east: And, behold, the glory of the God of Israel came from the way of the east: and his voice was like a noise of many waters: and the earth shined with his glory.*
>
> —EZEKIEL 43:1–2

This chapter focuses on restoring the East Gate. Church leaders can find incredible significance behind the restoration of the East Gate as it relates to strengthening the Christian church. Well grounded in traditional Jewish history, there is clear and convincing evidence that the East Gate was prophesied as the entrance gate through which the Messiah would return. Upon restoring the East Gate, church leaders will be challenged to accept the importance revealed by the mystery of Christ's return.

The East Gate restoration requires specific attention to the biblical instruction regarding Christ's return. Repairing the East Gate involves renewing every Christian heart and mind to embrace the reality of Christ's imminent return. As the church repairs the East Gate, believers begin to truly live each day as if it were their last. The necessity of repairing the East Gate is seen by the great number of Christians occupying themselves with trivial matters that have no eternal weight or significance. The lack of fervent teaching regarding Christ's return causes the Christian heart to grow sick, as from a hope that is deferred. Postponing the significance of the Lord's return in the hearts of Christians allows their lives to become easy spoil for the enemy. As church leaders approach the challenge to restore the East Gate, they need to refresh the church's understanding that in a mere twinkling of an eye Christ will return for His bride and take the church up to the heavens to abide with Him forever. In Nehemiah 3:29, the "East Gate" is mentioned during the process of restoration in the ancient city:

> After them Zadok the son of Immer made repairs in front of his own house. After him Shemaiah the son of Shechaniah, the keeper of the East Gate, made repairs.
>
> —NEHEMIAH 3:29, NKJV

Church leaders will be encouraged as they discover how God meant to leave a visible print and memorial for His people so that they would never lose hope. The East Gate is a constant reminder to God's people to live their lives with the earnest expectation of Christ's imminent and glorious return. God's people lived and taught that one day the King of glory would return, as a mighty conqueror to establish His eternal kingdom.

The historical significance for the existence of the East Gate in ancient Jerusalem was so widespread that conquering nations would purposefully close up and block any possible entrance to the city from this gate. To this day, the East Gate in Jerusalem remains closed and cemented with concrete blocks due to the fear of reprisal from a Messianic conqueror that would return and conquer the city. Many invading armies that entered Jerusalem would immediately order this gate closed upon learning of the prophecy that a great king would enter Jerusalem through the East Gate to deliver His people. The devil and his host have always hated the prospect of Christ's glorious return, so Satan would love nothing more than to obstruct the East Gate by blocking the entrance with huge stones. Historically there has been much controversy concerning this gate and the revelations of how a ruler is expected to return and subdue the city from foreign rule. The prophet Ezekiel wrote concerning the details that involved the Prince's appearance through this East Gate in the following passage:

> Then he brought me back the way of the gate of the outward sanctuary which looketh toward the east; and it was shut. Then said the LORD unto me; This gate shall be shut, it shall not be opened, and no man shall enter in by it; because the LORD, the God of Israel, hath entered in by it, therefore it shall be shut. It is for the prince; the prince, he shall sit in it to eat bread before the LORD; he shall enter by the way of the porch of that gate, and shall go out by the way of the same.
>
> —EZEKIEL 44:1–3

The accuracy of this prophetic account has powerful implications for those waiting for Jesus to return. The present state of disrepair regarding the East Gate within the Christian church involves having neglected the truth that lies behind the gate and the reason for its existence. A broken East Gate debilitates the Christian zeal affecting the passion of God's people by forgetting the hope realized in Christ's return. When the church loses this integral part of God's truth, Christians begin to miss out on the weight and motivation of God's design imparted to keep believers expectant, vigilant, watchful, and ready to receive the coming kingdom. When the East Gate is restored, the world will notice a vibrant church living as pilgrims and strangers anxiously awaiting the imminent return of their Redeemer.

The present apathy, seen in many Christian believers who linger without understanding that they are closer to the Lord's return today then when they first believed, creates a culture where the church becomes spiritually sluggish in their walk and service for the Lord. When the East Gate lies in ruins, the church is plundered of spiritual vitality, wealth, and strength inherent in embracing the truth regarding the Lord's return. Any church that is frail and hopeless, existing without the vibrant expectation of Christ's prompt return must quickly restore the East Gate from its fallen condition. The restoration of the East Gate will transform defeated churches into vibrant thriving churches that are renewed in their understanding of the Lord's return. Whenever a Christian church redefines their existence in the light of the Lord's imminent return, the Christian's heart is set ablaze knowing eternity is right around the corner.

Many Scripture passages addressing Christ's return speak of His coming from the East. In Zechariah 14:1, there is a prophetic message foretelling the Lord's return through the east side of Jerusalem. Hundreds of years before the coming of Christ, Zechariah wrote concerning the Lord's return:

> Behold, the day of the LORD is coming, And your spoil will be divided in your midst. For I will gather all the nations to battle against Jerusalem; The city shall be taken, The houses rifled, And the women ravished. Half of the city shall go into captivity, But the remnant of the people shall not be cut off from the city. Then the LORD will go forth And fight against those nations, As He fights in the day of battle. And in that day His feet will stand on the Mount of Olives, Which faces Jerusalem on the east. And the Mount of Olives shall be split in two, From east to west.
> —ZECHARIAH 14:1–4, NKJV

The Mount of Olives faces the East Gate. When the Messiah returns, He will appear on the Mount of Olives and will enter through the East Gate. Jesus warned His followers to expect Him as a light that cometh out of the East:

> For as the lightning cometh out of the east, and shineth even
> unto the west; so shall also the coming of the Son of man be.
>
> —MATTHEW 24:27

The Lord forewarned that from the East He shall come and the moment will be like lightning, beginning in the East and flashing toward the West. The East Gate's significance is the fulfillment of its God-ordained purpose: receiving the King of glory into His beloved city of Jerusalem. A healthy and revived church is one whose members have an earnest expectation of the Lord's return. When the East Gate is fallen and burned up in the church, Christians become lethargic, falling asleep and living in ignorance of the reality that Christ may return at any moment.

When the East Gate is functioning, there is bubbling anticipation that Jesus' return is just around the corner, and that the church should accommodate His priorities instead of theirs. When the church loses perspective of the urgency of Christ's return, they grow indifferent to the fulfilling of their call as His church. At the East Gate, church leaders are reminded of Jesus' last words:

> He which testifieth these things saith, Surely I come quickly.
> Amen. Even so, come, Lord Jesus. The grace of our Lord Jesus
> Christ be with you all. Amen.
>
> —REVELATION 22:20–21

The urgency with which these words were written carries an assurance that the Lord will not tarry in fulfilling His promise. The Lord wants His people to be aware that His coming will follow soon thereafter:

> And, behold, I come quickly; and my reward is with me, to
> give every man according as his work shall be. I am Alpha and
> Omega, the beginning and the end, the first and the last.
>
> —REVELATION 22:12–13

The church should be continually alert that Christ is on the verge of returning, and that His coming will take place quickly. For every believer, the return of Christ ought to represent a living hope resounding deeply in the heart each second of every day. Christian children should be continually reminded of Christ's instruction. The church should proclaim with a loud shout to the world that Christ shall soon return.

The apostle Peter warned the church that many mockers would rise in the last days questioning the veracity of Christ's promise to return:

> This second epistle, beloved, I now write unto you; in both which I stir up your pure minds by way of remembrance: That ye may be mindful of the words which were spoken before by the holy prophets, and of the commandment of us the apostles of the Lord and Saviour: Knowing this first, that there shall come in the last days scoffers, walking after their own lusts, And saying, Where is the promise of his coming? for since the fathers fell asleep, all things continue as they were from the beginning of the creation. For this they willingly are ignorant of, that by the word of God the heavens were of old, and the earth standing out of the water and in the water: Whereby the world that then was, being overflowed with water, perished: But the heavens and the earth, which are now, by the same word are kept in store, reserved unto fire against the day of judgment and perdition of ungodly men. But, beloved, be not ignorant of this one thing, that one day is with the Lord as a thousand years, and a thousand years as one day. The Lord is not slack concerning his promise, as some men count slackness; but is longsuffering to us-ward, not willing that any should perish, but that all should come to repentance.
>
> —2 PETER 3:1–9

What a blessing to know that if the Lord delays His return it is because of His righteous judgment and longsuffering. Christ's sincere desire is that no one should perish but that all should repent and have everlasting life. He is waiting for others to come along. Peter writes that some willfully forget that God has already destroyed the world once by water. God was faithful to proclaim the coming flood in the times of Noah. For hundreds of years, God warned those generations that He would destroy them for failing to repent of their evil ways. Only Noah and his family were able to prepare the ark for their salvation. Nonetheless, in the last days men walking after their own lust would willfully forget how God was faithful to fulfill what He had previously foretold in the times of Noah.

But God is not slow regarding His promise, for He desires all to repent and be found right at His coming. The Bible says that in the last days many will walk about in disbelief of Christ's return. These people will disregard any warning for preparation for that great day upon which Christ will return.

Many Christians claim to have been saved by the element of God's grace. But they fail to realize that when true grace is present, it is actively preparing and instructing believers to expectantly wait for the Lord's return. The true grace that leads to God's salvation includes the element of preparing and earnestly waiting for the Lord's return. The following passage in the Book of Titus, informs believers that the purpose for God's saving grace is nothing less than to prepare God's people so they patiently wait for the appearance of our Lord Jesus Christ. What does the grace of God ultimately do? Grace allows all believers to look for the blessed hope and glorious appearing of the great God and Savior Jesus Christ:

> For the grace of God that bringeth salvation hath appeared to all men, Teaching us that, denying ungodliness and worldly lusts, we should live soberly, righteously, and godly, in this present world; Looking for that blessed hope, and the glorious appearing of the great God and our Saviour Jesus Christ.
>
> —TITUS 2:11–13

A restored East Gate will allow the church to safeguard the reality that Christ shall return and establish His kingdom upon the earth. The grace of God has come so that the church can deny ungodliness and worldly desires, then they will be ready to present themselves worthy at the appearing of the Lord. Every single book in the New Testament is replete with promises about the Lord's return. Every writer in the New Testament warns believers to proclaim and encourage one another with words that concern Christ's return.

I did not know about the Lord's return until I was seventeen years old. My father before me had not heard about the Lord's return until he was forty-nine years old. I have met people as old as eighty-four who have never heard about the Lord's return.

Each gate in this book tells a story that reveals a little more about the heart of God. The East Gate tells the church there is an expectation that Christ will keep His promise. Many grow weary of waiting, but Christ warns the church that the day and hour of His return no one knows:

> But of that day and hour knoweth no man, no, not the angels of heaven, but my Father only. But as the days of Noe were, so shall also the coming of the Son of man be. For as in the days that were before the flood they were eating and drinking, marrying and giving in marriage, until the day that Noe entered into the ark, And knew not until the flood came, and took them all away; so shall also the coming of the Son of man be. Then shall two be in the field; the one shall be taken, and the other left. Two women shall be grinding at the mill; the one shall be taken, and the other left. Watch therefore: for ye know not what hour your Lord doth come. But know this, that if the goodman of the house had known in what watch the thief would come, he would have watched, and would not have suffered his house to be broken up. Therefore be ye also ready: for in such an hour as ye think not the Son of man cometh.
>
> —MATTHEW 24:36–44

The many warnings found in Scripture regarding the Lord's return are an awesome opportunity for the church to prepare so that they are not caught off guard; neither will they sleep or mismanage their time. The parable of the ten virgins that waited for the bridegroom's return is also indicative of a believer's responsibility to prepare for Christ's much anticipated return:

> Then shall the kingdom of heaven be likened unto ten virgins, which took their lamps, and went forth to meet the bridegroom. And five of them were wise, and five were foolish. They that were foolish took their lamps, and took no oil with them: But the wise took oil in their vessels with their lamps. While the bridegroom tarried, they all slumbered and slept. And at midnight there was a cry made, Behold, the bridegroom cometh; go ye out to meet him. Then all those virgins arose, and trimmed their lamps. And the foolish said unto the wise, Give us of your oil; for our lamps are gone out. But the wise answered, saying, Not so; lest there be not enough for us and you: but go ye rather to them that sell, and buy for yourselves. And while they went to buy, the bridegroom came; and they that were ready went in with him to the marriage: and the door was shut. Afterward came also the other virgins, saying, Lord, Lord, open to us. But he answered and said, Verily I say unto you, I know you not. Watch therefore, for ye know neither the day nor the hour wherein the Son of man cometh.
>
> —MATTHEW 25:1–13

Jesus constantly reminded His followers of the importance of this event. The warnings remain the same throughout Scripture: the church should be sober, vigilant, awake, and prepared. The apostle Paul warned the Thessalonians not to be ignorant in dismissing this day as insignificant. In 1 Thessalonians 4, Paul told the church:

> For this we say unto you by the word of the Lord, that we which are alive and remain unto the coming of the Lord shall not prevent them which are asleep.
>
> —1 THESSALONIANS 4:15

The Lord will descend from heaven with the voice of an archangel and the trumpet of God, and the dead in Christ will arise first—and thus, we shall always be with the Lord:

> But of the times and the seasons, brethren, ye have no need that I write unto you. For yourselves know perfectly that the day of the Lord so cometh as a thief in the night. For when they shall say, Peace and safety; then sudden destruction cometh upon them, as travail upon a woman with child; and they shall not escape. But ye, brethren, are not in darkness, that that day should overtake you as a thief. Ye are all the children of light, and the children of the day: we are not of the night, nor of darkness. Therefore let us not sleep, as do others; but let us watch and be sober. For they that sleep sleep in the night; and they that be drunken are drunken in the night. But let us, who are of the day, be sober, putting on the breastplate of faith and love; and for an helmet, the hope of salvation. For God hath not appointed us to wrath, but to obtain salvation by our Lord Jesus Christ.
>
> —1 THESSALONIANS 5:1–9

When the East Gate is restored, church leaders will be required to ask their church members the following questions: Are you sober? Are you awake? Are you vigilant? Has your family grasped the reality that Christ's coming is at hand? The Bible describes the unpredictable nature of Christ's coming as that of a thief that comes in the night. (See 1 Thessalonians 5:2.) Many times Christ taught His followers that no one could know the day or the hour of His return but the Father. The closest predictions concerning the Lord's return that can be ascertained are the ability to know the times and the seasons. Nonetheless, distant or near, Christians must adjust their understanding of life to include the Lord's imminent return. The Bible states that if the last days were not cut short, even the elect would be lost.

> And except that the Lord had shortened those days, no flesh should be saved: but for the elect's sake, whom he hath chosen, he hath shortened the days.
>
> —MARK 13:20

Many books have been written on the topic of the Lord's return. I remember back in 1988 there was a book titled *88 Reasons Why the Rapture is in 1988* that sold thousands of copies. When 1988 came and passed, people threw their books away and denied having ever bought them.

This generation has witnessed events that many people never thought they would ever see in their lifetime. My grandmother's generation stands in awe before the licentiousness and decadence of modern social standards. The elderly remain incredulous with the extent to which our youth culture has fallen into degradation in today's world. The trends today show an inclination toward wickedness and increasing depravity like never before. The previous generation has seen evil spread from chewing gum and cursing, to rape and murder. As the days grow more and more towards evil, the church must be prepared for the Lord's imminent return. Is the church awake? Are they living each moment ready to meet their Lord? The Bible states:

> And then shall appear the sign of the Son of man in heaven: and then shall all the tribes of the earth mourn, and they shall see the Son of man coming in the clouds of heaven with power and great glory. And he shall send his angels with a great sound of a trumpet, and they shall gather together his elect from the four winds, from one end of heaven to the other.
>
> —MATTHEW 24:30–31

Many people fail to understand the terrible nightmare that will befall the earth when all godly believers are raptured. Many will ask, "Lord, why was I left behind?" When the East Gate is restored, the church begins having a daily check with reality, breaking off with every temptation to compromise and never allowing the devil to grab a foothold through earthly priorities and entanglements. The tedious entanglements of temporal affairs on Earth such as business commitments and opportunities, along with career interests or future investments, can strangle the church's spiritual life. The East Gate breaks the bondage of earthly worries by prioritizing the Lord's business. When the East Gate is restored, Christians will not permit other interests to take preference. The church must be willing to tell the Lord, "I really desire things like getting married and having a family, Lord, but you come first," or "I want to pursue a career in such and such field, but you come first, Jesus. You're my priority," or "I desire to write books and travel the world, but if You come I want to go with You," or "I want to be ready at the very moment when You appear in the clouds." Failing to be prepared to meet the Lord will be the cause of much confusion and despair for many Christians:

> And the kings of the earth, and the great men, and the rich men, and the chief captains, and the mighty men, and every bondman, and every free man, hid themselves in the dens and in the rocks of the mountains; And said to the mountains and rocks, Fall on us, and hide us from the face of him that sitteth on the throne, and from the wrath of the Lamb.
>
> —REVELATION 6:15–16

There are several biblical passages that illustrate the Lord's return as a bridegroom coming for his bride. Paul wrote to the Corinthian church that he desired nothing more than to espouse the church to one husband, so that they may be presented to the Lord as a chaste virgin. (See 2 Corinthians 11:2.) Resembling a bride who is prepared to meet her groom, the church must walk in total commitment and purity with her Lord. The East Gate refers to the divine courtship between Christ and the church, reminding the church not to forget her prenuptial obligation to get ready and culminate this relationship in marriage. The church must realize that their relationship with the Lord is not a last-minute arrangement between two unknown parties. Many times the church leaders have forgotten that the church has been betrothed to Christ. The church has an invitation to come and commit her devotion and allegiance to Christ and Christ alone. As a result, the Groom has gone off to prepare a place for His bride:

> Let not your heart be troubled: ye believe in God, believe also in me. In my Father's house are many mansions: if it were not so, I would have told you. I go to prepare a place for you. And if I go and prepare a place for you, I will come again, and receive you unto myself; that where I am, there ye may be also.
> —JOHN 14:1–3

In the old Jewish tradition, the groom would extend an invitation to his bride and propose engagement vows requesting that she go with him. He would break a piece of bread and say, "This is my life that I want to share with you," and the bride would partake of it. This engagement ritual was repeated throughout Israel and is also seen at the last supper of Christ when Jesus ate with the disciples. That night, before Christ was crucified, He took bread and broke it, and extending an invitation to His disciples, saying, "I want to betroth you, I want the church to be wed with Me, so that the church might become one with Me for all generations," (author's paraphrase). In Jewish tradition, after the bride accepted this vow of engagement, the groom left to prepare a dwelling place to consummate the marriage. Meanwhile, the bride-to-be was to keep herself faithful, expecting and knowing her beloved would return in a moment's notice. Once the engagement was made, the young maiden could not entertain any other priority that would distract her from her commitment. The bride would wait for her groom day after day because he would appear at any second so that they might dwell together forever.

The wedding relationship between Christ and His church is further illustrated in ancient Jewish folklore. In ancient times, it was thought that young men who were in love became anxious, thus requiring the father's help to supervise the bridegroom's building of the new couple's dwelling. Until the bridegroom's father gave permission, the young man could not return to take up his bride. At the appointed time, the groom began his journey. During dark nights, the young bride would vigilantly stand outside her home and try to hear the bridegroom's voice. She would prepare her oil-burning lamp that could be seen at a good distance, and the groom would try to follow that lamp to his betrothed.

This is similar to how the church waits for Jesus today. He says, "No one knows the day, nor the hour. Not even the angels, nor myself, only my Father who is in Heaven. So, I am preparing this place for you." For this purpose, Christ gave Himself in order to present a glorious bride for marriage.

> That he might present it to himself a glorious church, not having spot, or wrinkle, or any such thing; but that it should be holy and without blemish
>
> —EPHESIANS 5:27

In other words, the church must prepare herself as a bride with a white dress not having spots, wrinkles, or any such thing, so that when Jesus returns she will be found blameless and no one will be left behind. (See 1 Corinthians 1:8, author's paraphrase.) Today, the church has forgotten that the Lord is about to return. When the Lord returns, there will be many who are going to be surprised— even those who call themselves ministers, pastors, apostles, evangelists, teachers, or prophets. If only God's people could see a glimpse into the heavenly realm of the angelic host preparing to usher in the culmination of End Time world events, many would change their course of direction.

The Lord will send some angels to gather and deliver His elect, and other angels to usher severe judgments upon the earth. The Bible states that God will send out His angels to gather His elect. The people who ultimately stay behind will experience the wrath and furies of God's judgments and suffer with other earthly inhabitants those things that will befall the earth. Upon the Lord's return, backslidden Christians will regret their indifference toward such a great salvation. I have been asked many times, "Do you really believe God would destroy everyone just because they weren't Christians? That doesn't sound like God. God is love." Well, God, who is the pure essence and embodiment of love, has already destroyed the inhabitants of the earth with water during the time of Noah. The church must understand that God has previously warned them in the second epistle of Peter that He intends to judge the earth again, but this time through fire. (See 2 Peter 3:5–7.) Every Christian has hope that just as God saved one family during the first destruction, He intends to save only a small remnant the second time—the family of God.

The East Gate challenges the body of Christ to live their lives in the light of the reality of Christ's coming. When God's people make decisions and plans that take into account the certainty of Christ's return their inclination is toward heavenly interests. Similarly, when God's people set aside the urgency of Christ's return, their thoughts and actions usually follow nonspiritual pursuits. The East Gate alerts the church that being prepared for the coming of the Lord is more important than staying behind and participating in the litany of End Time events.

Restoring the East Gate means that church leaders will rekindle and sustain the fire of the Lord's coming in each soul they minister to, making sure that this truth does not become solely intellectual information, but that the doctrinal truth becomes a vibrant, fiery expectation of consuming passion that generates godliness and zeal for the work of God. The following questions can awaken and stir up interest in the Lord's return:

> ➤ Wouldn't it be foolish for you to fall asleep spiritually?

> ➤ Wouldn't it be foolish for you to disregard the reality of Christ's coming?

> ➤ The Bible states Christians were not appointed to God's wrath.

> ➤ Christians were appointed to salvation through Jesus Christ.

The hearts of God's people must be saturated with thoughts of the Lord's coming so that it stands out as a reality for every Christian who attends a church. Think back to those families who stood outside Noah's ark announcing their much-belated concession, "Okay, we believe now." I am sure those who missed the opportunity to escape the coming judgment wanted nothing more than salvation after the door had closed and salvation was no longer available. The East Gate allows the church to proclaim that today the door remains open for all who desire to be found ready and blameless upon the Lord's return. Restoring the East Gate in the church inflames an inward groan awaiting adoption that should increase more and more to the very day of redemption. Paul writes to the believers in Rome, making them aware that the whole earth is longing for that day when Christ returns:

> For we know that the whole creation groaneth and travaileth in pain together until now. And not only they, but ourselves also, which have the firstfruits of the Spirit, even we ourselves groan within ourselves, waiting for the adoption, to wit, the redemption of our body.
>
> —ROMANS 8:22–23

This passage states that all of creation groans and labors in pain, desiring to see the sons of God set free in liberty. Creation wants the sons of God to rule and to reign, then the curse will be lifted from creation. By repairing the East Gate in the church, God will open the spiritual eyes of all to understand the importance of what will happen in the spiritual realm when Christ returns. The East Gate delivers every Christian from the need to worry about earthly affairs. Worrying about a faulty world can be a hindrance to the Christian faith. The cares of this life can only serve to choke the good seed and stifle the hope in Christ's return. The church needs to feel the heart of God telling His people to pray—pray that you might be accounted worthy to escape on the day of wrath:

> Watch ye therefore, and pray always, that ye may be accounted worthy to escape all these things that shall come to pass, and to stand before the Son of man.
> —Luke 21:36

Every believer must await the Lord's return with a burning passion. Prior to the Lord's return, they must occupy themselves with the Lord's work, faithfully carrying out biblical mandates. This is a time of preparation, for once the Lord returns His reward will be with Him to give every man according to his work. The East Gate restored means that the church's heart has opened a path awaiting the Lord's coming—to hear the voice of the beloved singing on His way back. The church leaders should pray that the convictions of this truth sink deeply into the hearts of God's people so that they might renew their commitment to Christ as if He were returning in the next second.

The enemy desires to cover up the latent message and significance of the East Gate because it provides a potent source of exhilaration for God's people. The East Gate carries a message that solidifies the urgency of the gospel. When Christians think upon the East Gate their thoughts should immediately turn toward God's timetable, knowing they have little time left to finish their work before Christ returns. The devil would rather oppose the church's restoration of the East Gate so he can continue to plunder the riches of God's people. By postponing Christian sentiment away from Christ's return, Satan is able to render many Christians sterile and unmotivated to live for God.

The body of Christ suffers a lack of vitality when the East Gate remains unrestored. When the East Gate is fallen, God's people lose their vibrant hope in Christ's Second Coming. The promise of Christ's imminent return creates a mind-set for Christians to live life more abundantly. The East Gate affects whether or not God's people will allow themselves to be trampled upon by the affairs of this temporal world and by the worries and the concerns of this life.

Modern times have failed to give worth and value to God's eternal realties. When Christian churches begin to place valid significance upon Christ's return then temporal matters become insignificant in the light of this glorious event. As the church gives way to the celebration of Christ's imminent return, they will squelch the noise of other matters that have no consequence.

For many years, I have lived in an area that is prone to experiencing furious hurricanes that annihilate structures with unrelenting force. Usually the local weather channels will give residents a few days warning to prepare. As the local community prepares to withstand the devastating nature and consequences of these winds, all other tasks are left unattended until after the storms have passed. Similarly, those who hear about the glaring announcement of Christ's imminent return should be more preoccupied preparing for such a date than attending to matters of less significance and importance.

As a young attorney, I once had the opportunity to experience the liberating power of living life in light of the Lord's return. At the time, I stored all of my financial information and important records on a computer in my office. During that time, the computer shut down, leaving me unable to retrieve or input any information. This obligated me to call a computer technician. When the technician arrived, he promised that without difficulty he would fix the computer and I would be back to work in no time at all. I mentioned to him how important the documents and information contained in the computer were, and that the entire law firm would be affected by their loss. After a while, I noticed he began to sweat, and I asked him, "What happened?" He replied, "I lost everything." Instantly I had the serious desire to vent my frustration and retaliate for the offense. I wanted to address him with my choicest words of displeasure and dissatisfaction. Instead, I found myself returning to my desk and praying, *Lord, if You were to come tomorrow this loss is insignificant and will mean nothing.* Suddenly, I was purged of every negative feeling and I was able to go back to the technician and tell him not to concern himself.

The Christian testimony is preserved by the restoration of the East Gate, which brings everything back into perspective. No matter what a Christian faces in life today, the Lord's return immediately heals the ills of every life occupied with earthly concerns. When believers realize that Christ's return is imminent, all else is considered to be of little or no regard.

Long ago, Christians customarily greeted each other with the hopeful word *maranatha*, which means "the Lord is returning soon." Dividing it as *marana tha* means "our Lord, come," while *maran atha* means "our Lord has come." This greeting reveals the expectant hope in which early Christians lived, watching for the imminent return of Christ. As the church delves into the proposition of restoring the East Gate, I pray that this early Christian greeting becomes the practice of our day. Early Christians were fascinated by the promise of the appearance of Christ, and it carried much influence in their daily lives. The apostle Paul wrote in his second epistle to Timothy that the Lord has a crown of righteousness for all those who loved His appearing:

> Henceforth there is laid up for me a crown of righteousness, which the Lord, the righteous judge, shall give me at that day: and not to me only, but unto all them also that love his appearing.
>
> —2 TIMOTHY 4:8

When certain people ask, "Aren't you worried about the things that are going on around the world? Look what is taking place!" The Christian will reply, "No! I'm not worried, I'm excited because my Lord is going to return and He has promised to deliver those who wait and love His appearing." As church leaders venture toward renewing their hearts in restoring the East Gate, I pray that all churches might be fortified in their preparation for the Lord's coming. The restoration of the East Gate will allow the body of Christ to reprioritize every religious agenda, ritual, and ceremony so that churches can begin to walk in the knowledge that at any moment, day, or hour when they least expect, the sky will open and the Lord of hosts will return for His church.

PRAYER APPLICATION

Father God! Help the Christian church restore the East Gate. Lord Jesus, while Christians seek Your face for earthly blessing and increase, never allow the body of Christ to lose perspective on the priority of getting prepared for Your coming. Holy Spirit, set every Christian heart ablaze with the fire of the Lord's coming so that each one will clearly prefer to leave with Christ over staying behind to hoard earthly treasure and gain. Help us Lord to yearn for Your return so that our hearts, minds, and souls are caught up in You and not in the affairs of this world. Lord, I pray that the church can always keep in mind that in one sudden moment the Lord Himself shall descend from heaven with a shout, with the voice of the archangel, and with the trumpet of God, and we shall all be changed in the twinkling of an eye.

10

THE INSPECTION GATE

> *And I saw a great white throne, and him that sat on it,*
> *from whose face the earth and the heaven fled away; and*
> *there was found no place for them. And I saw the dead,*
> *small and great, stand before God; and the books were*
> *opened: and another book was opened, which is the book*
> *of life: and the dead were judged out of those things which*
> *were written in the books, according to their works. And*
> *the sea gave up the dead which were in it; and death and*
> *hell delivered up the dead which were in them: and they*
> *were judged every man according to their works.*
>
> —REVELATION 20:11–13

This chapter focuses on restoring the Inspection Gate. The efforts at restoring the Inspection Gate require the serious awakening of each member of the body of Christ and the whole world at large that God has appointed a day to inspect and reconcile accounts by judging every life lived upon Earth. Restoring the Inspection Gate requires turning the heart of God's people to the reality that both the righteous and unrighteous shall be required to stand before God to be rewarded and held accountable in eternity for all their actions—whether good or bad.

The necessity of repairing the Inspection Gate is seen by the multitude of Christian believers who have forgotten the awesome reality that God is a consuming fire and soon will demand that all appear before Him to face the judgment of His divine scrutiny. As church leaders approach the challenge to restore the Inspection Gate, they need to understand that many believers have forgotten about Judgment Day. Most believers have become secularized by solely living for temporal rewards and earthly recognition. In Nehemiah 3:31, the restoration efforts culminate with this last gate called the *Miphkad* (Inspection) Gate.

> After him Malchijah, one of the goldsmiths, made repairs as far as the house of the Nethinim and of the merchants, in front of the Miphkad Gate, and as far as the upper room at the corner.
> —NEHEMIAH 3:31, NKJV

Culminating this journey to restore the church as God's most holy dwelling place, the final gate restored in old Jerusalem was the Inspection Gate. The significance behind the Inspection Gate reveals that God desires to inspect and hold His people accountable for their actions and behavior upon the earth. The Inspection Gate reveals that God intends to review and balance the weight of all hearts, every conduct, and thought to reward and recompense each person.

The Inspection Gate is also known as the Gate of Examination or the Gate of Judgment. Another Hebrew word used to describe this gate has been *miphkad* (muster, inspection, master), referring to God's judgment. The Hebrew word *miphkad* means "appointment, account, balancing, census, mustering." The word carries the idea of gathering troops and having them show up for review, inventory, examination, and to receive rewards upon returning from battle. At the Inspection Gate, church leaders learn that each soldier will ultimately be inspected to give an account for each and every thing they have done and said during their habitation away from home.

Knowing that God has set a divine appointment to judge His people, Christians should be aptly prepared to live lives that glorify God in everything they do so that they can be prepared and unashamed when they are inspected, examined, and judged in heaven. The very purpose of all human existence was to bring glory to God's name in all things. The will of God is that the whole earth might be filled with the glory of God through His creation. All things were created to bring glory to the Highest; so that all can see the splendor and magnificence of God's power. God's design is that the church becomes the joy of all the earth. In the same manner, the church is expected to live and move for the glory of God so that Christians serve as a witness to all who are upon the earth.

Nehemiah's footsteps have been closely traced in this incredible journey to restore the ancient gates that surrounded the old city of Jerusalem. First, beginning with the Sheep Gate and finally traveling all the way around to stand before the Inspection Gate, the city was enclosed and protected against their enemies. The very last verse in chapter three of Nehemiah concludes with the mention of the Sheep Gate. Historically, the Inspection Gate was the place where the rewards were handed out to the soldiers who had returned from their time at war. At the Inspection Gate, courageous soldiers were praised and commended for an admirable job. At the Inspection Gate, recognition and honor were given to loyal men who had paid the high price of service to defend their kingdom. The Inspection Gate will be the place of evaluation regarding a believer's service and duties before God. Everything a Christian accomplishes in the work of the Lord by serving Him will be rewarded and accounted for at the Inspection Gate.

If the church were without an Inspection Gate, church leaders would be in a serious problem because everyone would just be doing as they pleased without fearing that they will have to give an account for their lives one day. Failure to restore the Inspection Gate may cause many believers to be driven to a careless, reckless, and even negligent Christian walk. Proponents of mercy and grace who purposefully exclude teaching on biblical accountability and responsibility to avoid reprisal have watered down the biblical reality and truth of being judged by God. Many church leaders fail to understand and teach that every believer will be required to give an account for what he does while in the flesh.

When believers understand that all of their work shall be accounted for and rewarded, the church becomes revived and driven to serve the Lord with ultimate sacrifice. The Inspection Gate turns the Christian heart toward home, reminding the church to store up their treasure in the heavenly places where they can never be taken or corrupted:

> But lay up for yourselves treasures in heaven, where neither moth nor rust doth corrupt, and where thieves do not break through nor steal.
>
> —MATTHEW 6:20

When the Inspection Gate is left in ruins, the body of Christ is taught to lay up their treasures on Earth where all kinds of negative consequences follow. Great devastation takes place when Christian leaders fail to restore the Inspection Gate. Christians begin to forego any consideration for their actions, ignoring the fact that they are incurring serious eternal consequences in heaven. Restoring the Inspection Gate requires the church to adamantly forewarn and admonish every believer that, one day, they will stand before Jesus Christ and render accounts for what they have done or have not done, during their Christian walk. Having a broken Inspection Gate in the church allows ministers and members to operate in a manner that ignores and rejects the truth that they must give an account to the Lord. No longer does the church understand that their service and work will be given to the Lord to be inspected.

Failing to restore the Inspection Gate causes many church leaders to undermine the admonition in the Book of Hebrews, which says that they who watch over souls must do so as if they were to give account:

> Obey them that have the rule over you, and submit yourselves: for they watch for your souls, as they that must give account, that they may do it with joy, and not with grief: for that is unprofitable for you.
>
> —HEBREWS 13:17

Many people have begun to believe in the hope of reincarnation, with the false reasoning: "I'm doing so badly this time around; next time I'll do better." That is one of the greatest satanic lies, and many people are banking on it. Many people feel that they are going to have several opportunities—several "go-arounds"—but the Word of God clearly states the contrary:

> And as it is appointed unto men once to die, but after this the judgment.
>
> —HEBREWS 9:27

The Inspection Gate insists that the body of Christ understand one thing—they must get it right this time around. It is appointed unto men to die once, and then comes judgment. Every Christian needs to be sure that they understand they only get one bite of the apple. This life is the life in which God desires that His people set all things in order. Clearly, this passage does not say, "They have several chances to get it right as they continue to evolve." Men and women have an opportunity to live just once for God, and then they shall die and face God in judgment. This life is where God confronts every living being with the opportunity to walk in such a way that He might welcome them into heaven by saying, "Well done, thou good and faithful servant...enter thou into the joy of thy lord" (Matt. 25:21).

By the looks of things, the modern church has removed, broken, and failed to restore the Inspection Gate, thus encouraging believers to "live for the moment." Certain of these so-called "Christians" live their lives without weighing the long-term consequences and realities of an Inspection Gate. They ignorantly proceed in malice and wickedness living in the futility of their mind. The Inspection Gate constantly reminds each member of Christ's church that they are to live for the hereafter and for heavenly treasures, rather than for earthly temporal rewards. When the Inspection Gate is restored, the church will begin to aim their efforts toward heavenly rewards and prizes.

At the Inspection Gate, the church should know that God's goodness should lead every person to repentance so that he or she can avoid being confronted by the severity of God's wrath on Judgment Day. Many Christians have chosen to pursue a life that forgets the eternal consequences of prodigal living. The purpose of the Inspection Gate is to remind each believer of the importance to keep moving toward the ultimate goal. When persons are led to believe that there is no date of inspection or examination, they often react on the normal human tendency to procrastinate or postpone taking inventory of their lives and actions. Many of the greatest men and women who ever lived were those who fixed their eyes on eternity, knowing that every day counted as an opportunity to live in preparation to meet their Maker.

At the Inspection Gate, Christians can be greatly motivated to honor God at all times so that they are not embarrassed at the time of their inspection. The ultimate desire of God is that His bride be found blameless without spot or wrinkle. To know that God has determined to inspect and evaluate every man and woman upon their expiration obligates everyone to prime themselves to answer their Maker for what they did during their physical time in the earthly realm.

What a blessing to be forewarned that on the appointed day, no one will have reason to have forgotten the reality of God's final judgment. That means that nobody will be able to say, "But Lord, You came too fast. I thought I had more time. You came too soon." Not one soul will be able to say, "God, You are not fair. You did not give me enough time. No one told me." The Bible states that on that day when men look into the face of their Maker, many will be ashamed embarrassed, and some will say, "Lord, I knew You. In Your name I preached, I cast out demons, I prayed for the sick, I went to the hospitals, and I held funerals." (See Matt. 7:22.) But the Lord will say, "I never knew you; depart from Me, you who practice lawlessness!" (Matt. 7:23, NKJV). For this reason, understanding Judgment Day is critical.

The serious implications of this divine appointment require the church to take every opportunity to fix accounts. Long before Christians are to appear before God, He will have already bestowed the things needed to prepare coming before His presence. On that day, God expects His people to be found resiliently bright and shining as the noonday sun:

> So then each of us shall give account of himself to God.
> —ROMANS 14:12, NKJV

The purpose of revisiting the Inspection Gate is to acknowledge that every member of God's family is expected to prepare to give an accurate account of themselves before God. Recently, I met a gentleman who seemed to have a critical spirit that led him to point a judgmental finger towards others. He began to recall the many wrongful actions of various inept preachers, ministers, and others he had met who professed to be Christians. I told the gentleman that knowing about these wrongfully committed acts would allow him to easily put everybody on quick judgment—but more importantly, one day he, too, would stand before God to give an account for his own wayward conduct. It seemed that this gentleman needed to be reminded that while many weigh and render accounts for others, they often forget that on Judgment Day each one will give account of *himself* before God. After our conversation, the gentleman recognized the importance of taking care of his own personal standing before God regardless of how others might proceed. Restoring the Inspection Gate will allow each Christian to reflect upon the future day of their divine appointment before God:

> For we must all appear before the judgment seat of Christ; that every one may receive the things done in his body, according to that he hath done, whether it be good or bad. Knowing therefore the terror of the Lord, we persuade men; but we are made manifest unto God; and I trust also are made manifest in your consciences.
> —2 CORINTHIANS 5:10–11

The apostle Paul was conscious of the reality of having to appear before the judgment seat of Christ. Therefore he made it his aim, whether present or absent, to be well pleasing to God. (See 2 Cor. 5:9.) This declaration makes it evident that each person must be prepared to receive God's judgment according to what they have done— whether good or bad. The church must prepare itself to carry the incredible task of forewarning humanity concerning the realties of having to stand before the judgment seat of Christ.

In the above passage, Paul says that one motivating factor was that he knew "the terror of the Lord." In other words, Paul was diligent in persuading others to consider the realties and extent of God's wrath and the severity of His judgment upon those who walked unrepentant in continual sin and rebellion. While for some people, the judgment seat of Christ will be a time of accolades, merits, and rewards, for others the judgment seat of Christ will be a time of receiving shameful reprimand, rebukes, and eternal punishment.

Paul wrote in 2 Corinthians 5:11, "Knowing therefore the terror of the Lord, we persuade men." In other words, Paul is making every effort to tell all men that they do not want to be recipients of God's wrath on that day. Instead of being ill-prepared for their appointment, men should choose their eternal destiny by living a life that pleases the Lord. They should do this in advance of coming before God's throne for judgment where heaven and hell will be decided. Church leaders should know that the Lord is a consuming fire and each man's work will be tested in that fire. There is a somber illustration given to the prophet Isaiah that truly affords a glimpse into the serious nature of every sinner's dilemma:

> The sinners in Zion are afraid; fearfulness hath surprised the hypocrites. Who among us shall dwell with the devouring fire? who among us shall dwell with everlasting burnings?
> —ISAIAH 33:14

The Inspection Gate requires believers to confront the seriousness of their predicament facing a pure and holy God on the day of their inspection. Restoration of the Inspection Gate requires believers to weigh the consequences of shirking their responsibility to be prepared for their divine appointment. Once the church restores the Inspection Gate, each believer will carry an unwavering commitment to walk with godly character. The response given to the question of who can dwell with everlasting burnings is answered in the following verse:

> He that walketh righteously, and speaketh uprightly; he that despiseth the gain of oppressions, that shaketh his hands from holding of bribes, that stoppeth his ears from hearing of blood, and shutteth his eyes from seeing evil.
>
> —ISAIAH 33:15

This verse seems to indicate that only people purified from sin will be allowed to enter into God's presence, thus being able to endure the everlasting fires of judgment. On that day, everything will be consumed except that which is pure and transparent.

Every Christian has been called to work and build something for the Lord. The Lord will not allow anyone to show up and say, "Hey, what's up, Lord? Man, I've been waiting for You for a long time." The Lord will require much fruit and multiplication of talents and gifts according to the talent or gifts previously bestowed by Him. The fruit by proxy will not count on that day. The number of godly men and women who Christians were acquainted with will not suffice for God's inquiry. The Word of God instructs each person to bring forth his own fruit to be present to the Lord.

While salvation is not obtained by works—because salvation is the gift of God received by grace—Christians must acknowledge that genuine faith produces much fruit. The very fact that the body of Christ has received the free gift of salvation requires them to walk in the fear of God working out their salvation with fear and trembling. The fruits of the Christian walk with God will confirm that in Him the body of Christ is able to produce fruits that glorify His name. The Bible states that believers need to be vigilant and careful, lest they fall short of the grace of God or from their own steadfastness. The fact that God has sent the rain and the showering of His grace does not mean that grace alone will produce anything without the labor of those who cultivate the fields. While understanding that only God is able to give growth, it becomes clear that Christians must involve themselves with the plowing, sowing, watering, and reaping of the harvest:

> For the kingdom of heaven is as a man travelling into a far country, who called his own servants, and delivered unto them his goods. And unto one he gave five talents, to another two, and to another one; to every man according to his several ability; and straightway took his journey.
>
> —MATTHEW 25:14–15

When Christian leaders understand the necessity of restoring the Inspection Gate, they will the body of Christ to recall the demands of the Lord of the harvest. Upon acknowledging that a merciful God has given abundant talents and gifts, Christians must also recognize that He will expect a return on His investment and not be cheated by charlatans who refuse to produce a godly harvest. To receive God's amazing grace and total forgiveness without producing the godly fruit of gratefulness and faithfulness to the Lord would be sinful, especially for Christians who profess to have such great measure of God's mercy and love. The only reasonable response the Master could give to those who fail to restore the Inspection Gate is, "Depart from me, you wicked and evil servant. Go into the outer darkness where there is the gnashing of teeth and torment of fire." (See Matthew 25:26, 30.) After God has bestowed upon the body of Christ the grace of His salvation, the church should be fruitful and offer up glory to God with all of their strength:

> Herein is my Father glorified, that ye bear much fruit; so shall ye be my disciples.
>
> —JOHN 15:8

When the world can see godly fruit in the church, they will desire to glorify God. One day, all will come before God and say:

God, this is what I have been able to do. I was diligent with what You gave me. You gave me one and here I bring two.

While many Christians despise the numbers game, Jesus made it very clear that He was counting. His teachings were replete with numbers, figures, and amounts, making sure that His return was always worthy and honorable. If He gave one talent, His followers could not show up with one talent; they were required to generate increase. If Jesus gave two talents, His followers were required to improve and multiply for a good return. On the other hand, the wicked servants who failed to produce earnings with the Lord's talents violated His trust, and the Master sent the wicked servants into everlasting darkness. What were the excuses the servant gave the Lord? He said, "'Lord, I knew You to be a hard man, reaping where you have not sown, and gathering where you have not scattered seed. Lord, I knew You were a terrible Master and I was scared, so I planted. I hid my treasure, my talent" (Matt. 25:24, author's paraphrase). And the master responded, "If you knew I was so terrible, if you knew that I was so stern, so harsh, you should have at least put that talent in the bank so that it would have gained interest" (Matt. 25:26-27, author's paraphrase).

We need to understand that salvation is a gift of the Lord, but the Lord expects each member of the body of Christ to cultivate and invest their life because salvation was purchased by the blood of Jesus and belongs to God. The following passage illustrates the importance of repairing the Inspection Gate:

> Every man's work shall be made manifest: for the day shall declare it, because it shall be revealed by fire; and the fire shall try every man's work of what sort it is.
>
> —1 Corinthians 3:13

This portion of the apostle Paul's letter to the Corinthians sheds more light concerning the day of inspection. Despite the building material used by each Christian, whether wood, hay, or straw, Paul warns that every man's worth will become evident, for the day will declare it. When inspection day arrives and the church's work endures the fire of God's scrutiny, then they will receive their reward. Every Christian must realize that they will suffer loss if anyone's work is burned up upon inspection. On that day, many Christians are going to be surprised at what men will attempt to offer up as the work of God. They will put their work before the Lord and stand on top claiming it to be fully endorsed by God, but when the Lord begins to test their work with His eternal flames, they will be buried in a heap of ashes.

Many church leaders will be buried in ashes over their heads because all of their work will burn up as temporary trophies of their human wit and glory instead of being eternally tested treasure. When they stand before the Lord, their work will be tested by fire. After the purifying fire, the gold, silver, and precious stones will only increase in their value and worth. The precious minerals and stones are eternal. Some men forsake the eternal things of God in exchange for earthly building projects and tabernacles. God desires for His people to build a spiritual house utilizing living stones. The living stones are people, and Christian leaders must begin to build them up as God's edifice. Paul writes of his desire to "present you as a chaste virgin to Christ" (2 Cor. 11:2). Every work of Christian service must be prepared to withstand the test of God's consuming fire.

The time has come for church leaders to ask God to allow them to work toward those areas that are going to last forever. Many Christian leaders have spent their entire lives defending dogma and denominational bylaws only to realize that God was never involved. When they get to heaven, they will be ashamed of having spent so much valuable time on issues having no eternal impact or worth. Instead of winning souls for Christ and furthering the kingdom of God, these men lived their lives for personal pride to further their own interests.

Years ago in a small mission in Mexico, the missionaries were very much concerned about the physical effort and labor needed to build the concrete structures and buildings. When I saw the anguish and distress suffered by their efforts, God reminded me of all the great Christian men I had known who had lost their physical buildings and property due to persecution and financial hardships. At that moment, I was led to encourage the missionary pastor to concentrate his efforts in building up the spiritual lives of the people, and not invest so much energy and frustration with the physical concrete and wood. Physical sites will fall and fade away, but souls are eternal and everlasting. Christian leaders must value the lives of God's people, because the little girls and boys of that missionary village will still be around after the present ministers are long gone. I have witnessed Christian leaders so zealous about their physical building programs and temple fundraisers that they have destroyed church families and congregations.

Often when church leaders are doing the work of the Lord, they are more concerned about the physical dwelling, yet they are despising the souls of men and women or the issues that have an eternal consequence. The Inspection Gate turns our focus to the eternal works of God. On that day, Christian leaders will confess saying, "Lord, You entrusted us with this work and we can face you unashamedly knowing that we did our best and stand to receive eternal rewards and crowns." Having full confidence to stand before the judged is a very good reason for the body of Christ to live productive and godly lives with all diligence and discipline. Every decision made by a Christian leader should be made in the light of the eternal consequence, making sure that they are not building anything that will not hold up on the day of inspection. The Inspection Gate allows the Christian church to know that God stands prepared to inspect every man's work; to reward some and chastise others.

Through the Inspection Gate, the body of Christ can replace the complacent attitude that leads some to believe that solely because they are Christians everything is going to be okay. The church must begin to warn others that simply saying, "I have accepted Jesus and confess to be a Christian," is not sufficient. Jesus made sure that His followers had a glimpse of eternity in Matthew 25:31. The following parable of the sheep and the goats depicts the manner in which God will judge between the righteous and unrighteous:

> When the Son of man shall come in his glory, and all the holy angels with him, then shall he sit upon the throne of his glory: And before him shall be gathered all nations: and he shall separate them one from another, as a shepherd divideth his sheep from the goats: And he shall set the sheep on his right hand, but the goats on the left. Then shall the King say unto them on his right hand, Come, ye blessed of my Father, inherit the kingdom prepared for you from the foundation of the world.
> —MATTHEW 25:31–34

In this passage, the Lord allows His followers the benefit of seeing a glimpse of what will take place in eternity. Similar to a dress rehearsal, no participant is left to wonder what will happen. Jesus does not keep anything hidden. He reveals all things. I love those words. What an invitation—what a green light opportunity so that all are without excuse:

> "For I was hungry and you gave Me food; I was thirsty and you gave Me drink; I was a stranger and you took Me in; I was naked and you clothed Me; I was sick and you visited Me; I was in prison and you came to Me." Then the righteous will answer Him, saying, "Lord, when did we see You hungry and feed You, or thirsty and give You drink? When did we see You a stranger and take You in, or naked and clothe You? Or when did we see You sick, or in prison, and come to You?" And the King will answer and say to them, "Assuredly, I say to you, inasmuch as you did it to one of the least of these My brethren, you did it to Me." Then He will also say to those on the left hand, "Depart from Me, you cursed, into the everlasting fire prepared for the devil and his angels: for I was hungry and you gave Me no food; I was thirsty and you gave Me no drink; I was a stranger and you did not take Me in, naked and you did not

clothe Me, sick and in prison and you did not visit Me." Then they also will answer Him, saying, "Lord, when did we see You hungry or thirsty or a stranger or naked or sick or in prison, and did not minister to You?"

—MATTHEW 25:35–44, NKJV

Apparently, some think that they are attending to the Lord's work only to discover the frightening prospect that on Judgment Day they will be counted by the Lord as goats. The Inspection Gate allows God to saturate people with the reality of His inspection and judgment, particularly on those who engage in self-righteousness while forsaking true acts of kindness and mercy. When Jesus gave this example, He said that some who call Him "Lord" will ask, "When did we see You hungry or thirsty or a stranger or naked or sick or in prison, and did not minister to You?" (v. 44). Here both of these groups claimed to know Jesus as Lord, but on that day one was found to be lacking before the Lord. The other received a welcome with open arms. The first was acting under a different self-serving spirit and was not led by the Holy Spirit.

Another important aspect of restoring the Inspection Gate is found throughout several passages of the New Testament. The teachings given by Christ reveal that there will be many witnesses expecting to testify against believers on Judgment Day. Noah condemned the whole world by being obedient to God, and therefore placed the rest of the world under judgment. God will be asked to render His judgments according to past measures of judgment. All the residents destroyed in the fiery judgment of Sodom will be present as witnesses on Judgment Day. Even the Queen of the South, who traveled deserts seeking God's wisdom and truth, will sit there as a witness against many people who dislike traveling to church because they find it too far or difficult. Many could be asked on Judgment Day, "Did you faithfully attend church?" Perhaps, some might respond saying, "It was too far, three whole blocks away," or, "I only went three times every year because I was busy." While the Queen of the

South looks on, others will testify saying, "Well, I live about forty minutes away, and You know Lord, my car's air conditioning system gets too cold and I freeze on the way over."

The following passage in the Gospel of Matthew refers to this incident and is a clear indication that God expects His followers to begin to eliminate all the lame excuses:

> The queen of the south shall rise up in the judgment with this generation, and shall condemn it: for she came from the uttermost parts of the earth to hear the wisdom of Solomon; and, behold, a greater one than Solomon is here.
> —MATTHEW 12:42

This woman who came from the farthest ends of the earth to hear the wisdom of Solomon is going to hear what some Christians will offer as an excuse. Some in the body of Christ must be out of their minds to come up with meager excuses before the Lord. Another group of witnesses who will rise in judgment are the men of Nineveh who repented upon hearing Jonah's proclamation:

> The men of Nineveh shall rise in judgment with this generation, and shall condemn it: because they repented at the preaching of Jonas; and, behold, a greater than Jonas is here.
> —MATTHEW 12:41

This passage of Scripture reminds the world that Jonah went into Nineveh and proclaimed a word, and the whole city repented. In comparison, Jesus came into the world and proclaimed the good news of repentance with all the signs He performed including resurrecting the dead and laying down His own life. The people of Nineveh will say, "Wait a second, we did not have so much, we just had an angry reluctant man who smelled real fishy who simply said, 'Yet forty days, and Nineveh shall be overthrown'" (Jonah 3:4). The men of Nineveh didn't have more than that, and they made quick efforts to repent and obeyed the instructions of Jonah to get right before God.

God expects every generation to hear and receive Jesus as He proclaims God's Word for all men to repent. The proclamations of Christ come with great signs and wonders—the laying down of His life and rising from the dead on the third day. Indeed, a greater one than Jonah is here. I believe that those who ignore the words of Christ will not fare so well on Judgment Day. Many will try to formulate good excuses for their disobedience, but they are not going to be adequate:

> Woe unto thee, Chorazin! woe unto thee, Bethsaida! for if the mighty works, which were done in you, had been done in Tyre and Sidon, they would have repented long ago in sackcloth and ashes. But I say unto you, It shall be more tolerable for Tyre and Sidon at the day of judgment, than for you. And thou, Capernaum, which art exalted unto heaven, shalt be brought down to hell: for if the mighty works, which have been done in thee, had been done in Sodom, it would have remained until this day. But I say unto you, That it shall be more tolerable for the land of Sodom in the day of judgment, than for thee.
> —MATTHEW 11:21–24

Throughout the Bible, God is constantly preparing His people for this examination date because He does not want anyone to fail. God has a righteous tract record of judging generations, nations, and peoples. The Bible states that the judgment of God is righteous. (See Romans 2:5.) He is going to hold everyone accountable, just as He has in the past. There are very few Christians who truly believe that there is going to be an actual Judgment Day on which they will render an account of their lives. We should already have a clear familiarity with God's judgment based on previous dealings.

As a practicing attorney for many years, I had many clients ask, "Have you been before this judge before? What is he like?" Generally, I would mention a few anecdotes of decisions that the judge had made in past court cases. Sometimes, I would advise a client to wear their best outfit to show respect and honor before the presiding judge. In the same manner, Christians do not want to find themselves before a holy righteous judge wearing garments of unrighteousness. The Inspection Gate shows the body of Christ the important reminder of having to stand before God one day to answer for every detail of their earthly existence. A particular verse of the Bible that is often overlooked reveals that God's scrutiny will address even the smallest and most insignificant expressions coming from our heart:

> But I say unto you, That every idle word that men shall speak, they shall give account thereof in the day of judgment.
>   —MATTHEW 12:36

This may seem too outlandish for some in the body of Christ but only because the church has not properly taught God's truth. The reason this passage is mentioned in the Gospel of Matthew is because the Master does not want His people to be idle speakers. Rather Jesus is preparing His followers to be ready for that day when they will be weighed in the balance scales of His justice, even to the extent of their careless words. Every work will be brought into judgment. Every secret thing will be revealed. Nothing remains hidden. Nothing shall be covered up. Every secret word that was spoken in darkness shall be heard. Every word that was spoken, even in closets, shall be proclaimed. Every idle (or careless) word that was spoken they shall render account for it.

Some people complain that the church is too judgmental and this is why they no longer attend any congregation. They fail to realize that this aspect of the Christian church is needed to assist believers in coming within the purview of God's acceptance. One of the secrets to repairing the Inspection Gate is found in 1 Corinthians chapter 11:

> For if we would judge ourselves, we should not be judged. But when we are judged, we are chastened of the Lord, that we should not be condemned with the world.
>   —1 CORINTHIANS 11:31–32

God has designed the church to be our home away from home. Every true Christian should seek some kind of accessibility to a manner in which they can enter into accountability. One should get as close as one can to the measure by which they will be examined in heaven so that their daily walk and life are not lacking when they appear before God. Every Christian should attend a godly church so their daily walk is able to be inspected and examined by a godly family of believers. This way, on Judgment Day, they are not surprised and unprepared. In other words, the secret to preparing for Judgment Day is for Christians to show their life to other godly believers here on Earth so that their conduct is examined and corrected before they enter into eternity.

The question is often asked, "How will I measure before God?" At church, every member of the body of Christ has an opportunity to hear and learn the weights, limits, and measures of God's verdict as He rules. For many this is a difficult process because they despise correction and reproof causing them always to run from any semblance of judgment. While others pray that God will continue to reveal hidden areas that do not please Him and need to be corrected. While Christians continue upon Earth they can learn to ask God to examine their lives now. King David often prayed asking the Lord to judge his walk and thoughts here on Earth:

> Judge me, O Lord; for I have walked in mine integrity: I have trusted also in the Lord; therefore I shall not slide. Examine me, O Lord, and prove me; try my reins and my heart.
> —Psalm 26:1–2

Every Christian should pray, *Lord, bring me to purity in my thoughts, in my mind, and my heart, Amen!* This transparent posture will allow each member of the body of Christ to come through the Inspection Gate to receive eternal rewards. The Bible states that there is no condemnation for those who are in Christ; that God through Christ has paid the price of all rebellion and sin. (See Romans 8:1.) Now, all

Christians have to do is receive glory and honor and begin to walk in submission without sin:

> But we are sure that the judgment of God is according to truth against them which commit such things. And thinkest thou this, O man, that judgest them which do such things, and doest the same, that thou shalt escape the judgment of God?
>
> —ROMANS 2:2–3

The judgment of God is according to His truth. God is not going to use anything other than His Word. Understand this—He will not use sympathy, pity, compassion, or clemency. Christ will hold every person accountable to the truth of His Word because God does not lie. The following text instructs every human on Earth to not despise knowing the goodness of God that leads to repentance:

> Or despisest thou the riches of his goodness and forbearance and longsuffering; not knowing that the goodness of God leadeth thee to repentance? But after thy hardness and impenitent heart treasurest up unto thyself wrath against the day of wrath and revelation of the righteous judgment of God; Who will render to every man according to his deeds: To them who by patient continuance in well doing seek for glory and honour and immortality, eternal life: But unto them that are contentious, and do not obey the truth, but obey unrighteousness, indignation and wrath, Tribulation and anguish, upon every soul of man that doeth evil, of the Jew first, and also of the Gentile; But glory, honour, and peace, to every man that worketh good, to the Jew first, and also to the Gentile.
>
> —ROMANS 2:4-10

On that day, God will be in total disgust toward the lukewarm. With total indignation He will spew out of His mouth those who were unable to decide with all deference for godliness and well doing.

Upon that day, God will make no exception of persons. For with God there is no partiality. To those who claim, "Lord, I come from the line of Abraham," or, "Lord, I have come through the dispensation of grace": no partiality. If church leaders expect to see the Lord, they must pursue true holiness, regardless of their spiritual lineage or extraction because God will hold all people to His righteous measure of His holiness:

> Follow peace with all men, and holiness, without which no man shall see the Lord.
>
> —HEBREWS 12:14

In Revelation 20, there is an "insider's view" of the moment when the platform is set for the final day of judgment before God's great white throne. Just before the church prepares to rule and reign with Christ for all eternity, God will gather every nation, tribe, and tongue before the great white throne of judgment. This prophetic message foretells the manner in which the world will stand before its Creator to give account of all their doings while they were in the flesh:

> And I saw a great white throne, and him that sat on it, from whose face the earth and the heaven fled away; and there was found no place for them. And I saw the dead, small and great, stand before God; and the books were opened: and another book was opened, which is the book of life: and the dead were judged out of those things which were written in the books, according to their works.
>
> —REVELATION 20:11–12

Dictators like Adolph Hitler, Saddam Hussein, and philosophers such as Nietzsche, Marx, Darwin, Buddha, and Socrates will on that day have to come before the Lord's throne. They will have to give an account before their Maker, and they will be judged out of the things written in the books:

And the sea gave up the dead which were in it; and death and hell delivered up the dead which were in them: and they were judged every man according to their works.

—REVELATION 20:13

Restoring the Inspection Gate requires a proclamation that God would be tremendously unfair if He judged the world without first telling them that there was going to be a date of inspection. The Inspection Gate, when repaired and restored, will enable the church to prepare for the great and glorious day when the books will be opened to judge from those things that are written:

And, behold, I come quickly; and my reward is with me, to give every man according as his work shall be.

—REVELATION 22:12

PRAYER APPLICATION

Father God! Help the Christian church restore the Inspection Gate. Lord Jesus I purpose to weigh each one of my thoughts, words, and actions in the light of Your Word so that I am not condemned with the world and rendered unqualified to receive entry into Your heavenly kingdom. Holy Spirit, continue to send a strong conviction to reprove the world, with regard to sin, righteousness, and judgment according to Jesus' promise. Lord from this day forward, I pray that the body of Christ begins to live in such a manner that shows they are concerned of one day standing before you face-to-face to answer for all their ways so that the world can also believe in Your righteous judgment.

CONCLUSION

> *O God, the heathen are come into thine inheritance; thy holy temple have they defiled; they have laid Jerusalem on heaps.*
>
> —PSALM 79:1

Restoring the Gates That Prevail is not intended to solve every infirmity or dilemma facing the modern church. The purpose of this book is to encourage church leaders and ministers entrusted with the care and supervision of God's work to rise up and teach by example those aspects of God's truth that are foundational to the church's success. I believe Christian leaders everywhere will be blessed and refreshed by the practical application of God's hidden mysteries behind each gate. I sincerely believe that Jesus intended for His followers to participate as active members of an overcoming and glorious church. Jesus promised to build a church with the power and strength to prevail against the gates of hell.

As church leaders revisit each ancient gate in the Book of Nehemiah, they can begin to restore the spiritual truths represented behind each gate using the same zeal and tenacity in their ministry. Every paragraph in this book emanated from a sincere desire to assist leaders in the body of Christ to present the church as a chaste virgin to Christ, without spot or wrinkle. Ultimately, church ministers and leaders bear the responsibility to restore the church from its present state of disrepair so that the body of Christ is no longer plundered and abused.

Many church leaders claim to have a ministry anointed by the Holy Spirit, yet fail to produce fruit worthy of that anointing. For many years ministry leaders have confirmed the existence of God's anointing upon their ministries by quoting the following passage of Scripture:

> The Spirit of the Lord GOD is upon me; because the LORD hath anointed me to preach good tidings unto the meek; he hath sent me to bind up the brokenhearted, to proclaim liberty to the captives, and the opening of the prison to them that are bound; To proclaim the acceptable year of the LORD, and the day of vengeance of our God; to comfort all that mourn; To appoint unto them that mourn in Zion, to give unto them beauty for ashes, the oil of joy for mourning, the garment of praise for the spirit of heaviness; that they might be called trees of righteousness, the planting of the LORD, that he might be glorified.
>
> —ISAIAH 61:1–3

The preceding passage of Scripture is familiar to ministry leaders that serve the body of Christ. However, many fail to realize that a true anointing of God's Spirit shows forth in fruits of restoration, rebuilding, and renewing ruins and devastation of former generations. I believe this book will help redefine what some consider the legitimate anointing and power of the Holy Spirit. The anointing of God's Spirit has come upon those willing to restore and repair the ruins of many generations. I pray that this book will serve as a godly encouragement to church pastors, ministers, and youth leaders to measure the effectiveness of their anointing with the tangible fruits that strengthen the church. The willingness to understand God's true anointing will be tested, as leaders reflect on Isaiah 61:4, remembering that anointing should birth the fruit of restoring, renewing, and rebuilding ruins and places long devastated:

> And they shall build the old wastes, they shall raise up the former desolations, and they shall repair the waste cities, the desolations of many generations.
>
> —ISAIAH 61:4

The ministry of God's Spirit and His anointing should always direct the lives and efforts of His leaders in order to enrich and add weight, substance, direction, and purpose to the local church. Every church must possess the willingness and effectiveness to lift up ruins in the place of God's dwelling where His people have suffered devastation for many generations. I believe that any desire to participate in an anointed ministry must address the issues found in this book.

I pray that churches everywhere will use this book as a blueprint to motivate their leaders to rebuild, restore, and renew the ruins and desolations found in the Christian church for generations. This work of restoring and rebuilding the ruins of the church is not limited to an elite special taskforce or a group of elected, choicely anointed apostles. It is for each individual member within the body of Christ. God promised to pour out His anointing and Spirit on all flesh so that the body of Christ can walk in the power of total restoration:

> And it shall come to pass in the last days, saith God, I will pour out of my Spirit upon all flesh: and your sons and your daughters shall prophesy, and your young men shall see visions, and your old men shall dream dreams: And on my servants and

on my handmaidens I will pour out in those days of my Spirit; and they shall prophesy: And I will shew wonders in heaven above, and signs in the earth beneath; blood, and fire, and vapour of smoke: The sun shall be turned into darkness, and the moon into blood, before that great and notable day of the Lord come: And it shall come to pass, that whosoever shall call on the name of the Lord shall be saved.

—ACTS 2:17–21

As the church addresses the subject matter found in this book, they can expect to see things change for the glory of God. For generations, the church has suffered great loss and now continues to experience an identity crisis because leaders have failed to rebuild, restore, and strengthen many aspects of the local church ministry.

While writing this book, I often wept bitterly for the condition of the local church and the present state of desolation and continual loss suffered in the body of Christ as a result of unscrupulous leaders. The devastation occurring within the body of Christ all over the world is intensely severe, and it is the product of wayward teaching and ministry. The abominations performed and continuing to exist within the body of Christ are beyond my ability to withstand without raising my voice to cry out for total restoration and reparations of church walls and gates. As leaders study the concepts presented in *Restoring the Gates That Prevail* their indifference and apathy will turn to passion and zeal to protect the house of God. Securing walls, repairing the breach, and fixing the gates shall ensure that the body of Christ becomes a people who prevail standing in their call to be a glorious church.

Restoring the Gates That Prevail is not a new revelation. God and His Spirit have always taken great offense at the atrocities taking place within His city's gates. The passage of Scripture recorded in the Old Testament Book of Ezekiel, reveals God's heart and instructions addressing the abominations committed within His holy city:

> And the LORD said to him, "Go through the midst of the city,
> through the midst of Jerusalem, and put a mark on the fore-
> heads of the men who sigh and cry over all the abominations
> that are done within it."
>
> —EZEKIEL 9:4, NKJV

Upon further examination of Ezekiel 9, church leaders can witness that those marked by God were preserved, and only those who sincerely wept for the evil committed in the city of God were preserved from the fury of God's wrath and judgment. *Restoring the Gates That Prevail* is a call to arms in order to encourage and strengthen those who carry the burden and anguish of things done wrong among the people of God. The church must dispense with the fanfare circus environment and entertainment and return to sound doctrine and legitimate ministry that benefits those gathered within the body of Christ. Tragically, the recent fanfare and mockery found in today's churches and Christian ministries can only be compared to that of worldly gimmicks and all the abominations of the nations. Christian leadership must consider with all due seriousness whether the ministry efforts they further equate to the "abominations of the nations" that defile the house of the Lord:

> Moreover all the leaders of the priests and the people trans-
> gressed more and more, according to all the abominations of
> the nations, and defiled the house of the LORD which He had
> consecrated in Jerusalem.
>
> —2 CHRONICLES 36:14, NKJV

The present generation has witnessed the absence of truly anointed ministries that serve to restore, rebuild, enrich, strengthen, and protect the church. If the church continues to allow the existence of fallen walls and burned gates, the body of Christ will become a heap of ruins. Consequently, the young men will be spiritually castrated, young virgins will be unprotected, the aged will suffer dishonor, and the weak and vulnerable believers shall be taken captive. Many families have lost their sons and daughters as a result of wayward church leaders being unwilling to restore the sanctuary of God. The instruments and vessels from the house of God, great and small, the treasures of the house of the Lord, including leaders, worshipers, and ministers, have been lost in confusion and sin for too long. When the body of Christ has suffered destruction and loss of their most precious possessions and families, the time has come to admit that the gates are broken and the walls have fallen.

God is calling the church to raise a generation of godly leaders and servants willing to fight for and strengthen the walk of all those in the body of Christ. If the church confesses to have the mind of Christ and the wisdom of God, they should equip the body of Christ so that the church begins to show forth these virtues. The Christian church's inherent calling is to "proclaim the praises of Him who called [us] out of darkness into His marvelous light" (1 Pet. 2:9, NKJV).

Christians cannot cultivate nor experience the fruit of God's Spirit in the midst of destruction and defeat. The church cannot continue to claim victory while evidence of defeat is prevalent. In Psalm 137:4, the psalmist inquires, "How shall we sing the LORD's song in a strange land?" While God's people were held captive, their enemies would ask them to sing their joyful songs of victory. They responded that to sing songs of victory was impossible because of the terrible and unpleasant realties of their captivity. How can Christians continue to sing to the Lord songs of mighty victory and omnipotence while they sleep surrounded by defeat in a heap of ruins day after day? The church cannot be expected to sing joyful songs of deliverance to a great God while experiencing captivity and suffering devastation like the ungodly. Christians cannot expect the church to hold itself out as favored people, strong and glorious, when they continue under the unbearable weight of sin, guilt, shame, chains, and desolation.

The body of Christ will not experience the joy, peace, and righteousness of God's kingdom if they are continually plundered by ungodly insurgents. Churches that prevail must remove all worldly influences or perspective and replace them with God's truth. The outward manifestation of the church shows the body of Christ stricken with pestilence and plagues such as divorce, teenage pregnancy, rebellion, disobedience, unfaithfulness, alcoholism, covetousness, greed, idolatry, body piercing, tattoos, and poverty because leaders have failed to establish the truth of God in the hearts of His people. As church leaders begin to restore the gates and build up the walls of godly standards in the Christian church, the body of Christ will begin to prevail at such a degree that Christians who are brought back from worldly captivity will think they are dreaming:

> When the LORD brought back the captivity of Zion, We were like those who dream. Then our mouth was filled with laughter, And our tongue with singing. Then they said among the nations, "The LORD has done great things for them."
> —PSALM 126:1–2, NKJV

Finally, I pray that the body of Christ begins to enjoy the fruits of courageous, godly leaders who are willing to minister with true spiritual anointing, zeal, and passion. Undoubtedly, the grace of God abounds towards leaders like Nehemiah and Ezra, who make themselves available to restore and rebuild the ancient ruins of God's city. God is able to move the hearts of godly men and women so that the next generation of Christian families can enjoy a glorious church without spot, stain, or wrinkle. After such a long period of nightmarish captivity for the body of Christ, many will believe that the restoration of the church is a possible dream come true.

EPILOGUE

> *And I looked, and rose up, and said unto the nobles, and to the rulers, and to the rest of the people, Be not ye afraid of them: remember the LORD, which is great and terrible, and fight for your brethren, your sons, and your daughters, your wives, and your houses.*
>
> —NEHEMIAH 4:14

The impartation of God's grace is essential to the achievement of every God-given task. Without God's grace, God's people cannot expect to fulfill God's plan. After reading this book, church leaders may desire additional resources to continue the restoration needed in the local church. God has given the church apostles, prophets, evangelists, pastors, and teachers so that the saints would be perfected for the work of the ministry, and for the edification of the body of Christ.

Every ministry that can speak the truth in love will contribute to the growth of the body of Christ. Every Christian is required to pay the price of walking and living as a true member of the church as God's household. The church has been called to support God's truth in obedience like a pillar that upholds a structure for the benefit of every believer. The whole world yearns to see the truth of God's work in the church. Ministers have been accused of superficially proclaiming the knowledge of God's Word without producing the tangible evidence of its fruit. The church must manifest the wisdom of God in every aspect of its work—things said and done—as the genuine earthly representatives of God's truth.

Church leaders must endeavor to cultivate in every Christian heart the desire to honor and glorify the name of Jesus. Christians need to be filled with wisdom and truth from the praises of Him who has called them out of darkness and into His marvelous light. The Christian calling—to be the head and not the tail—is only possible by shining forth as godly examples to all the nations.

Church members must realize the awesome responsibility to be godly examples and lead lives filled with God's peace, joy, and righteous order. The church has been given "exceedingly great and precious promises, that through these [we] may be partakers of the divine nature, having escaped the corruption that is in the world through lust" (2 Pet. 1:4, NKJV).

Every believer having received God's grace should attest to the existence of this gift of grace by walking in the power to resist ungodly lust and worldly influence, and continue to live soberly and righteously in this present age. (See Titus 2:11–12.)

The final and remaining truth is that the church as the bride of Christ is destined to prevail and take her place upon His glorious throne. To all the cynical opponents who wickedly assert that the Christian church will never prevail: God has promised in the Bible that the church will make herself ready, and that she will be "granted to be arrayed in fine linen, clean and bright, for the fine linen is the righteous acts of the saints" (Rev. 19:8, NKJV).

TO CONTACT THE AUTHOR

To order more books or to obtain additional resources on church leadership and ministry, as well as scheduling speaking engagements, seminars, or conferences, write to:

Changing the World
c/o Dr. Joaquin G. Molina
P.O. Box 654338
Miami, FL 33265

Web site: www.solmiami.org

E-mail: jmolina@solmiami.org